Understanding Research

BECOMING A COMPETENT AND CRITICAL CONSUMER

Second Edition

Jeffrey Kottler and Laurie A. Sharp

Bassim Hamadeh, CEO and Publisher
Kassie Graves, Acquisitions Editor
Leah Sheets, Associate Editor
Christian Berk, Associate Production Editor
Jess Estrella, Senior Graphic Designer
Alexa Lucido, Licensing Coordinator
Don Kesner, Interior Designer
Natalie Piccotti, Senior Marketing Manager
Kassie Graves, Director of Acquisitions and Sales
Jamie Giganti, Senior Managing Editor

Cover image copyright © 2014 iStockphoto LP/TaiChesco.
    copyright © Depositphotos/SergeyNivens.
Chapter opener image source: https://unsplash.com/photos/aJTiW00qqtl.

Printed in the United States of America.

ISBN: 978-1-5165-2625-3 (pbk) / 978-1-5165-2626-0 (br) / 978-1-5165-4533-9 (al)

Understanding Research

BECOMING A COMPETENT AND CRITICAL CONSUMER

Second Edition

Brief Table of Contents

Detailed Table of Contents

Chapter 8: Doing Research: Accountant, Explorer, or Both? ...155

Chapter 9: What Do You Want to Know, and What Do Others Already Know? ...171

Preface

Whether it is acknowledged or not, the reality is that most practitioners and students who must take basic research courses as part of their academic degree programs have little interest, nor inclination, of designing and carrying out a research study in the near future. For those who do intend to pursue such a noble path, there is advanced-level training available, both on the job and in advanced graduate degree programs. However, there is a limited amount of time in a single course to teach the basics of research for practitioners in the education, health, helping, and social sciences professions. Moreover, there are limits to what a student can meaningfully digest and personalize. That is one reason why many students may dread such a course, why they often postpone it for as long as possible, and why they approach the experience with such apprehension. Another reason is that the subject matter is typically viewed as extremely complex and difficult and considered largely irrelevant to their professions and lives. "I don't want to be a researcher," we have heard over and over again, "I just want to help people."

Most contemporary textbooks on the basics of research are rather large, ponderous volumes, loaded with much valuable information. But, they are also daunting because of their dual tasks—to teach students about research and how to make sense of it, and then to teach them how to do their own studies. Yet, many research courses are designed primarily to accomplish the first goal, that is, to help novice professionals become literate, knowledgeable, and competent in making sense of research. In other words, the primary objective of *Understanding Research* is to help you read research in an informed and critical manner so that you can make sense of the material, evaluate its usefulness, and, most importantly, to apply the results to your work and life.

The overriding goal of this text is to help you become proficient in finding information and resources that you need to do your job and live your life more effectively. Whenever you feel stumped by a problem or situation, or are looking for innovative strategies, or find yourself searching for information about a particular area of interest, you must be able to locate the sources that will be most useful. Just as importantly, you must be able to read the sources you found, digest it, critically evaluate it, and decide which parts might be most relevant. Moreover, you must be able to make sense of the material and examine for yourself whether the researchers followed procedures that lead to valid results—otherwise, you will be relying on faulty data or conclusions.

Features of the Text

Understanding Research is thus a different kind of textbook in that the territory covered is both realistic and relevant for most practitioners and students. Because the focus is primarily on the *consumption* of research, practitioners and students may quickly develop the skills to read, evaluate, and apply the material. In other words, the same skills that will help you to read research competently will also help you in other areas of your life, especially when it comes to thinking through problems and proceeding in an orderly and logical manner. In this text, we take you systematically through a process that helps you to read or examine any document with a critical eye so that you can determine for yourself whether it has usefulness in your life and work. If we are able to deliver this promise by the time you finish reading the text, it means that you will develop new skills and competencies that will permit you to pick up most any journal article or research report and read it as if you were fluent in another language—and you will be!

There are several other unique features of this text that we would also like to bring to your attention:

1. *There is an active process.* Rather than reading about research, you are required to learn, integrate, and apply skills that will be useful to you in deciphering studies. Furthermore, you will be engaged with thinking critically and analytically about relevant problems and issues. Activities, exercises, and practical examples are inserted throughout the pages to help you to personalize the material and apply the concepts to your work and to your life.

2. *Engagement is critical.* How hypocritical is it for supposed experts in the field—those who are supposed to know all about learning and how it operates—to not follow their own wisdom? It is difficult to learn any subject if the learners are bored, disengaged, or otherwise not motivated to study what is offered. Through the use of humor, practical applications, and dialogue with you, the reader, we hope to keep you involved as partners in this learning process.

3. *Attention to content and process.* All subject matters have content, the material to learn, as well as an underlying process. For example, economics has concepts such as supply and demand, but also introduces a means by which to make predictions. Research, as well, has lots of content and ideas that address concepts like reliability, validity, and so on. But there is also a *process* that organizes this material in a way that is designed to help you develop skills of critical thinking, problem solving, and finding information you need to know.

Ancillaries That Accompany the Text

We have included ancillary materials to further reinforce and support the learning goals of *Understanding Research*. These include the following:

- Evaluation tools to appraise the Introduction, Methods, Results, and Discussion sections included in journal articles and research reports for quantitative and qualitative studies.

- Example complete evaluations for a quantitative article and a qualitative article.

- An overview of American Psychological Association (APA) style to assist with reading and writing academic research reports.

Acknowledgments

First and foremost, we would like to acknowledge the ideas and work of Dr. Paul Jones who coauthored the first edition of this text in 2006 with Jeffrey Kottler. After receiving such a positive reception for *Understanding Research*, Paul and Jeffrey discussed ideas for a second edition. Unfortunately, Paul passed away and these efforts halted. Paul's expertise from the first edition of *Understanding Research* has been an excellent springboard for the ideas and information we present in this text.

We also offer our sincere thanks to our editor and muse, Kassie Graves, who provided insights and help whenever needed. We greatly value the courteousness, professionalism, and responsiveness from Kassie and the entire team at Cognella Academic Publishing.

Finally, we offer special thanks to university faculty who have reached out and shared their positive experiences with *Understanding Research*. These communications confirmed the need for a text that supports students and professionals who are learning about research. We also repeat our thanks to our students for sharing their honest thoughts on research and how to make learning about research engaging.

About the Authors

Jeffrey A. Kottler is one of the most prominent authors in the fields of counseling, psychotherapy, health, and education, having written more than 90 books about a wide range of subjects. Some of his most highly regarded works include *On Being a Therapist, Creative Breakthroughs in Therapy, The Mummy at the Dining Room Table: Eminent Therapists Reveal Their Most Unusual Cases and What They Teach Us About Human Behavior, Bad Therapy, The Client Who Changed Me, Divine Madness, Stories We've Heard, Stories We've Told: Life-Changing Narratives in Therapy and Everyday Life, The Therapist in the Real World, Relationships in Counseling and the Counselor's Life, Therapy Over 50*, and *On Being a Master Therapist*.

Jeffrey has been a counselor, therapist, supervisor, and educator for 45 years, having worked in a variety of settings: a preschool, middle school, mental health center, crisis center, hospital, nongovernmental organization (NGO), university, community college, private practice, medical school, and disaster relief settings. He has served as a Fulbright scholar and senior lecturer in Peru and Iceland, as well as worked as a visiting professor in New Zealand, Australia, Hong Kong, Singapore, and Nepal. He currently lives in Houston where he works on projects related to refugee trauma and is Clinical Professor in the Menninger Department of Psychiatry and Behavioral Science at the Baylor College of Medicine. Jeffrey is also Professor Emeritus of Counseling at California State University, Fullerton.

Laurie A. Sharp is a rising scholar within the field of education. She has authored or coauthored numerous publications that report empirical findings and describe best practices for practitioners and scholars at the K-12 and higher education levels. Laurie's publications cover a wide range of topics for all levels of learners, including the preparation of preservice teachers, the continued development of practicing educators, literacy and content learning instructional methods, use of digital technologies, fine arts education programming, online learning strategies, and differentiated instruction for diverse learning needs.

Laurie has been a public educator for more than 15 years, having taught in K-12 public schools and higher education. Currently, Laurie is the Dr. John G. O'Brien Distinguished Chair in Education at West Texas A&M University in Canyon, Texas. In this position, Laurie works in collaboration with school districts and university faculty colleagues to identify and coordinate research for current issues in education relating to best teaching practices.

CHAPTER 1

How This Book Came to Be

CHAPTER CONCEPTS

Perceptions about research

Personal and professional experiences with research

Premise of research

Introduction

This is a rather unusual textbook written by two co-authors who have very different backgrounds, interests, attitudes, and experiences related to the subject of research. Laurie teaches a graduate-level education research course on a regular basis and is absolutely passionate about the subject. She knows that most students are apprehensive about the course she teaches because the content is unfamiliar. Thus, students begin the course feeling extremely underprepared and overwhelmed. Laurie enjoys helping students overcome their initial apprehension toward research by designing engaging instruction to facilitate meaningful learning experiences.

Jeffrey, on the other hand, has devoted most of his career to teaching applied courses for prospective and practicing social workers, psychologists, counselors, teachers, and medical students. He has written dozens and dozens of books that rely mostly on comprehensive literature reviews and qualitative research methodologies (those that rely on interviewing and observing people). Although many years ago he studied research as part of his doctoral program, he has since focused primarily on clinical issues, especially as they relate to advocacy, social justice, and leadership. Although he relies heavily on research in his work, he has never taught the subject, at least in a systematic way.

More than 20 years ago, a colleague of his, Paul Jones, asked Jeffrey to co-author an earlier edition of this book, not because of his expertise on the subject but precisely because he tended to avoid it whenever possible. Whereas Paul, like Laurie, was a specialist in research, Jeffrey was a pure writer on the team, known for making complex ideas accessible. Jeffrey's job, therefore, was to make research far more interesting and enjoyable for readers and students rather than a subject to be dreaded or feared.

After Paul died several years ago, the book languished in obscurity even though a few dedicated instructors (like Laurie!) continued to require the book in their courses precisely because it was so different and engaging. When Laurie approached Jeffrey about doing a new version of the text, one that would retain the flavor and style of the original, this new, improved edition was born.

Perceptions About Research

In this introductory chapter, we introduce you to the subject of research in a personal and engaging manner. We have the ambitious goal not only to teach you to read and understand research, as well as to undertake systematic studies useful in your work, but also to enjoy the experience. We understand that you may feel a bit suspicious of this goal and perhaps even doubt whether it can be attained. We'll revisit this challenge again at the end of the chapter, but we ask that you move forward with an open mind. After all, if you expect to influence others in constructive ways—by taking risks, accepting new challenges, facing apprehensions and fears, taking on difficult tasks—then you must also be willing to do so.

An Overheard Conversation

"So," one student addressed her friend, "which classes are you taking next semester?"

"Ugh," he grunted. "I have to take that stupid research class."

"Poor thing. Maybe you can postpone it or something. That's what I'm doing. Maybe they'll change it as a requirement," the young woman thought out loud wistfully.

"No such luck," he said with a shrug. "I figured I might as well get it over with." His tone resembled that of an inmate beginning the long walk to their execution.

"Excuse me?" a professor interrupted. "I couldn't help but overhear your conversation." They had been standing right outside his office door.

The students laughed nervously and felt slightly embarrassed. After all, there was no secret that the research class was the one most students dreaded, avoided, and vilified.

"Sorry," the young woman began, "we didn't mean to… "

"No, no, that's okay," the professor reassured them. "I'm just curious though—what is it about this class that you dread so much?" He was especially curious because he was scheduled to teach the class for the first time.

"How much time have you got?" the young woman cracked.

"Are you kidding?" the other student jumped in. "It's a total waste of time. It's just some university requirement or something. I think you guys get together and plot ways to make us do stuff—you know—get through obstacles in order to get out of here. It has absolutely no connection to what I'm doing now or what I plan to do after I graduate!"

The professor was taken aback by the vehemence of the feelings. He knew from his own experience, first as an undergraduate and then as a graduate student, that research courses could be a little dry—okay, even a bit scary—but could some students really not see how critical the material was?

"Let me ask you a question," he said to the two students who were now leaning against the wall in comfortable positions. It was clear this conversation was important enough to them that wherever they had to go, they were willing to wait. He was even surprised that that they had temporarily put aside their mobile devices to provide their full attention. "How would you feel if the class had a different name?"

"What do you mean?" they both answered cautiously. They wondered if this was some sort of trick question. They had both encountered professors who were very skilled with catching students unaware and turning their words around.

"Look," he explained further, "we all know that the very word 'research' strikes fear in some hearts. You have these uneasy associations with the term, right?"

"Of course," the young woman answered. "You have to do these calculations and stuff. I hate math. When I was. ..."

"Actually," the young man interrupted, "they've got software that does that stuff now. I don't think we actually have to calculate things."

"But still," she countered, "it's just boring and irrelevant." Then she turned to face the professor. "You just make us learn it because you had to do it once upon a time." Half-joking, she looked at him as if this occurred in the last century (which it did).

"She's got a point," her companion agreed. "I'm going to be a teacher and coach, and maybe a school administrator someday. I need to learn as much as I can about getting through to kids and making learning as fun as I can. But research? It not only takes the fun out of what I'm learning, but it creates so much added stress. I mean, have you seen the text we use?"

The professor nodded his head in sympathy. He *had* seen the assigned book. It was big—huge actually. With very small print. But it wasn't the size alone that was so off-putting. The content and presentation were equally uninspiring. He himself was feeling a little trapped because most of the faculty members in the department had agreed to use this same text even though he found it daunting.

He thought to himself about how many students were so hungry for hands-on experiences. They wanted to do a better job preparing for their planned professions. They wanted to make connections to the content and understand it deeply. They wanted to change the world, and they couldn't see how studying research fit into the equation.

"Have you seen the table of contents in the text?" the young man continued. He pulled the book from his backpack and flipped to the table of contents. "I mean, just look at this stuff: quasi-experimental designs, formulating hypotheses, stratified random sampling, phenomenology, nonparametric statistics, inductive and a priori codes—I'm supposed to get excited about this stuff? And, can I ask you, how exactly does this relate to me and what I plan to do?" He shut the book and jammed it back into his backpack with a look of defeat on his face.

The professor nodded his head in agreement. He couldn't help but understand their resistance to a requirement that didn't appear directly connected to their life and career goals. He realized, with a degree of defensiveness and regret, that his department wasn't really practicing what they had hoped to teach developing professionals—that learning should be relevant and meaningful in their lives. Students could easily see how a class on finance and budgeting prepared them to be organizational administrators, or a class on interpersonal skills helped them as future practitioners, or a class about change and learning processes helped them to better understand human behavior—the connection between these courses and their prospective professions was quite explicit as to how the content will prepare them to do their jobs better. But it was much less obvious to students how studying research would help them in any significant way, if at all.

"So," the professor tried again, "let's get back to my question. I was wondering how you'd feel if the class was named something else."

"What do you mean, like 'Stupid Things You Ha[ve]" students laughed.

The professor smiled. "Well, kind of similar. Wh[...] 'How to Find Out Stuff You Need to Know?' Because [...] is all about. It's just a way to discover the answers t[...] about something that puzzles you."

"Yeah? Then why does it take this huge book," he [...] if it was the central piece of evidence in his case, "jus[...] this kid I'm working with right now can't seem to g[...] got part of the story, but he's got some learning disab[...] figure out. He lives in a shack with no heat. He can't [...] adults who often stay there—who knows where his [...] night. This kid doesn't have a clue what's. ..."

"But that's exactly my point!" the professor interru[...] research class could help you to find out what is going [...] of your other students for that matter? What if research was really just a way to look at challenges and problems in a systematic way and then search for things that would be helpful to you in working out an effective strategy?"

Both students appeared to be thinking. "Well," the young man started, "that would be pretty cool."

"Exactly!" The professor felt like he was a mountaineer who had just reached the summit.

This is a conversation that we have overheard, or participated in directly, more times than we would care to admit. It might be the most frequent reaction that students have when they review their program of studies and see the elusive re-quired research course. They aren't necessarily surprised that research is included in their plan of study, and they often equate it to be one of the necessary evils in

I mean, it still doesn't help - the guy just listed most of the issues without taking the research class ...

life that can't be avoided, such as taxes or rush hour traffic. But students around the world, in almost every discipline, often don't often have a clear understanding of what research is all about and how it can improve the effectiveness of their work and quality of their lives. We could even make a case (and we will) that there is no other subject that is more necessary and useful for success in life.

 Reflective Exercise 1.1

In small groups of three to four individuals, engage in a discussion about some of your fears and gripes about studying research. Because this is the last time that you are going to be allowed to complain freely about your apprehensions, get it all out of your system. Create an exhaustive list that describes your past negative associations with learning about research, as well as any unknown aspects that cause feelings of anxiety and stress. The more you can add to the list within your small group, the better.

Once the list is complete, review it and suggest categories to group similar ideas together. For instance, if the group created a list of foods most hated, potential categories might be: Fruits and Vegetables, Starches, or Meats. A more creative labeling of potential categories might be: Chewy Foods, Green and Purple Foods, or Foods Mom Made Us Eat. Use this same methodology with your small group lists to categorize fears and apprehensions related to learning about research. Try to create a minimum of three to five categories.

After categories have been identified, share the "research" your small group just conducted with the other groups. Compare findings and arrive at a consensus as a whole group as to what the main areas of resistance are regarding learning about research.

After the small and whole group activities, reflect on this process individually. How do you follow a similar strategy every week, if not every day, in your life?

Personal Stories: How the Authors Came to Know Research

Because we wish to make the subject as personal and relevant as possible, we thought we might introduce ourselves to you by sharing our personal stories of how we came to respect and enjoy the research process so much. Before you roll your eyes or skip this section altogether, we urge you to keep an open mind as we share our personal stories and consider the multitude of ways that research has affected your lives.

The sort of personal narratives that we use to introduce ourselves are not unlike a particular kind of research you will study later in which interviews are used to elicit personal stories. Themes are then identified in the narratives that can be used to understand a phenomenon at a deeper level.

Jeffrey's Narrative

When I was a kid growing up during the hot, humid Michigan summers, the neighborhood swimming pool was not only a social arena, but the main way to stay reasonably refreshed. The only thing that ever stood in the way of cooling off was the dreaded "Eat and You Drown Commandment." This was a rule enforced by our parents, without exception, that proclaimed that unless we waited a certain amount of time (to be determined by the parent on duty) after eating, we would immediately die of a stomach cramp if we went into the water. The negotiations went something like this.

"Mom, can I go in the water now?"

It was a sweltering day. Even the mosquitoes were too hot and languid to bother flying around much.

"What did you have to eat?" my mother would ask with rapt concentration. In fact, this is about the only time that I can recall my mother would pay much attention to me (but that's another story).

"Aw, just a peanut butter and jelly sandwich and a few fries." I could see her doing the calculations in her head and it didn't look good, so I quickly added, "But, I didn't eat the crusts of the bread."

"I see," she answered imperially, but it was clear I would definitely not be getting much time off for leaving the crusts. "Did you have ketchup with those fries?" she asked, already far too knowledgeable about my eating habits.

"Yeah," I said cautiously. Surely she wouldn't be charging me time for ketchup.

"And how many fries did you have exactly?"

"I don't know," I said more impatiently than I intended. But it was so darn hot out and I couldn't wait to jump in the pool. "Maybe 10 or 15."

"Which is it? 10 or 15?"

"I guess 15."

"Okay then. That'll be 40 minutes."

"Aw, Mom. 40 minutes!"

There was no sense appealing the decision. That was it. I was sentenced to spend the next 40 minutes sitting on the edge of the pool, dangling my feet in the water. Occasionally, a friend would swim by and tease me, but I was basically a kid serving the waiting sentence and was left alone to suffer in silence. In looking back, it felt like I spent most of my childhood summers sitting on the edge of the pool entertaining nightmares of what would happen if I accidently slipped into the water. We all knew there was no more agonizing death than drowning of stomach cramps.

Now, fast forward 15 years later. I am in a scuba diving class and we have begun our final briefing before we do our open water test dive the next morning. So far we've been through the litany of all the ways you can die underwater—something to do with Boyle's Law, Charles' Law, and all those other physics ideas that say if you go up or down too fast bad things happen.

"Remember," the diving instructor reminded us as a final piece of advice, "Eat a big breakfast tomorrow before you show up at the boat."

"Ah, excuse me," I said in a rather scolding voice that I recognized as my mother's. I raised my hand, waving it to get his attention. "But if we eat some-thing, *anything*, before we go in the water, won't we get bad stomach cramps and die?"

The instructor thought this is very funny but I couldn't figure out the joke. "Oh," he explained when he saw the look on my face, "that's just an old wives' tale. Actually, eating something before you go in the water helps to maintain your body temperature and prevent hypothermia."

"Wait a minute," I insisted. "You mean to tell me that all that time I spent as a kid dangling my feet in the water I could have been swimming?"

"That's right," the instructor answered gently, seeing that I was on the verge of tears.

I just knew that stupid rule never made sense. It was the same thing in gym class in those days. We weren't allowed to drink any water while exercising, no matter how thirsty we were, because supposedly it would make you sick. We now know, of course, that it's imperative to drink as much water as you can to prevent dehydration.

Once I discovered how misinformed supposed experts (like parents) can be, I resolved then and there that I would do my own research and not rely solely on the advice of others. Ever since then I've approached most every problem I face with an open but critical mind, and a willingness to investigate further what may be lying under the surface.

Laurie's Narrative

As a young child, I was driven by the perpetual question that so many young children ask, "Why?" I lived in a constant state of inquiry and thoroughly enjoyed learning as much as I could about topics that piqued my interest. I'm quite sure I asked, "Why?" more times than my parents care to remember, and I would be extremely frustrated with vague responses, such as, "Because." I possessed an innate sense of curiosity and sought explanations that provided facts about information.

During my early elementary school years, I continued to question things, searching for answers by reading as much as I could, and if my interest in the topic had not yet waned, I conducted "experiments" on my own. I was fortunate to have supportive parents who indulged my scientific interests, and some of my most cherished birthday and Christmas gifts were a human eye model, a chemistry kit, and a leather-bound *Encyclopedia Britannica* set. However, I was also an impulsive child who occasionally engaged in spontaneous and unplanned studies. For example, I remember dusting the fireplace mantle one day and became curious as to what would happen if I poured Liquid Gold dusting fluid onto the lit kerosene space heater. Needless to say, experiences such as these reinforced the importance of safety equipment (definitely a fire extinguisher for the above-referenced incident!) and procedures. Despite my developing interests in research, I did not view myself as a researcher.

During my later elementary and junior high school years, I had the privilege of attending public schools that cultivated opportunities to engage in age-appropriate research during science fairs. One year, I remember conducting an experiment with four plants to explore the effect of adding different vitamins to plant soil (my independent variable). I placed each plant in a different pot and provided each with the same amount of sunlight and water during the experiment. I did not add any vitamins to the soil of one of the plants (Plant A: the control group), and I sprinkled the same amount of crushed vitamins (Vitamins B, C, and D) onto the soil of the other three plants (Plants B, C, and D: the experimental group). As the "researcher," I kept a journal and logged my daily observations and measurements of each plant's growth (my dependent variable). Although I cannot recall the specific outcome of this particular experiment, I clearly remember the level of commitment I had while carrying it out, as well as the feelings of accomplishment and pride when I presented my findings during the science fair. However, I still did not see myself as a researcher.

Approximately two decades later, I was a 30-something fourth grade classroom teacher enrolled in a graduate program. I had reached the pivotal point in my studies where I was required to meet with my advisor and indicate whether I would take the comprehensive exam or complete a thesis. During this meeting, I did not feel strongly about the decision one way or the other and was leaning a bit toward the comprehensive exam because it seemed like a much easier path. Alas, my advisor informed me, without negotiation, that I would do the thesis.

I look back at this moment and am extremely grateful for my advisor's guidance and wisdom. I can honestly say that earning advanced degrees and becoming a researcher were not even on my radar at the time, but she must have sensed this potential. Thus, my role as a researcher matured from conducting an experimental design with plants and vitamins to performing an action research study with real people. Specifically, I used research strategies to explore my professional teaching practices systematically and determine which ones were most effective among students. For the first time in my life, I considered myself a researcher.

Acknowledging my identity as a researcher was a significant point for me personally and professionally. If I had been asked as a child to describe what a researcher looked like, I probably would have described a White male in a lab coat with crazy hair who resembled Albert Einstein. As a teenager and young adult, my description would have evolved into a more refined male who had earned his university degrees from Ivy League institutions and became affiliated with well-known scientific organizations or universities. In spite of the support and opportunities provided by my parents and schools, my initial perceptions were largely influenced by deeply ingrained societal views that convinced me to believe research was reserved for an elite and privileged group of older men. However, I now realize that research is essentially a quest for finding information that provides answers to questions. Moreover, if a person were to now ask me to describe what a researcher looks like, I would simply say, "Look in the mirror."

 Reflective Exercise 1.2

Write your own personal story that represents a close association with research and how it affected your life in a significant way. After composing your personal story, exchange stories with a peer partner.

After reading exchanged personal stories, communicate with your peer partner about what you learned about each other, as well as yourself.

A Synthesis and Road Map of What Will Follow

If you believe that knowledge is power, then you have already accepted the primary premise for research. Research isn't about mindless data gathering or senseless analysis. Research is simply about finding out things that you want or need to know.

Some questions can be answered with information already available, stored in libraries, electronic databases, and a variety of other venues accessible both in print and electronically. Our first task together involves how to critically evaluate that information and identify not only what the evidence is, but also what exactly can be appropriately inferred from it.

For many of the important questions in the education, health, helping, and social sciences professions, the evidence is far from sufficient. We are faced daily with questions for which evidence to guide our actions is simply not available.

That will be our second task together, how to design and conduct studies in authentic, real-world settings to provide such guidance.

Sharing our personal stories was intended, in part, to begin a relationship with you. We are real people with real strengths and weaknesses who share with you a commitment to learning and to using our skills to enhance the quality of life around us. Perhaps most relevant is that we are two curious folks willing to spend inordinate amounts of time plowing through pedantic texts, but also likely to scan the tabloids when checking out at the grocery store or conduct a Google search to find updates for a breaking news story. We are so motivated to understand ourselves, to make sense of the behavior of others, and to come to terms with the complex world around us that we devour every piece of information we can. Our life's journey is one long tour of research.

We should point out that there are potential pitfalls in research-based decision making. Sometimes the information people use to make decisions is simply incorrect, as evidenced in Jeffrey's example of swimming cramps. Sometimes there is insufficient attention to what is already known or new ways of thinking. And, sometimes the error is in how a question was initially phrased, how a research endeavor was designed and implemented, or how collected data were analyzed and interpreted.

Successful trial attorneys often follow a practice in which they try to address the weaknesses of their case, as well as the biases that the jury might have, before the opposition has the chance to do so. You are likely to have noticed that we began our journey together by doing just that—openly acknowledging the reality that many students have mostly negative feelings about research in general and introductory research courses in particular.

We recognize that there is probably nothing you will find in this text that is not available somewhere else. We are pleased and flattered, though, to be your guides and lead you on a path that we believe is both exciting and interesting. In the content that follows, we hope to earn both your respect and your trust in such a way that you catch some of our enthusiasm for the subject at hand.

Summary and Closing Thoughts

We conclude this chapter with a preview of our journey. The structure of our text is divided into three sections and based on a principle of meaningful redundancy. In other words, we are intentionally going to travel in a circle and, at times, repeat important points. Throughout the remainder of this first section, we take a closer examination as to why so many students appear to dislike research.

Our journey continues in the second section by examining the steps needed to critically evaluate published research reports. Whether or not you actually become motivated to conduct your own research studies (and we truly hope this will be an outcome of our journey), there are ongoing needs to review and critique what others have already done. To be honest, some of those needs come only because of course-related requirements. But, the importance of informed research evaluation skills extends far beyond your training programs. There are answers available in the research literature for many of the questions you confront in the practice of your profession, as well as in your everyday lives. But, all of us have found apparent contradictions in the abstracts or sound bites of those studies, such as when we are being informed about what foods we should or should not be eating to maintain a healthy lifestyle.

In the second section, we first begin by exploring tools that can be used to make sense of conflicting recommendations. Specific factors used to comprehend and evaluate published research reports will be examined one by one, beginning with how to find and evaluate the research objective in a published study and how to determine whether the literature review provides a solid foundation.

Next, we examine factors to consider in deciding whether the researchers have selected a research sample from which an answer to the question could even be anticipated. We also identify features to consider in assessing whether the researchers have selected an appropriate research design with which the study's participants could provide an answer to the question, and whether the data collection tools used in the selected design were sufficient to generate sought information.

We then investigate how to identify and evaluate findings conveyed in published research reports. For many, a particularly off-putting element in published research reports is a Results section that appears to have been written in a foreign tongue, such as the language of statistics in quantitative research studies. Some understanding of this language is crucial because simply skipping over the reported findings is not a viable choice when evaluating whether the stated conclusions are actually supported by the reported results. However, coping in a setting with a different language does not necessarily require one to be absolutely fluent in the language being used. If you've traveled in a country where English is not the first language, you no doubt already know that there are key phrases, such as "Where is the bathroom?" and nonverbal signals that suffice to meet basic needs.

The second section of the book then concludes with an examination of factors to use in evaluating the actual usefulness of the findings in a given research report. Primary attention will be given to how to evaluate the significance of the study, as well as implications noted by the researchers. This part of our journey is important. In the process of learning how to do something you most likely will have to do, such as evaluate published research studies, you will have also acquired the essential foundation for the activities that we truly hope you will now be motivated to do—design and conduct your own research studies.

The final part of our journey begins in the third section with an examination of the researcher's perspective. Curiosity is obviously a key element. Creativity, however, is of equal, perhaps even greater importance. Doing good research requires the mind-set of both an accountant and explorer. Like an accountant, organization and attention to detail are necessary research skills. And, like an explorer, doing good research requires a person who is motivated to expand their personal boundaries and courageously take risks associated with travel in only partly charted territory.

Deciding where you want to go is the most important part of the exploration process. Once that decision is made, there are some basic, simple, and mostly commonsense guidelines for the trip, and those form the remaining chapters in the third section of this book. We examine how a researchable question is framed, including the role and presentation of prior research studies. We also examine in some detail the factors involved in selecting an appropriate research sample and general methods associated with the different research designs for you to achieve your research objective.

We end our shared journey in the final chapter by addressing possible ethical issues researchers may encounter. A particular challenge for research studies in the education, health, helping, and social sciences professions is that our inquiries involve other human beings. There are legal safeguards necessary to protect the rights of persons who agree to be subjects in research studies. We examine those features and offer specific suggestions in the form of do's and don'ts. On the practical side, we provide novice researchers with some guidelines about scholarly writing so that findings may be shared with a wider audience.

CHAPTER 2

Why Many Practitioners/ Students Think They Dislike Research

CHAPTER CONCEPTS

Design of research
Myths and misconceptions about research
Negative feelings toward research
Purposes for research

Introduction

Just after the end of World War II, a physician by the name of Sidney Farber was agonizing over his sense of helplessness in treating children who were dying of an incurable disease. During this time, leukemia was a major mystery, a malady that appeared to spread throughout the body, absolutely impervious to any intervention available to medicine. Farber had already been able to determine that this condition resulted from mutated white blood cells, which was a major breakthrough, but he and others had yet to discover anything that would stop—or even slow down—the relentless, uncontrolled growth. When a colleague, Lucy Wills, found that anemia could be cured by folic acid, a vitamin ingredient of Marmite (a yeast spread favored in Australia), Farber wondered if it would have a similar effect on another blood disease. Farber formulated a hypothesis, which is the starting point for most experimental studies. He reasoned that introducing folic acid might cure, or at least block, the spread of leukemia.

Farber next recruited several children infected with the disease (the experimental group) and compared their progress with those who didn't receive the folic acid treatment (the control group). The results of his investigation were indeed dramatic. Unfortunately, the subjects receiving high doses of synthetic folic acid actually had the malignant cells spread much more quickly throughout their bodies and the children died. Obviously, the experiment was a disastrous failure and Farber was almost fired for this terrible error in judgment.

But wait! If folic acid had such a powerful effect on leukemia white blood cells, Farber questioned what would happen if he could develop an antifolic drug that might impede the production of more toxic blood? In other words, although his initial hypothesis was clearly wrong, and his experiment was a disastrous failure, the results provided new information that helped him form an alternative plan that was the exact opposite of what he originally conceived. It turns out that this was the first documented clinical trial demonstrating that remission of this type of cancer was indeed possible. Farber's investigation also provides a powerful example of how one type of research design is typically conducted:

1. An idea pops into your head that you wish to test to determine whether it might be sound.
2. You consult existing literature to identify previous research efforts, as well as unexplored areas related to your idea.
3. You make a prediction about what might occur if you introduce an intervention or treatment.
4. You select an appropriate research design and identify the research methods.
5. You carry out the investigation, collect data, and perform data analyses.
6. You formulate conclusions that confirm or refute your prediction.

Our goal in sharing this story is to reinforce that research is simply a systematic process of findings answers to questions.

Did you enroll in a research course for which this book is required with a sense of anticipatory delight? Would you have taken a research course had it not been required? Did you select this book on your own as a tool with which to engage in continuous personal or professional learning? Would you have picked this book from the shelf to read just for pleasure and enlightenment? For most people, the odds suggest answers of, "No," "Definitely no," and "Are you crazy?" In fact, if you answered, "Yes" to any of those questions, you might want to just skip this chapter and move on to the rest of the book.

It's not that we wish to be defensive or apologize for subjecting you to something that you may wish to avoid, but we wish to be open and honest with you from the outset to win your trust. We recall being required to study subjects that we never understood why they were really necessary. We are not saying that these courses weren't useful and included as part of our educational journey for very good reasons—just that it was assumed, from the outset, we had already accepted that we were forced to spend time and money studying the content presented in these courses.

When you finish reading this chapter, we hope to have persuaded you that studying research is worth your time and effort. Moreover, we hope to show you how research will help you to do your job, and perhaps even live your life, more effectively. How could one hate something like that?

The first question to consider is, "Do students really dislike research or just think that they do?" There is obviously some logical inconsistency in that question (if I think that I hate something, then I hate it). We propose, though, that in most, if not all cases, what's really going on is a need to examine, and perhaps reconstruct, the meanings associated with the words "research" and "hate."

We believe that, quite often, such negative associations arise from incomplete, if not erroneous understandings of what really is involved in doing research. Furthermore, we believe that feelings associated with the word "hate" are often actually just ill-disguised fears.

Did we just accuse you of being an uninformed coward? Obviously that's not a great way to initiate what we hope will become a shared and positive relationship during our journey together. But, we do believe that because research is such a naturally rewarding process, negative feelings about the topic must have roots in misinformation and misunderstanding (and that this, too, is often the result of how the material is presented).

We predict that you may be somewhat skeptical. You have been told many times before, by many other so-called experts like us, that certain things are good for you, such as tofu, Brussels sprouts, flu shots, and enemas. But, they still don't taste, smell, or feel very good. Is research really just another one of those bad-tasting medicines that is supposed to make you feel better? Or, in the case of certain subject matters—mathematics, philosophy, Latin—is research supposed to give you a foundation that allegedly makes subsequent studies easier? Skepticism is understandable and, in fact, is an attitude that serves you well in working with research. To tell you the truth, we were skeptical as well.

Reasons Why People May Think They Dislike Research

Among the reasons we've often heard about why people have some negative feelings about research include the following:

- "It's not why I got into this field."
- "It's boring."
- "It's irrelevant."
- "It's too hard."
- "I've never been very good at math."

Let's examine each of these reasons a bit more closely. A few of them do have merit and a few others are based on myths and misconceptions that we hope to correct.

It's Not Why I Got Into This Field

What drew you to your profession in the first place? If you are a teacher, you may have imagined yourself standing before a group of children who were utterly spellbound by your wisdom and wit, your caring attitude, and your deep level of commitment to them. If you are a mental health professional, you may have experienced difficulties in your life and want to be the beacon of light and ray of hope that you either had or wish you had to others who experience similar difficulties. With these professions and so many others, you likely never deluded yourself into thinking that you would get rich, but you have probably entertained dreams of changing the world, or at the very least, the small corner of it that is contained within your domain.

When you considered what it would take to become an exceptional professional in your field, you may have made a mental list of things you would need to learn. As you began your professional studies, you likely wanted to master the knowledge base related to the profession, including useful theoretical models and essential concepts. Of course it's important to be able to respond to questions that others direct your way, whether they are from clients, patients, students, employees, or curious community and family members. You would want to speak with wisdom and authority about your discipline and understand how to apply ideas to solve problems and serve others. To achieve this goal, certainly you would have to devote yourself to the diligent study of content related to your domain that would be critical for you to perform well in your job.

You might have also been hungry for information concerning practical applications—the techniques, strategies, and methods for achieving objectives in your field. As a student, you've had enough lousy or mediocre teachers in your life to know that being wise, smart, or knowledgeable isn't nearly enough. Unless you have learned the ways to structure these understandings in meaningful ways for others, then what you know is relatively useless. Thus, you are probably motivated to learn the skills, methods, and structures that are most effective in promoting lasting change. (It turns out, by the way, that it is research that ultimately allows you to discern what works best and what doesn't, but we'll get to that later.)

There might even be some required foundational information that you were not crazy about learning, but, you were still able to ascertain a connection, albeit a loose one, between taking those courses and being a better informed practitioner. Surely you understand that effective professionals are those who perform well and also have strong rationales to explain why they make certain choices and behave in particular ways.

You might add to your list of valuable study areas those that deal with cutting-edge technology, especially in a world is changing so quickly. It seems that every decade the tools at our disposal are rendered obsolete eventually, and we are required to reinvent the ways we do our jobs. With advances in augmented reality, social media, deep data mining, wireless energy transfer, artificial intelligence, nanotechnology, and even quantum teleporting, it is clear the world will be a very different place every few years, requiring us to operate and adapt very flexibly. Such technology training may seem daunting at first, but you likely see a clear connection between commitment to learning and profitable results.

Finally, we come to the part of your educational journey that addresses concepts related to research, including methods, measurement, and evaluation. Why in the world would this information be a necessary part of your professional training?

We think you'll agree that, at least once upon a time, there was a solid rationale for everything that was included in your professional training, either mandated by accreditation standards, licensure requirements, or specialists in the field. But that doesn't necessarily mean that these reasons still hold true or even that you would agree with them.

Perhaps the simplest and most direct reason we could give you is that if you ask a question about almost anything, and then look for answers, you are automatically doing research. You might not be very rigorous in your methods or systematic in your strategies, but you are still conducting a basic study. Of course, if you are relying on some type of systematic assessment or evaluation process, more likely than not, you will end up with "better" answers to your questions.

It's Boring

You're right. Research *is* boring. Or rather, it can easily be tedious if it isn't introduced in a way that emphasizes its more exciting and useful features.

Imagine you are a student who has just spent an obscene amount of money to purchase, rent, or access a textbook that you already know you don't want to keep one minute after the class is finished. In its printed form, the hardcover version weighs a ton. You turn through the pages and see there are more than 700 pages, for goodness sake! And, the majority of the text is in small print!

You thumb through the pages and hope there are at least pictures and cartoons—after all, this couldn't possibly all be words. You find the good news—there is indeed some content other than words. However, the bad news is that these alternatives consist of incomprehensible graphs, tables, and formulas.

Next, you turn to the table of contents. Reading through the content in this book is even more discouraging. Did someone actually imagine that readers would be interested in this stuff? Surely there must be one chapter that looks a little interesting. "Sampling and External Validity?" Nope. How about "Research Criteria to Optimize Observation Constraints?" No way.

Completely disheartened, you close the textbook. The class has not yet begun, but you already dread it. This could be the most amazing professor you've ever had and the most interesting course you've yet experienced, but you have already given up hope. A more interesting course would be "How to Find the Love of Your Life," or

"How to Get Rich," or "101 Ways to Make Healthy Meals in Less than 30 Minutes." But, a required research course? What could possibly be exciting about that?

In addressing this question, it is very important not to confuse the messenger with the message. The messenger, which in this analogy is a required textbook, may well be too long, excruciatingly uninspiring, and essentially incomprehensible. Some of them certainly seem to be so (although we suspect you would agree that research texts are not the only ones that meet these criteria). Remember, though, that the book is only about research. It isn't actually representative of what it is really like.

While waiting in the checkout line at your grocery store, do you ever glance over at the headlines in the magazines and tabloids? Most of us do because we are curious. Do media stories, even those about events unlikely to ever happen to you, draw your attention? Again, the answer is usually "yes," and the reason is because we are curious. Although tempted to digress into the evolutionary utility of information-seeking responses as a way to preserve our safety, if not our lives, a simpler proposition would seem to suffice. We are curious creatures, and research, at its core, is simply a way of satisfying one's curiosity. After all, why are people riveted by violent movies, slow down to take in the aftermath of traffic accidents, or seem drawn to movies and stories about zombies, vampires, apocalypses, or terror attacks? This isn't about a morbid fascination with the dark side of behavior. Rather, it is a means of doing research to anticipate and protect ourselves about imagined threats.

It's Irrelevant

Worse than boring is irrelevant. You can tolerate something that is boring if, down the line, it is going to be useful in some way. But, you may have yet to be convinced that you will ever use research on a regular basis. When you consider all the things that you will be doing as part of your job, much less all the things you want to do, research is likely toward the bottom of the list.

Consider those times when you have been stuck in some way, desperately in search of some answers, long before you thought about doing a research study, or even consulting professional literature. What did you do—call or text a friend? Consult with a trusted colleague? Ask a supervisor? With this in mind, the question becomes whether you want to have to depend on others for help all the time or whether you would like to be able to check things out for yourself.

In the chapters that follow, we make every effort to use illustrations that reflect real problems in daily work and life. With relevance as a primary goal, we focus first on the tasks you are most likely to encounter, evaluating a published research report, and then move to the steps for actually designing and conducting your research study, even if on an informal basis.

It's Too Hard

Well, if we're going to be honest with you, sometimes research *is* hard. But, then most things in life that are important and worth doing are difficult. Even though studying research, or any new discipline with its own language and elaborate concepts, is indeed challenging, it is not so hard that you can't master it with enough commitment and motivation.

You will find, in fact, that, apart from a new vocabulary, most research designs involve little more than just the application of logic and common sense. Consider the following scenario as an example.

A professor taught two sections of a history course during a specific semester (Section 1 and Section 2). As in most history courses, students were required to read assigned passages in the course text prior to attending class. At the beginning of each class, the professor gave a short quiz about the assigned reading and posted earned grades. At the end of the first week, the professor observed that the majority of the students were not scoring well on the quizzes.

Based on this data, the professor decided to try something new. In Section 1, the professor provided students with a study guide that they could complete along with the assigned reading. The study guide included vocabulary exercises, as well as questions about important concepts in the assigned reading. After one week, the professor noticed that quiz scores were higher in Section 1 when compared with quiz scores in Section 2.

So, did the study guides make the difference? The professor thought about this question and recognized that although this is possibly true, there are lots of other things that might have led to the improved quiz performance with students in Section 1. Maybe the students in that section were unusually bright and capable. Perhaps the time of day affected the outcome. Or perhaps the professor inadvertently did some things differently in one of the course sections. So, during the third week, the professor did something to sort this out. Students in Section 1 no longer received study guides. Rather, the professor provided study guides only to students in Section 2. After one week, the professor observed that quiz scores in Section 1 declined, whereas quiz scores in Section 2 increased.

This "experiment" provided the professor with some rather useful information. It became evident that students needed the assistance of a study guide to be able to demonstrate their understandings of assigned readings in the format of administered quizzes.

There was nothing especially complicated in this activity—it was simply good instructional practice. Trying the study guides with one class and then the other is just common sense. Keeping track of student performance through quizzes is also nothing out of the ordinary. What may be new, however, is the realization that the professor just conducted a quantitative study that employed an experimental research design. Later, you will learn why this activity warranted this designation, and you will learn research techniques that further strengthen the quality of the information provided from such studies.

I've Never Been Good at Math

Another assumption that people often have about research is that it demands a lot of number crunching and a deep understanding of things like calculus, trigonometry, quantum mechanics, and superstring theory. (We just threw the latter in because this physics theory is so complicated that even physicists don't understand it!)

We don't want to lie. Some grasp of quantitative concepts is essential both to read and conduct research studies. Understanding the formulas used in statistical analyses does involve the mastery of high school algebra. We do wish to stress, however, that research isn't really about numbers. Rather, research is about what numbers represent. A complete mastery of statistical formulas is not a prerequisite for either evaluating quantitative studies or doing them.

There was a time, not so very long ago, when computers were the size of trucks, or even buildings, rather than the mobile devices of today that you can hold in your hand or wear on your wrist. There was a time when you might have had to use a slide rule, a calculator, or even write computer programs to perform a decent analysis of data collected. At one time, lengthy calculations played a major role in conducting most research studies. Yet most researchers today probably can't remember the last time any hand calculations were required during their analysis of data. Nowadays, researchers only need to enter numbers into a computer program. That's it.

It is essential, however, to become somewhat literate in the language of statistics to evaluate the work of others or your own results. You're not starting from point zero, though. Some parts of the language are already in your repertoire, such as understanding the concept of mean, or average, of a group of numbers. Think back to your high school algebra course, and you may recall that a standard deviation represents a series of numbers in terms of their location to one another. Knowing how to calculate most statistics is not nearly as important as understanding what they mean.

Consider the following:

> On a 40-item test, I believe that all of my students will do well. If I am correct, which of the following combinations of mean (M) and standard deviation (SD) is more likely?
>
> a. $M = 95$, $SD = 2$
> b. $M = 95$, $SD = 5$

    c. $M = 85$, $SD = 2$
    d. $M = 85$, $SD = 5$

Because I believed that my students would all do reasonably well, the best answer would have to be either "a" or "b" because each of these answer choices has the higher mean (M) score. However, believing that all of my students would do well makes "a" the best choice because the scores would be closer together, as indicated by the smaller standard deviation (SD).

In the chapters that follow, a variety of statistical terms will be introduced and described. The underlying quantitative concepts are no more difficult than the ones in the example above, and not nearly as difficult as the quantitative concepts involved in learning to tell time, a task you successfully accomplished with much less mental fire power than you have now.

 ### Reflective Exercise 2.1

Consider the most common reasons as to why practitioners and students in the education, health, helping, and social sciences professions dislike research. Either individually or in a small group of three to four individuals, compile a list of reasons. When your list contains 10 or more reasons, review the list and select the reason that you identify with the most. Individually, compose a reflective response that describes why you agree with the selected reason.

After composing your response, share your ideas with a small group of peers. Then, engage in a discussion about ways to overcome negative perceptions associated with reasons practitioners and students dislike research.

Even We Thought We Hated Research

We don't wish to give you the impression that it is all that unusual that you might have some concerns or apprehensions about research. We were once students ourselves and, like many generations before us, we thought we dreaded learning about research, along with the best of them. You will notice that we keep inserting the word "thought" in the discussion because, as it turned out, we didn't really dislike research at all. Our perceptions were based on erroneous facts, misguided interpretations, and poorly executed learning experiences in the classroom and with our assignments.

Jeffrey's Personal Story

Numbers always scared me. I had a math phobia that can be traced back to my first algebra class. Actually, it must have started way before that time with long division—I could never line up the numbers correctly under the appropriate columns. But, my greatest trauma was during algebra when we had to walk up to the board and do equations. This usually involved X's and Y's and moving things from one side of the equal sign to the other.

What was never clear to me then (and even now) was what this had to do with anything important in my life. In order of importance, my priorities at the time were getting girls to like me, making more friends, stopping my parents from fighting so much, becoming a professional baseball player, and some day upgrading my mode of transportation from a bicycle. If by moving around the numbers any of these goals could have been reached, I would have devoted myself to the task with single-minded passion. But alas, neither algebra nor geometry, and later analyses of covariance, were explained in such a way that they were anything other than some sort of cognitive exercise.

Supposedly, math and statistics were going to teach us how to think logically and critically, and maybe they did, but the experience was certainly not much fun. For me, most of the time it was downright terrifying. This was the legacy that I brought to my research training during my first course as an undergraduate psychology major and later as a graduate student.

It wasn't until years later that, first as a psychologist, and later as the founder of a NGO (nongovernmental organization) focused on preventing child trafficking, that I had some burning questions that befuddled me. At the time I began my career, there was little written in the area of ethics. I tried to find some literature to guide my practice, but there was little available. This discovered "hole" has been the guiding principle in the research that I do—I become aware that what I'm looking for isn't there. Likewise, when a group of colleagues and students joined me in a project to identify and protect at-risk girls in Nepal who were in danger of being sold as sex slaves, we had to provide data to demonstrate that our methods were sound and that the programs were both cost-effective and successful.

Here's a more specific example. I realized that I was treating a disproportionate number of troubled children who were extremely difficult kids who were neither motivated to learn, nor cooperative with my agenda. I looked in "the literature," which means I checked journal articles and books that have been written on the subject of working with difficult and resistant children. Strangely, I discovered there was very little research done on this subject at the time. I found articles in nursing journals about working with difficult patients. I located articles in medical and dental journals about GOMER (Get Out of My Emergency Room) patients. I perused psychology, social work, family therapy, and education journals and found that whatever literature was available focused mostly on what's wrong with these people to make them so ornery, but little literature was available on how to deal with them.

This led to a journey (and research is very much a journey) in which I began interviewing teachers, counselors, nurses, and other helping professionals about their most difficult clients, students, or patients. I then began a parallel investigation talking to current and former challenging children to hear their side of the story. What I learned from these interviews and from reading just about everything written on the subject, is that many students don't come to us as difficult—we sometimes make them that way. In other words, my research changed from a study of difficult people to an exploration of difficult helping relationships. What resulted for me (and hopefully for others) were a series of guiding principles that are useful in working with so-called difficult and resistant people.

I have repeated this process a few dozen times since then and each time I follow a similar procedure. I have trouble resolving a conflict with a colleague, and this leads to a study of such relationships. I start thinking about all the weird things I do when I'm alone, and this leads to a study of what people do when nobody is watching. I wonder how I can be more effective in promoting lasting change, and this involves an investigation of that phenomenon. I think about my attachment to material things, and so I do a study of acquisitive desire.

I have found that I no longer fear research, but I embrace it as the means by which to explore the issues and questions that concern me most passionately. I have watched other professionals become burned out while I continue to flourish. I think one big reason for this is that because I see my job as continually evolving, constantly being informed by new research conducted by others and myself.

Laurie's Personal Story

When I reflect upon previous negative perceptions I held about research, I am first reminded of the dreaded, required research paper from high school. Completion of this research paper was a heavily weighted English grade, as well as a graduation requirement. The high-stakes nature of this project created a great sense of fear and stress among my peers and me. We literally felt that our futures were dependent on our performance with this research paper!

Although I had earned an excellent grade on my research paper (as you might have guessed, I actually held onto this evidence of excellence until I was in my 20s!), I despised the entire experience. Every single step of the process—topic selection, consultation of sources, creation of note cards, composing the draft, providing evidence of revisions and edits on the draft with crazy-looking symbols, and the production of a final copy—was prescribed, formulaic, and quite boring. There was little room for independent thought because every single component had a specific structure. I felt absolutely no personal connection to my assigned topic, which was an analysis of language in the works of William Shakespeare. For me, it was difficult enough to read and analyze his writing, but thanks to this research paper, I had the distinct pleasure of spending a month of my life immersed in researching and writing about it! This unfortunate initial experience with a comprehensive research endeavor had a strong influence on my perceptions toward the subject.

After high school, I approached research tasks at the university with a jaded attitude and the driving question of, "What do I need to do to get an 'A'?" To me, research was completely teacher-driven and one of the necessary evils required in my professional training. Thus, I became quite skilled with the art of fluff writing.

However, my perceptions toward research changed significantly during my graduate studies. In my master's program, I specialized in learning how to teach writing in Grades K-12. During one of my classes, I learned how to engage elementary-aged students in meaningful research endeavors that are personally relevant, inspire passion, and nurture curiosity. Like many other graduate students who are also full-time working professionals, I tested these teaching practices with my fourth grade students. While implementing these practices, I observed positive results that were contradictory to my own personal experiences. My students were motivated learners who were excited to learn about research and passionate about their self-selected topics. Every student completed the same common components—creation of research plan, gathering relevant sources, synthesizing information, and organizing and presenting ideas. But, the research process itself was not prescriptive and rigid. Rather, it was flexible, individualized, and personally meaningful. I remember thinking, "What if *all* teachers and professors taught research this way?"

From this point forward, I perceived research very differently. I no longer viewed it as a boring, irrelevant, necessary evil. I saw it as an opportunity to learn more deeply about a topic of significance. In looking back at my research experience in high school, I realize that the issue was not necessarily with the process, but it rested with the manner in which it was imposed.

Throughout the remainder of my graduate studies, I looked forward to completing research tasks. If I was not immediately interested in an assigned research topic, I would ask the professor if I could complete the same task using a different topic. To my surprise, almost every single professor I approached responded favorably.

Now, as a professor and researcher, I currently play a dual role: (1) I teach students about research, and (2) I design, conduct, and share findings from my own original research endeavors. If another person asked me how I felt about my work, I would firmly and promptly declare, "I absolutely LOVE my job!" I love helping my students recognize that their previous experiences have conditioned them to view research poorly. Confronting and examining these experiences is a crucial step in fostering more positive views toward research. Additionally, I thoroughly enjoy facilitating their learning experiences with research. My students often comment that their experiences with research are challenging yet enjoyable.

I believe that positivity is contagious, and there is considerable research to support this statement. Therefore, if teachers and professors seek to expose students of all ages to experiences with research that are encouraging, then the long-standing negative perceptions will dissipate. In this same manner, we, as researchers, have a responsibility to share our positive experiences with others. We do this perpetually with vacations we took, restaurants where we dined, books we read, and movies we watched. We share these experiences enthusiastically and with a genuine smile, which convinces other people that the endorsed experience would make their lives more fulfilling. Should we not also share our experiences with research in the same way?

Why Research Really Matters

Throughout the ages, a lot of very bright minds have advocated strongly that research skills are critical for most any professional. It is the principal way that we advance disciplines, test theories, and publicize what was learned. Research is nothing more, nor less, than formalized methods of curiosity. It is a way of finding out things you want to know. "If we knew what it was we were doing," Albert Einstein once said, "it would not be called research, would it?"

Research is more than just something you do to satisfy your curiosity or demands of your institution. It serves a number of significant purposes that may ultimately matter to you. First of all, you don't know nearly as much as you think you do. Without straying too far into the philosophical realm of epistemology and how we know what we know (believe it or not, philosophers have written thousands of books trying to answer that question), let's just say that "knowing" is a matter of confidence in the evidence available. In mathematics, for example, scholars can actually know something at the highest level—they can prove things (or say they can) based on carefully developed propositions and numerical values. For the rest of us, however, we are stuck with a world where things such as "truth" are often just figments of our imaginations, or at the very least, individualized perceptions of reality.

We wish to be clear, from the outset, that what you think you already know is really just a set of assumptions you have, and myths that you subscribe to are simply based on your evaluation of evidence. You read an article in the paper that says eating more brown rice will prevent certain health problems. Do you believe this? Do you think that this statement is based on reliable and valid data? More importantly, will learning this change your eating habits?

There are a lot of things that you know, or rather think you know, that are based on data that is flawed, biased, inaccurate, or just plain misguided. In some cases, you might have incomplete information or didn't get the whole story. In other instances, you may have misread the data or misinterpreted the results. In most cases, you probably took the word of the author because it was published in a reputable source. We hope to wean you of this bad habit, and as such, teach you to be a more critical thinker. And that happens to be the first important reason why research matters—it helps you to discover new things systematically and critically so you can have great confidence in what you know and have access to more accurate information from which to operate.

Let's review what you think you already know. If we consider only core beliefs that underlie your profession, there are likely a few dearly held beliefs to which you subscribe. How do you know these assumptions are true, or at the very least, helpful to you in the work that you do and the life that you lead? You may have accumulated this information from a number of sources. You could have read it somewhere. Someone whom you believe is pretty smart told you they were true. Or, your own accumulated experiences may have informed you. Regardless of the source, you walk around pretty certain that some things are true and others are not.

So, what are we trying to say here? Just three major points:

1. You don't know as much as you think you do.
2. What you do know comes from research efforts.
3. If you want to know more information that is reliable, useful, and will work consistently, you had better learn to be skilled at doing research.

 ### Reflective Activity 2.2

In small groups of three to four individuals, engage in a discussion related to the ways in which research has improved your personal and professional lives. Within your small groups, identify specific examples with detailed explanations. For example, you may refer to research related to seatbelt safety and share a personal experience where use of a seatbelt saved your life or the life of a loved one.

After each person has contributed, work within your small groups to identify ways that research can improve your personal and professional lives. For example, a group member who is a social worker might describe a current issue that they are encountering in their professional role. Based on this issue, they should then conjecture about possible research inquiries that might help them overcome this issue and perform their duties better.

After each person has contributed, reflect on the discussion that you just participated in individually. In what ways, both personally and profession-ally, does research matter?

Summary and Closing Thoughts

Before you begin the next section of the book, we wish to mention two main goals. One is for you to become a more intelligent and critical consumer of pub-lished research—that is, for you to be able to read and understand better what you see in popular and professional journals and online sources. An important part of this endeavor is for you to be able to use what you read and apply it in your work and life. All too often, we read interesting information that may present an alternative understanding, yet we continue on in our lives with a "business as usual" approach.

Secondly, we will teach you how to do research. We don't necessarily mean that you have to undertake massive studies and publish the results in academic journals. Our goal is to prepare you to be able to conduct a systematic study relevant to your discipline to learn more about what you do and identify possible ways to improve your practice.

CHAPTER 3

What Is the Question, and Why Is It Important? Evaluating the Introduction of a Research Report

CHAPTER CONCEPTS

Conceptual framework

Context and significance
of research topic

Directional hypothesis

Discussion section

Holistic design

Hypothesis

Introduction section

Linear design

Methods section

Mixed methods study

Nondirectional hypothesis

Null hypothesis

Objective statements

Primary sources

Qualitative study

Quantitative study

Research bias

Research questions

Results section

Review of relevant literature

Secondary sources

Skepticism

Theoretical framework

Introduction

C ritically reviewing a published research study requires some basic skills, core attitudes, and a little experience. The task is essentially an exercise in problem solving in which you ask a series of well-constructed questions and search for answers in the article. In some cases, you might consult other sources to validate information presented, as well as corroborate your interpretations. The process is similar to how a police officer investigates a crime.

In this chapter, we explore the specific elements that should (and should not be) apparent in the Introduction section of published research. You will first encounter an easily used rule of thumb to identify whether the manuscript you're evaluating is quantitative, qualitative, or a mixture of the two. Next, we will present some general information about content you might normally encounter in the Introduction and describe how to conduct a rigorous review of this content for studies that utilize, or emphasize, different research designs. Finally, we will conclude with a description and recommendations for a skeptical mind-set that we believe is useful for evaluating things you read critically.

When this chapter is completed, you can expect enhanced ability to

- analyze and critique information provided in the introductory section of published research reports; and

- use that analysis to (1) screen out research reports that may not warrant further attention from you, and (2) identify research reports that provide essential information to meet your needs.

A Quick Review

Before we begin, let's quickly review the overall organization of this text. In this section, your role is that of a consumer, an evaluator, and a critic of research studies published by others. In the next section of the book, we will revisit this topic with you in a new role—as an active investigator in which you will be the one completing a study and others will be scrutinizing the quality of your work. Both roles, consumer and researcher, are vital in research-informed professional practices. Remember, as the title of this text implies, good research leads you to find out information you need to know to do your job better (not to mention leading a life more accurately informed by relevant, accurate, and useful information).

In your professional role, most of your involvement with research will likely be related to using published research reports as guides for your professional practice. Learning the keys to being an effective consumer will also provide invaluable information for you to design and conduct research studies to investigate questions that are perplexing and interesting in a systematic manner. However, you can't very well undertake such a mission until you have first examined what others have investigated previously.

We anticipate that you may already be in some form of professional practice or are in a training program to prepare for such practice. Let's assume, for illustrative purposes, that you are functioning in the role of an instructor in some capacity, whether in the classroom or mentoring others. Imagine these examples of circumstances in which you might need to evaluate published research critically:

1. You have an idea for a new instructional strategy. Before you use it you'd like to know if others have tried it previously and how well it worked in other settings.

2. You have just attended a workshop and were impressed by the dynamic speaker who recommended a significant change in the way you operate. Dramatic results were promised, but implementing the change requires a great deal of your effort and time.

3. Your employer is implementing a new initiative that involves the use of common practices. You have been asked to serve on the committee that will develop and approve the new practices. To ensure that other professionals are well-prepared, data generated from implementation of these new practices will drive future decision making.

All of these examples are situations in which a professional will want to evaluate research effectively. In the first example, you have an idea and wonder, "How many others have already experimented with this strategy? What were their results? What were the limitations of the method?"

Using the work of others to guide your own practice is equivalent to having a personal consultant available at your beck and call. When you are feeling lost, confused, uncertain, or when you are hungry for new ideas, delving into existing research literature will provide you with material that is not only informative, but also supplies the means by which to judge its usefulness and relevance to your situation.

In the second scenario, it is quite likely that the workshop presenter made statements along the lines of, "Research has shown… ," or "Research studies support… ," or similar verbiage. Arguably, almost any idea can claim to be supported by a research study of some kind. As an astute professional, you know that findings from research studies may be misinterpreted, intentionally or unintentionally. In extreme situations, reported findings may be the result of scientific misconduct. Therefore, you decide to explore the claims made by the workshop speaker further, guided by the following questions: Who conducted the research studies? Who were the participants and where were they located? What was the design of the research study? What were the procedures? How were data collected and analyzed? Were interpretations accurate? Rather than accepting research claims made by others at face value, your evaluation efforts may reveal inaccuracies, flaws, or deceptions.

Lastly, in the third example, you and your colleagues will work collaboratively to develop professional practices intended to improve outcomes. Similar to the first example, you understand the importance of being informed by existing research that is useful and relevant to your situation. Moreover, as in the second example, you recognize that research claims should be evaluated critically to ensure that they are reliable and valid. In other words, we are asking you to continuously ask yourself two questions: (1) What is the evidence? and (2) What is the quality of this evidence?

 ### Reflective Exercise 3.1

Consider how research could have been helpful in your personal life or professional practices. Individually, list and describe examples of times in which you have thought about trying a new approach or technique. This can be something you've developed on your own, or perhaps something that was recommended by others. After you have identified three to five examples, share your ideas with a small group of peers. After everyone has shared their examples, discuss the barriers and challenges that have limited the use of research data in your life.

Parts of the Whole

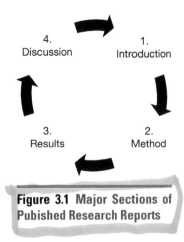

Published research reports are usually comprised of several easily identified major sections as illustrated in Figure 3.1. Following an Introduction, that may or may not have a heading, you will typically find a section called Methods that describes the procedures that were employed to investigate the phenomenon. This section will often have identified subheadings in which the researchers describe the research sample of participants used in the study, the research design, instruments and procedures used to collect data, and the analyses of data that processed the findings.

Figure 3.1 Major Sections of Pubished Research Reports

Quite logically, a Results section would follow in which—you guessed it—the findings of the study are described, often in the form of both a narrative description and a summary of the data. Depending on the research design, data may be reported in numerical (quantitative) or word (qualitative) form. The research report then ends with a section frequently identified as the Discussion in which the researcher has the opportunity to talk about the results reported in the previous section, including interpretations, meanings, and applications. This section summarizes the main themes and key points, offers recommendations for further research in the area under study, and addresses possible limitations of the research study.

We want to emphasize that although these are typically the major sections of a published research report, this is not necessarily a universal format. Sometimes, publishers and journals require a slightly different structure and format. Other times, researchers might use different names for headings and subheadings that are comparable for reporting their research.

To illustrate how these four major sections may appear in a published research report, we selected an article that was published recently in the peer-reviewed scientific journal *Emotion*. In Example 3.1, we present excerpts from each major section, as well as commentary regarding additional information that the researchers included.

Example 3.1 Major Sections of a Research Report

Introduction

A substantial and growing body of research has investigated the importance of wealth to subjective well-being. Most of this work has revealed a small, but discernible, relationship between income and well-being (for reviews, see Clark, Frijters, & Shields, 2008; Diener & Biswas-Diener, 2002; Diener & Oishi, 2000). Superficially, it appears that wealthier individuals—or at least, those who have sufficient wealth to meet, or marginally exceed, their basic needs (Kahneman & Deaton, 2010)—are also happier … we used objective, bank-reported measures of income and wealth.

Explanation

Author's commentary: The Introduction of a research report (often without a heading) begins with information about the context and importance of the study and ends, as above, with the researchers' objective statements, research questions, or hypotheses for the study.

Methods

Participants were customers of a large national bank in the United Kingdom who were recruited by e-mail in late 2014 to complete a survey about their financial attitudes and behaviors, as well as their life satisfaction. …

Explanation

Author's commentary: In the Methods section, the researchers provide detailed information about the research sample, data collection tools, and specific procedures used in the study. The detail is expected to be sufficient to allow another researcher to repeat (replicate) the study with a different group of participants.

Results

A path analysis was conducted to test whether the relationship between liquid wealth and life satisfaction was mediated by perceived financial well-being. …

Explanation

Author's commentary: The Results section usually uses both words and numbers to communicate findings from the study with specific attention to how they relate to the research objectives.

Discussion

Our results suggest that having a buffer of money available in checking and savings accounts confers a sense of financial security, which in turn is associated with greater life satisfaction.

Explanation

Author's commentary: A typical study ends with the Discussion section, which includes several paragraphs that address a summary of the findings, implications, limitations, areas for future research, and a conclusion.

Reference

Ruberton, P. M., Gladstone, J., & Lyubomirsky, S. (2016). How your bank balance buys happiness: The importance of "cash on hand" to life satisfaction. *Emotion, 16*(5), 575–580. doi:10.1037/emo0000184

What to Look for

We're now ready to begin the evaluation of the introductory material in published studies. There are usually three identifiable components in the Introduction section:

1. a general description of a specific problem, including its context and significance;

2. a review of relevant literature; and

3. objective statements, research questions, or hypotheses.

The information at the beginning of the Introduction has a singular purpose—to set the stage for what follows in the rest of the report. The researchers provide the reader with a broad sense of what is being investigated and why it's important.

In the next part of the Introduction, the authors describe relevant scholarship that has previously explored the problem under study. In some published articles, this is a summary of connected scholarship that provides a justification for the study being reported. In other published research reports, this may be addressed as a separate section with a heading, such as Review of Literature or Literature Review. Again, keep in mind this is sometimes labeled and structured in a variety of different ways even though the same content is covered.

In the last part of the Introduction, the researchers describe what their study was intended to accomplish. This is typically quite brief and may be written in the form of objective statements, research questions, or hypotheses that clearly identify the goals for the research study.

We also want to point out that you may encounter a theoretical or a conceptual framework in the Introduction of a published research report. Like the review of relevant literature, however, the researchers may address this framework in a separate section. A theoretical framework explicates the existing theory (or theories) that underpinned the entire research inquiry. By situating the problem under study in a theoretical context, the authors provide a conceptual foundation for how they understood and viewed the problem. On the other hand, a conceptual framework identifies key concepts for the phenomenon under study and explains how they are related. Along with narrative text, researchers may use a figure to visually depict the theoretical or conceptual framework for their study.

Example 3.2 Theoretical and Conceptual Frameworks

The following excerpt is from an article that was published in a scholarly journal. As you read the excerpt, try to identify the theoretical framework that was favored. Then, compare your findings with the explanation we provide at the end of the chapter.

Technology Acceptance Model

The theoretical background for this research draws from the Technology Acceptance Model framework. Inspired by theories from the psychology literature, mainly the Theory of Reasoned Action (Ajzen & Fishbein, 1980), the Technology Acceptance Model states that acceptance of technology is formed by a causal relationship constituting external variables, perceptions about technology, attitudes toward technology, and intentions to use technology. Two perceptions, namely, perceived usefulness and perceived ease of use, are the central operating variables that determine an individual's attitudes toward using a particular technology, which in turn, influences the behavioral intentions to use the technology. It must be noted that latter studies have dropped the attitude construct due to its weak role as a mediator between the perceptions and behavioral intentions (Venkatesh & Davis, 2000).

Perceived usefulness refers to the degree to which an individual believes that technology will enhance his/her performance in an efficient and productive manner. Perceived ease of use is the degree to which technology use is free of effort. Within the Technology Acceptance Model, perceived ease of use plays a key role in explaining the variance in perceived usefulness. These two constructs play a strong role in behavioral intentions, an individual's subjective probability to perform a specified behavior. Studies deploying the Technology Acceptance Model typically examine the mediating role of perceived ease of use and perceived usefulness between external variables (e.g., individual characteristics) and behavioral intentions.

Prior literature has endorsed the Technology Acceptance Model for its robustness in predicting adoption of technologies (King & He, 2006). A plethora of studies have applied this theory to various information services, technological products, and other innovations. For instance, the application of the Technology Acceptance Model was used to explain the acceptance of Internet (Porter & Donthu, 2006), e-commerce (Pavlou,

2003), e-government (Lin, Fofanah, & Liang, 2011), e-banking (Pikkarainen, Pikkarainen, Karjaluoto, & Pahnila, 2004), mobile phones (Kim & Garrison, 2009), and healthcare information systems (Kim & Chang, 2007). Although the Technology Acceptance Model has received considerable attention for its predictive ability of technology acceptance, it is still essential to assess the validity of the Technology Acceptance Model using a range of external variables to identify its influence on the Technology Acceptance Model constructs. As Legris, Ingham, and Collerette (2003) noted, external variables need to be tested in conjunction with the Technology Acceptance Model to increase external validity of the Technology Acceptance Model. Its due diligence is necessary to evaluate the chain of influence that external variables have on the Technology Acceptance Model constructs. Our study is the first to investigate technology acceptance among kindergarten teachers in early childhood education settings. We assessed the model using three external variables: computer self-efficacy, subjective norm, and personal innovativeness in education technology. Those variables are frequently applied along with the Technology Acceptance Model (Schepers & Wetzels, 2007; Teo, 2009; van Raaij & Schepers, 2008). Moreover, in the cited studies, the variables explain a significant amount of variance for the Technology Acceptance Model constructs.

In essence, the decisions you make evaluating the Introduction of a published research report should form the basis for your judgments. We do want to emphasize that the evaluation of a research report is not an all-or-nothing process. You may find flaws with some aspects of published research reports and value with others. For example, while analyzing the Introduction of a specific journal article, you might determine that it is not a useful research report in its entirety because the research problem was poorly defined, the significance of the study was unclear, or the context surrounding the research problem was too broad. However, this article may present an informative review of relevant literature. Thus, the article itself may not be useful in achieving your purpose, but it may provide information that leads you to other, more helpful resources.

The First Step: Quantitative, Qualitative, or Mixed Methods

The general information we provided above about what to expect in the Introduction of a published research report can be applied to most studies. Some differences in specific criteria for evaluation are needed, however, depending on the type of research design that was used in the study—quantitative, qualitative, or mixed methods.

We are confident that by the end of this text you will not only be able to quickly differentiate between the three types of research designs, as well as speak fluently about aspects of each (these skills come later in the book). For now, what is needed is a quick rule of thumb to decide which set of criteria to use in evaluating the material in the Introduction.

Fortunately, there is a relatively easy way to differentiate between research reports that utilized pure quantitative and qualitative research designs. In quantitative designs, the problem being studied will be defined, presented, and summarized using numerical data. Qualitative designs, in contrast, place emphasis on verbal descriptions (stories, direct quotes, experiences) of the problem under investigation. This is not to say that finding a number in the research report automatically excludes it from the qualitative category (and obviously you are going to find verbal descriptions in quantitative studies). But, for example, when stress levels among students are reported in a research report as a mean score of 31.4 with a standard deviation of 3.55, you probably have a quantitative study. A qualitative study of stress levels would be expected, instead, to provide detailed narratives about this phenomenon, such as descriptions of stressors, coping mechanisms, or its effect on daily living.

In some studies, the researchers tell you clearly in the Introduction whether their research design was qualitative, quantitative, or mixed methods. When the research design is not explicitly identified, you can simply look at the Results section of the report. If the primary focus in the Results section is numerical, and especially if those results are presented in equations, you will want to use the criteria for quantitative studies in your evaluation of the Introduction. On the contrary, if the findings are reported primarily using verbal descriptions, you will want to use the criteria for qualitative studies.

It may strike you as strange to think of data as something other than numbers or equations. However, data includes all of the information obtained systematically with data collection tools, whether those are surveys, assessments, observations, or interviews. In a quantitative study, the "raw data" collected are generally reported in numeric form. What this means, then, is that to differentiate between quantitative and qualitative studies, all you have to do is look in the Results section of the article to see how the researchers have primarily presented their data—in numbers or words.

Reflective Exercise 3.2

The titles in the boxes on the left and right were selected from recent issues of two different scholarly journals associated with the social sciences. Review the article titles for each journal. Then, respond in writing individually or discuss in small groups of three to four individuals each of the questions below.

Journal A	Journal B
• Learning from Others: An Auto-Ethnographic Exploration of Children and Families Social Work, Poverty and the Capability Approach • Black Mothers' Ethno-Theories of Moral Development: A Client-Centered Approach • Supervision: A Contested Space for Learning and Decision Making • Emotion Work in a Mental Health Service Setting • "All Teenagers Have Problems, Whether They're Adopted or Not:" Discourses on Adolescence and Adoption among Parents of Transnationally Adopted Teens	• Political Economy of Family Life: Couple's Earnings, Welfare Regime and Union Dissolution • Attention-Deficit/Hyperactivity Disorder Severity, Diagnosis, and Later Academic Achievement in a National Sample • Reducing Children's Behavior Problems through Social Capital: A Causal Assessment • Societal Inequality and Individual Subjective Well-Being: Results from 68 Societies and Over 200,000 Individuals, 1981–2008 • Understanding Trends in Concentrated Poverty: 1980–2014

1. Which of these journals appears to publish research reports that use quantitative research designs? Why?

2. Which of these journals appears to publish research reports that use qualitative research designs? Why?

3. Which articles appear to be targeted for practitioners? Why?

4. Which articles appear to be targeted for researchers? Why?

Reference

Jeong, H. I., & Kim, Y. (2017). The acceptance of computer technology by teachers in early childhood education. *Interactive Learning Environments, 25*(4), 496–512. doi:10.1080/1049 4820.2016.1143376

Introductions in Quantitative Studies

You have identified a journal article in a scholarly journal that may provide information regarding a new technique that you are interested in implementing into your professional practice. As we described above, you must first identify whether the primary focus of the research report is quantitative or qualitative. After skimming the Methods and Results sections, you determine that the extensive use of numerical descriptors signals the use of a quantitative research design. After this determination you can now focus on the extent to which the researchers have provided an appropriate foundation for their quantitative study.

Evaluating the Context and Significance

Before a study appears in print, several qualified professionals have already made judgments that the topic warranted the investigation. Once researchers have written a research report and submitted it to a scholarly journal for publication consideration, the editors of the journal decide whether the study is sufficiently important to send to reviewers. The reviewers are peer professionals who have some expertise in the general area. If the research report is sent out for peer review, it is typically "blinded," meaning all identifying information about the authors has been masked, and sent to multiple reviewers. Each reviewer uses specific criteria, often in the form of a rubric, to conduct an independent evaluation regarding the quality of the research report and make a publication recommendation: reject, revise and resubmit, or publish. After reviewers submit their independent evaluations to the editors, they compare reviews, which may not be unanimous, and make final determinations. Most of the time, authors are provided with specific and detailed feedback to make at least minor revisions.

You should know that the motivation to undertake research is not just driven by altruism and the search for truth. There is a personal context to the research piece, as well as a professional one. Scholars often keep their jobs, as well as earn promotions and pay raises on a myriad of factors, including their research productivity. This means that they must conduct empirical studies and publish research reports in refereed journals, that is, those that have a peer review process.

We do not mean to imply that most of the research studies you will read were completed solely for selfish reasons of job retention or pay increases. Quite the contrary, because anyone functioning in academic life for very long has to enjoy doing research to some extent. But, we do want you to understand that scholars are under extraordinary pressure to demonstrate their productivity by conducting research and sharing their findings.

What all this means is that when you are reading a published research report, you are looking at a piece of work that not only advances knowledge in the field, but also advances the careers of the researchers. This is certainly true for us as well—we have written this book because we believe it is important and useful for creating a more engaging and illuminating presentation of the subject, while also serving personal (providing extra income) and professional professional (career advancement) needs.

It is also important to keep in mind that when you evaluate the context and significance of the Introduction, you are not only checking the work of the researchers, but also of individuals associated with the journal. Those individuals include the editors and reviewers, who are usually faculty and staff members at various institutions, rather than employees of the publisher. When a research report is initially accepted for publication by a journal, the editor and reviewers almost always require the researchers to perform extensive rewrites of specific areas within the report. The final version of the research report that appears in the published journal, which may be in print or online, is actually a collaborative effort of several individuals.

There are two primary factors to use in this part of the evaluation:

1. How important is the topic?
2. To what extent is the presentation clear and objective?

The first question, importance of the topic, is actually twofold. Do the researchers provide a sound rationale that there is a good reason for the problem to be investigated? Do the researchers provide a broad societal context for the problem?

Importance of topic is also a personal decision, and whether the general topic of a research study matters to you will depend on a number of factors. Are you looking for help with a particular problem in your practice? Are you interested in broadening your knowledge about other human service areas? Maybe you're just curious. Perhaps you are just interested in learning more about a particular facet of human behavior, learning, or some unexplained phenomenon.

We make personal relevance the initial factor in the evaluation of the Introduction. A fair degree of concentration and commitment is involved in reading carefully, scrutinizing, and making sense of a research study. Given a choice of the following items on the nightstand by your bed—a professional scholarly journal, a riveting piece of fiction, or an electronic device installed with social media apps—which would you reach for first?

The Introduction provides your first real opportunity to learn what the research study is really about. The article title and abstract may not necessarily be dependable signals about what is actually in the research report. It is only by reading the

Introduction that you can make the best determination about whether the topic is of sufficient interest and significance to justify your time and effort.

Assuming that the research report has passed the relevance test, your next task involves evaluating the clarity of the presented information, which is again a twofold question. First, writing style is a part of the consideration, but you should look for more than just engaging prose. As you begin reading the report, do the words clearly portray the general intent of the study? Is the general problem area quickly evident, or do the researchers appear to be rambling around a variety of topics?

You also will want to look for evidence of bias in the language chosen by the researchers. This will be a value judgment and is a bit tricky. Researchers are human. They bring to every study their beliefs, values, attitudes, and even biased views.

The rules of science do not prohibit a researcher from having prior beliefs or even anticipated outcomes. What you are looking for is evidence to suggest that the researchers may have such strong beliefs that, either purposefully or inadvertently, may have been slanted toward their desired outcome. In this instance, the editorial and peer review processes employed by the journal may not be of help—editors and reviewers may also exhibit a preference for certain outcomes and professional views.

You may find it helpful to picture the complete Introduction of a quantitative research report as a series of concentric rings, with each defining increasingly specific boundaries for the study (see Figure 3.2). At the beginning of the Introduction, the researchers begin with the outer circle, the world of knowledge, and complete the first circle, carving out a general description for the problem under investigation from within that world. After reading the beginning of the Introduction, you must determine whether the researchers presented a sound rationale for their study in a clear manner.

Evaluating the Review of Relevant Literature

Although the review of relevant literature in quantitative research studies may bring back memories of writing lengthy term papers, the objective is quite different. The obligation of the researchers is to provide the foundation in prior research on which their specific research questions or hypotheses rest. They narrow the scope of the investigation, in effect, drawing a circle inside the first one with more limited boundaries (see Figure 3.3). Although the prose is usually quite dense, this abbreviated summary of what was previously written about the subject is absolutely critical before advancing future knowledge.

There are four primary factors to use in evaluating the review of relevant literature:

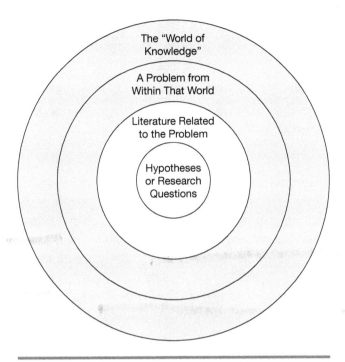

Figure 3.2 Boundaries for Context and Significance

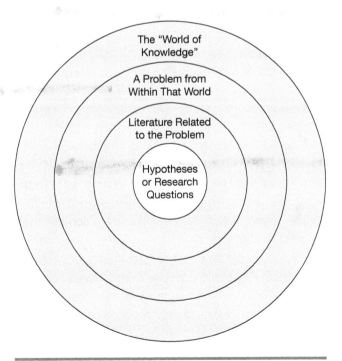

Figure 3.3 Boundaries for the Review of Relevant Literature

1. To what extent is the viewpoint balanced and appropriately comprehensive?
2. How has attention been given to both historical precedent and more recent work?
3. How coherent is the theme of the review of relevant literature?
4. Where did the researchers appear to emphasize primary, rather than secondary sources?

Balanced viewpoint. The purpose of the review of relevant literature is to make the case that the problem under study is important and supported by previous research. Thus, it is neither surprising nor problematic to find that most of the works cited support the beliefs of the researchers. Objectivity, however, is a critical element in quantitative research, and it would be hard to think of any important topic in which all previous studies pointed in the same direction. You can reasonably expect that the review of relevant literature should include some disparity with findings from previous research efforts.

Appropriate time frame. The time frame from the initiation of a research study to its final report being accepted and published is usually a period of two or more years. With this in mind, it is not necessarily a weakness for the most recent citation in a review of relevant literature to be dated a few years earlier than the article was actually published. However, when the most recent citation is five or more years old, you should expect the researchers to provide some explanation for why more recent studies were not included.

There is another side to this same coin. The quantitative research tradition is built on the basis of accumulated knowledge. When all prior research cited in the review of relevant literature are relatively recent, you have reason to question if the authors did their homework and considered historical precedents for their investigation, maybe even the possibility that their exact research design had been used in a prior study.

In addition to the earliest and latest citation dates, you should also be concerned about any lengthy unexplained gaps in the dates. If, for example, the review of relevant literature cited studies published in the 1970s and studies published in the year 2000 with nothing in between, it is legitimate for you to wonder why this is the case. There may indeed be an explanation because sometimes a topic receives a great deal of attention for a period of time and then interest in it appears to wane. But, it would be the researchers' responsibility to acknowledge any gaps in time and provide some possible explanation for it.

Coherent theme. Consider two scenarios. In the first, the objectives of the research study were chosen by the researchers after careful and extensive review of previously published work. These objectives appeared to be extensions of previously published work. In the second scenario, the researchers first conducted a research study and then searched previously published research reports that appeared to be related.

Scenario 1 gets a grade of A, whereas Scenario 2 gets a grade of F. Surveying the literature after a study has already been completed is not an acceptable way to conduct quantitative research. The rules for qualitative research are quite different because there is recursive or circular process involved in which the researcher is continuously exploring a question that may lead to unexpected directions.

Clarity in writing style is extremely important, and skilled writers may have the ability to make Scenario 2 look as if the literature was consulted prior to conducting the study. Most often, though, we believe that the "after the fact" or incomplete review of relevant literature will be evident in the way the researchers present the material. Some of us have been accused of using commas in our writing the way we use salt with our dinners—just sprinkle one in every once in a while. In a similar manner, if it appears that citations have just been sprinkled in for effect, you have evidence of a poorly conducted survey.

Primary sources. Primary sources are firsthand accounts, original documents, or research reports written by those who conducted the study. Secondary sources are descriptions provided by others who were not the original observers, authors, or researchers. As part of a review of relevant literature, primary sources are preferred.

Using secondary sources is permitted and may have been the researchers' only choice. Some sources are difficult to find, and a new wrinkle, aptly labeled as "web rot," has exacerbated the problem when information is published solely on the Internet. The latter phenomenon occurs when electronic files are intentionally or inadvertently deleted or moved, which results in broken or missing links.

Relying on secondary sources is dangerous and weakens ideas that researchers present in the review of relevant literature for one important reason. How do you know that the secondary source provided an accurate description, either intentionally or unintentionally, of the original source?

Evaluating the Objective Statements/ Research Questions/Hypotheses

This part of the Introduction typically comes just before the specific techniques and procedures of the study used are described in the Methods section. It is often only a paragraph or two in length and introduced with an assertion, case, or justification that the problem under study is important. The researchers may cite previous research that supports the reasonableness of the specific focus in their study. This becomes, in effect, the third and final ring (see Figure 3.4). When you

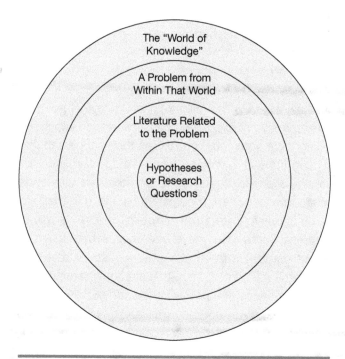

Figure 3.4 Boundaries for Objective Statements/Research Questions/Hypotheses

finish this section of a research report, you should have a clear picture of exactly what the study was intended to accomplish.

There are two primary factors to consider in your evaluation of this part of the Introduction:

1. To what extent were the objective statements/research questions/hypotheses clearly stated?

2. How has the review of relevant literature supported development of the objective statements/research questions/hypotheses for the current study?

Before we look at these questions in more detail, let's quickly review the underlying premises in the scientific method and the role of the hypothesis. The basic idea is that of an ongoing process. Each new research study adds to, clarifies, or disputes the findings of earlier research, incrementally adding to knowledge of the literature base for a specific topic. Each researcher, in effect, is expected to stand on the shoulders of the researchers who came before.

Despite the portrayals of scientists and researchers we see in past and present mad scientist movies—*Back to the Future, Frankenstein, Dr. Jekyll and Mr. Hyde,*

Underworld—real scientists and researchers are not superior creatures who just mess around with stuff until something remarkable happens, even though that has happened on occasion and resulted in the discovery of Velcro, antibiotics, X-rays, microwave, and cornflakes. They are not always misunderstood and shunned by society (and, they don't necessarily live in castles where the darkness is frequently shattered by thunder and lightning storms).

Researchers are mortal humans who begin an investigation with a prior belief or prediction about its outcome, which is called a hypothesis. They subject this belief to a data-based test and then modify their beliefs based on the outcome of the study. We realize that you may already have past associations with the term "hypothesis," but further precision with the definition may be useful. Essentially, a hypothesis is just an educated guess about what will result if a certain action is taken. Now why, you might ask, would anyone want to predict the results of a study before it has even been done?

There are at least two ways to address that question, one practical and one more philosophical. The practical answer is that this step is the tradition-bound expectation in a quantitative research study: first the context, then the review of relevant literature, then the hypotheses warranted by prior research. (We realize, by the way, that "because you are supposed to" doesn't really answer the question.)

From a more practical perspective, predicting what will occur does not necessarily mean that is what is desired. Instead, making such a prediction informs the reader that the researchers do, in fact, know enough about this topic to generate plausible predictions. Regardless of the outcome, something new will be learned. One could argue that a researcher who doesn't know enough about a topic to form a sound hypothesis probably doesn't know enough about the topic to be doing the study in the first place.

Let's try to answer the question once more, this time from a more philosophical viewpoint. Is there anything in the world about which absolutely nothing is known? The perspective of the quantitative researcher is that the answer to that question is a resounding, "No." Obviously, how much is known about different topics varies dramatically. The tradition of quantitative research is that all new studies are to be informed by the results of information obtained from prior studies. With access and comprehension of that information, it is possible to form a plausible prediction about the outcome of a related research endeavor.

Research hypotheses. There are three types of hypotheses that researchers use to predict the outcome of a research study:

- directional,
- nondirectional, and
- null.

In a directional hypothesis, the researchers believe that there will be differences between the groups being compared on some variable or that there will be a significant relationship between two or more variables. The directional hypothesis also predicts the direction of the difference or relationship, as shown below.

- Female graduate students are more likely than male graduate students to participate in course-related, closed social media groups.
- There is a significant positive relationship between the amount of time spent studying and earned scores on final examinations.

Simply put, researchers use a directional hypothesis to predict that something significant is going to happen, and they know which way it will go.

A nondirectional hypothesis is quite similar. As illustrated below, the researchers believe that there will be a difference between groups or a relationship between variables, but the expected direction is not specified.

- There is a gender difference among graduate students who participate in course-related, closed social media groups.
- There is a significant relationship between the amount of time spent studying and earned scores on final examinations.

Notice that the difference between the directional and nondirectional hypotheses associated with study time and final examination scores is only one word. The word "positive" in the directional hypothesis says that the researchers believe that more study time results in higher exam scores.

With the nondirectional hypothesis, the researchers suggest only that there is some relationship between the two variables of study time and exam scores. The nondirectional hypothesis would thus be supported with findings that showed either (1) more study time was associated with higher grades, or (2) more study time was a predictor of lower grades.

The null hypothesis, as you would expect, predicts that there will be no difference between the groups or that there is no relationship between the variables. The null form of the example hypotheses above would be:

- There is no gender difference among graduate students who participate in course-related, closed social media groups.
- There is no relationship between amount of time spent studying and earned scores on final examinations.

More and more often, researchers choose to end the Introduction of a quan-titative research report with stated objectives or research questions, rather than listing specific hypotheses. These alternate forms to hypotheses are primarily a matter of style, not substance. Therefore, it is reasonable to infer that stated objectives or research questions have roots in hypotheses formulated by the researchers. For example:

- How do male and female graduate students participate in course-related, closed social media groups?
- What is the relationship between the amount of time spent studying and earned scores on final examinations?
- The purpose of the present study was to investigate the relationship between gender and participation in course-related, closed social media groups among graduate students.
- The purpose of this study was to explore the relationship between amount of time spent studying and earned scores on final examinations.

In lieu of hypotheses, when researchers use objective statements or research questions in the Introduction, it will be difficult to identify whether the research-ers' predictions were directional, nondirectional, or null. In effect, objective statements and research questions typically just assume the characteristics of a null hypothesis.

You've now come to the end of the Introduction of a quantitative study. The researchers have provided a context for their study and cited prior research that is directly related to the problem being studied. The researchers have also identified specific objectives for the study, perhaps written in the form of hypotheses, but more likely presented as objective statements or research questions. How do you evaluate the quality?

The first, and most important factor, is clarity. What are the researchers at-tempting to accomplish with their study? This part of the research report isn't going to tell you how the research study was conducted—that comes later. But, after you finish reading the end of this section, the objectives of the study should be completely clear.

The second evaluative factor is whether the objectives of the study were supported with the review of relevant literature. This factor is a little harder to determine. Unless you have some expertise with the problem being investigated, it will be difficult to know whether appropriate relevant literature has been cited. You may have to retrieve and review the literature cited by the researchers in order to make this determination.

To summarize, the Introduction to a quantitative research report is linear by de-sign. It is assumed that general knowledge about a topic (world of knowledge) led the researchers to (1) identify a specific problem and ascertain knowledge about that problem from prior studies; and (2) formulate specific objective statements, research questions, or hypotheses to investigate the problem. Each element should be completed and reported in a set order.

 Reflective Exercise 3.3

This is a good time to take a break and decide if the quantitative/qualitative categorization is as clear as we have claimed. Either on your own, or with a partner, access a recent issue of a scholarly journal from your discipline. Skim each article published in the issue and identify which articles are research reports for original studies, as opposed to conceptual papers or literature reviews. Among these studies, identify whether they employed a quantitative research design, qualitative research design, or mixed methods design with either a quantitative or qualitative emphasis.

Introductions in Qualitative Studies

Earlier in this chapter we suggested a simple technique to classify a research study as primarily quantitative or qualitative. You will recall that quantitative studies emphasize numerical descriptions, whereas qualitative studies usually report verbal descriptions. The differences between these two approaches, however, are much deeper than just the format of the data presentation. Although the same general elements are used for evaluating the Introduction section of a qualitative research report, there are differences that require attention to some of the special features with qualitative research designs.

We suspect you will immediately notice that this section is significantly shorter than the material you just finished. In part, this is because some of the evaluative criteria are quite similar and can be presented with less detail. The more important reason for the shorter length, though, has to do with some basic characteristics of the qualitative method. Most individuals find qualitative reports much easier to read than research reports that describe quantitative studies because they more closely resemble stories we read. Settings and context are described using rich details. For example, thorough depictions of the participants make them become real to you.

We want to emphasize that one research approach is not better than the other. Rather, each approach is designed for a different purpose, makes use of different methodologies, and is based on different assumptions. You will want to be "fluent" in reading, understanding, and critically evaluating both kinds of studies, as well as those that combine both approaches.

The qualitative approach is, in essence, a different way of knowing about things. Qualitative researchers follow a somewhat different set of rules in both doing and reporting their research, and there other expectations associated with the information reported in the Introduction.

In contrast to the linear requirement in quantitative research reports, qualitative research reports are holistic by design. Research questions emerge during the study, and these may be modified in light of what researchers discover along the way. The review of relevant literature is ongoing throughout the study—as researchers collect data, their questions evolve, which leads to continued reading, followed by altered questions. Thus, qualitative research does not typically consist of a series of discrete steps that must be completed in a specific order. The qualitative researcher has more flexibility to adapt their investigation to fit specific needs in much the same way that a practitioner may make adjustments in their practice for a particular individual or setting, based on data gathered and analyzed.

One example might begin with a qualitative researcher investigating the ways that organizational and corporate leaders apply particular strategies to empower and motivate their teams. During initial interviews, one leader revealed that he tests new ideas by applying them in her daily life. "This one time," she shared, "I thought it would be interesting to make a more deliberate effort to compliment people for the ordinary things that they do—at a checkout line or a service desk. I started to notice changes, not only in the ways that they responded, but also the ways I felt about myself. So, that gave me an idea that maybe I should start doing that more at work."

Once the researcher transcribed the interview and considered the data above, he changed the focus of his study to explore more about how leaders use their knowledge and skills in daily life and how such experiences better inform their professional functioning. This also led him to review new literature on this subject, one that he found little systematic research that had thus far been undertaken. In turn, this encouraged him that he had stumbled upon a significant new area for further investigation.

The holistic focus does not, however, suggest that qualitative researchers can be haphazard or less rigorous in conducting or reporting findings from their studies. Qualitative research reports have specific features that you can use in your evaluation of the Introduction.

As with quantitative research reports, the Introduction of qualitative reports is usually the text that precedes the Methods section. In this initial section, you should be able to identify a general statement about the problem being studied, its overall context and significance, and a review of relevant literature. In some qualitative studies, the researchers may even discuss their personal motives for doing the study as a way to locate themselves and disclose any potential biases. For example, in a study of aggressive teenagers and how they respond to different treatment interventions, the researchers may not only mention that they were motivated to pursue this study because of their work with this population, but also because of very personal experiences that took place within their families. As you can readily see, whereas objectivity is a primary value in quantitative studies and subjectivity is the enemy, one's personal motives, perceptions, and subjective experiences are acknowledged and even embraced in qualitative studies.

Another feature unique with qualitative research reports are the reviews of relevant literature are far more comprehensive, interdisciplinary, and encompassing than those presented in quantitative reports. For example, researchers in a health profession, such as nursing, might include previous studies from counseling, history, the humanities, and the social sciences. For instance, in an investigation of the phenomena of crying, researchers may interview people about the ways they "speak" in the language of tears. This might involve covering literature not only in the psychology of emotional expression, but also in anthropology, sociology, fiction, endocrinology, biochemistry, linguistics, gender studies, and evolutionary sociology. In order to understand such a complex phenomenon as to how and why people leak water out of their eyes when they are emotionally aroused, it would be necessary to present a rich and complete context for the present study to examine crying as a form of interpersonal communication.

Evaluating the Context and Significance

The Introduction of a qualitative article begins with the statement of a problem or issue that is to be explored. Although quantitative studies test hypotheses, measure comparisons between groups, and collect specific data about differences, qualitative studies are ideal for exploring relatively new phenomena, as well as how people experience them. Nevertheless, just as you would with any research endeavor, your first objectives are to assess the relative importance of the study, as well as its overall clarity.

Blatant bias in language used should raise doubts about the researchers' willingness to be guided by the data. But, when evaluating a qualitative research report, some caution is needed regarding how you apply this criterion. This approach, by design, is research in which the investigators are typically involved with, rather than attempting to stand apart from, the problem being studied. A style of writing with a more personal approach does not in and of itself signal a biased researcher. What you are looking for is any evidence that the researchers were so involved with their initial beliefs and preferences that they would be likely to identify and report only the findings consistent with them. Value-laden terminology will often be more evident and is not necessarily unacceptable, particularly when a credible resource is cited.

A warmer, less distant tone is usually evident in qualitative research reports. Consider, for example, the opening vignette presented at the beginning of the qualitative report in Example 3.3.

Example 3.3

In a colonia along the U.S.–Mexico border, some parents rely on other people to help them pay their bills and read mail because they cannot read. Domestic violence often goes unreported or unaddressed by authorities, much of it occurring within sight of children in small one- or two-room homes constructed of cinderblocks or wooden pallets. Violence, extortion, government malaise, and corruption are common and viewed by some as normal or unalterable. Public schools have a 4-hour school day and classrooms with 40 to 50 students. By sixth grade many children drop out in order to work to help support their families. Raw sewage erodes unpaved streets, electricity is taken from power lines using car jumper cables, and trash accumulates alongside streets and in alleyways. Parents in the colonia laughed at Mrs. Donna when she initially talked with them about cofounding a school to prepare children for middle school, high school, college, and professional careers.

Reference
DeMatthews, D. E., Edwards, Jr., D. B., & Rincones, R. (2016). Social justice leadership and family engagement. *Educational Administration Quarterly, 52*(5), 754—792. doi:10.1177/0013161X16664006

The excerpt in Example 3.3 illustrates the more personal writing style typical in qualitative research reports. At the beginning of the Introduction in this particular qualitative report, the researchers opened with a vignette to remind readers that the research study involves real people who experience real challenges. To further assist with this communication, direct quotations from participants are used extensively throughout the research report and often help to quickly engage readers.

To evaluate the beginning of a qualitative research report, our prior visual of a ring with boundaries will again work quite well. A significant difference, however, is that in the qualitative approach, the concept of concentric rings with increasing specificity does not always apply. Rather, the interior boundaries might not be sharply drawn at all. Although remaining within the same general area of the problem under investigation, qualitative research is characterized by continuing interactions among data gathering, reviews of relevant literature, and research questioning. An initial outer circle may indicate the general parameters, but what happens inside this boundary remains open to change throughout the investigation.

Evaluating the Review of Relevant Literature

Differences between qualitative and quantitative approaches are especially evident with the review of relevant literature. Qualitative researchers typically provide a preliminary review of relevant literature in the Introduction, but that initial review, which includes relevant citations, is expanded upon as the study evolves and may continue throughout other sections of the research report.

You will be looking for clues that indicate that the review of relevant literature was balanced and sufficiently comprehensive, that it included contemporary and historical studies, and that the researchers tied outcomes from these studies together with some form of summary. Also, as with the quantitative approach, there should be an emphasis on primary sources.

Evaluating the Research Questions

Significant differences between qualitative and quantitative research reports are also evident in the final part of the Introduction. In qualitative reports, it is typical for the researchers to begin with only a preliminary identification of a guiding research question. This content serves as a general framework, not a specific statement, to guide the study initially. Researchers anticipate revisions to guiding research questions in qualitative studies as they gather and analyze data.

Thus, the criteria appropriate in evaluating the research questions in quantitative studies are essentially reversed when evaluating this part of a qualitative research report. Research questions in quantitative reports should be limited and specific, whereas research questions in qualitative reports should be sufficiently open-ended to facilitate exploration of themes that emerge during the study.

Compare the two research questions below:

- Do students in technology-rich classrooms have higher scores on standardized achievement assessments than those in classrooms without such technology?
- How do technology-rich classrooms affect the educational process?

The first research question above suggests a quantitative study. The second question would be more appropriate for a qualitative study because it identifies a general framework that can be reformulated as data are gathered during the study. In this proposed study, a deeper, richer question might evolve further asking, "How do students experience technology-rich classrooms?"

The Skeptical Mind-set

You may have been surprised earlier in this chapter by the statement that you are best served by an extremely skeptical mind-set when reading a published article. The proposition may seem particularly odd because having an open mind is a primary value associated with the research enterprise. Yet during these times of alleged "fake news" and bold-faced lies perpetuated by people who have agendas, it is more important than ever that we all become more critical, skeptical consumers of published information, especially those that are not based on solid evidence.

We do not believe that most research studies are conducted with a nefarious agenda. It is true that some studies, including those involved with human services, have obviously been slanted to support either the researchers' biases or a specific product, but these are not the norm. It seems reasonable to assume that most published research is instead intended to extend the frontiers of knowledge and increase the information available to practitioners working in the field so that they might operate more effectively.

So, why the admonition about presumed guilt? In any published research report, quantitative or qualitative, there are a remarkable number of assumptions based on trust that the reader must make. The researcher claims that participants were randomly assigned to two treatment conditions. Were they? The researcher reports that participants who received Treatment X had an average score of 25, whereas participants who received Treatment Y had an average score of 45. Were those the actual scores? And if those were the true results, what proof is there that one group wasn't given assistance that the other one was not?

A listing of assumptions and questions like those above could go on and on. You weren't there when the study was being conducted. You don't know, with absolute certainty, whether participants were actually randomly assigned to experimental groups. You don't have the actual test data—just the summaries provided by the researchers. You don't really know if a study was conducted at all. You don't know, the journal editor doesn't know, and the individuals who conducted peer reviews of the research reports and recommended its publication don't know either.

A promising cancer researcher at Duke University, Anil Potti, and several of his colleagues published 10 different research reports in prestigious medical journals during the years 2006 and 2009 regarding a personalized genomic technology application used among lung cancer patients (Barbash, 2015; Stancill, 2015). In their research reports, Potti and his research team claimed that use of the genomic technology they developed produced a personalized "fingerprint" capable of predicting with significant accuracy how lung cancer patients will respond to different chemotherapy treatments. The work of Potti and his team was initially viewed as revolutionary, referred to as the "holy grail" of lung cancer treatment, and supported with millions of dollars of federal funding. However, researchers were unable to replicate their work, which eventually prompted many questions regarding the credibility of their reported findings. The Office of Research Integrity conducted an investigation and determined that Anil Potti "engaged in research misconduct by including false research data" in published and submitted research reports, as well as grant applications seeking funding (U.S. Department of Health and Human Services, Office of Research Integrity, 2015, para. 2).

A prominent Harvard psychology professor, Marc Hauser, was a star researcher of cognitive neuroscience and evolutionary biology (Johnson, 2012, 2014). His work demonstrated advanced, sophisticated, and human-like cognitive abilities among primates and led to the publication of research reports in top scholarly journals, the production of popular books, and much media attention. However, after Harvard conducted an internal investigation, followed by an inquiry conducted by the Office of Research Integrity, Hauser was found responsible for several instances where data was falsified or fabricated (U.S. Department of Health and Human Services, 2012).

Did Potti and his research team outright fake their cancer research data to gain fame? Or, were they just careless and kept records haphazardly in a rush to have their work published? By the way, Potti was the only researcher who was held responsible for egregious scientific misconduct.

Did Hauser invent and misrepresent his data intentionally to achieve fame and notoriety? Or, was he simply overworked, which led to his oversight with important details, as he claimed? As things have evolved, the real answers to these questions remain uncertain. What is clear, however, is that caution in interpreting and accepting research data as reported is continually warranted.

Our premise is simple. If the information that is verifiable is found to be flawed, then it is reasonable and prudent to have serious doubts about the information that we are being asked to assume. The language in the Introduction of a research report, for example, might clearly indicate to readers that the researchers had strong biases about the outcome. Did this lead to the researchers' manipulation of the data to support that bias? We can't know that for sure, but we propose that if there are known mistakes, the unknowns should most definitely not be taken at face value.

In suggesting such a strong filter, we recognize that this may result in many otherwise legitimate research reports being eliminated from consideration. In the illustration above, the researchers may well have been completely objective and accurate in conducting and reporting the results of their study. Completely honest researchers may have omissions or make errors in writing the report. It is important to recognize that a poorly written report does not, in and of itself, demonstrate that the research study was poorly conducted. But this point remains clear—a mistake in what can be known casts a cloud on the probable accuracy and veracity about the things that must be assumed.

Your personal life experiences support this premise. If you have an acquaintance or friend who tells you something that you happen to know is not true, then you are hardly likely to trust other things they tell you, at least without healthy skepticism. If research data is to have much value to you, then you must be able to trust that what is offered is true as it was reported and keep in mind that truth is often subjective, and some scholars say it does not even exist.

On a practical level, this strong filter might be more difficult to implement if there were few research reports available for consideration. The reality, however, is just the opposite. The number of reports published each year, magnified by the number available in an online modality, is overwhelming. A vast number of research reports are published that do, in fact, meet the criteria presented here and in subsequent chapters.

Summary and Closing Thoughts

Implicit in this chapter is our belief that not all published research studies warrant more than just a cursory glance. Our objective was to provide specific guidance for critical evaluation of the Introduction section of published research reports.

In both quantitative and qualitative studies, the ending boundary of the Introduction will almost always be a section with a heading of Methods. This lets you know you are about to move into the realm of what was actually done, rather than just how this study was conceived conceptually. The Introduction is usually presented without a heading or subheadings, but you can expect to be able to identify content that addresses

1. a general description of a specific problem, including its context and significance;

2. a review of relevant literature; and

3. objective statements, research questions, or hypotheses.

Because the specific criteria to be used in critique of the Introduction are not identical in quantitative and qualitative studies, your first step is to identify which of these two approaches was used, or emphasized, in the investigation. The questions to be asked during your evaluation are quite similar, but some of the desired answers will depend on the approach. If the researchers do not label their approach (and, many do not), look through the article and decide whether the things being studied are principally defined with numbers or with extended verbal descriptions.

In the Introduction of a research report, from the vast scope of what could be studied, both quantitative and qualitative researchers first identify a boundary, in effect drawing a circle surrounding the general problem area. In a quantitative study, concentric rings are drawn inside the initial circle. Inside the first ring are the results of prior research related to a segment of the broad problem area. Then, based on the prior research, a second ring further limits the area to a specific focus of investigation for the study being reported. In a qualitative study, the area within that circle remains pliable throughout the investigation.

Finally, we have provided specific questions to assist you with critically evaluating the content provided in the Introduction of a research report. Despite the fact that we would classify ourselves as essentially warm and friendly people, we have suggested that you take a very rigorous approach in your critique. If a report fails to meet the criteria for evaluation at any point along the line, our guidance is to move on to another study.

Explanation

In this excerpt, the researchers described the theoretical framework in which they situated their research study: the Technology Acceptance Model. The researchers provided an overview of this theory, including its two key variables (perceived usefulness and perceived ease of use), and previous validating literature. They then identified the three variables that constitute the conceptual framework of their research study: computer self-efficacy, subjective norm, and personal innovativeness in education technology.

References

Barbash, F. (2015, November 9). Scientist falsified data for cancer research once described as 'holy grail,' feds say. *The Washington Post*. Retrieved from https://www.washingtonpost.com/news/morning-mix/wp/2015/11/09/scientist-falsified-data-for-cancer-research-once-described-as-holy-grail-feds-say/?utm_term=.9606d4e8b003

Johnson, C. Y. (2012, September 5). Former Harvard professor Marc Hauser fabricated, manipulated data, US says. *Boston Globe*. Retrieved from https://www.bostonglobe.com/news/science/2012/09/05/harvard-professor-who-resigned-fabricated-manipulated-data-says/6gDVkzPNxv1ZDkh4wVnKhO/story.html

Johnson, C. Y. (2014, May 30). Harvard report shines light on ex-researcher's misconduct. *Boston Globe*. Retrieved from https://www.bostonglobe.com/metro/2014/05/29/internal-harvard-report-shines-light-misconduct-star-psychology-researcher-marc-hauser/maSUowPqL4clXrOgj44aKP/story.html

Stancill, J. (2015, November 9). US says Anil Potter, former Duke doctor, falsified research. *The News & Observer*. Retrieved from http://www.newsobserver.com/news/local/education/article43885173.html

U.S. Department of Health and Human Services, Office of Research Integrity. (2012). *Findings of research misconduct* (Notice Number: NOT-OD-12-149). Retrieved from https://grants.nih.gov/grants/guide/notice-files/NOT-OD-12-149.html

U.S. Department of Health and Human Services, Office of Research Integrity. (2015). *Case summary: Potti, Anil.* Retrieved from https://ori.hhs.gov/content/case-summary-potti-anil

Evaluation Tools for the Introduction Section

Quantitative Study

Context and Significance

Consider

1. How important is the topic?
2. To what extent is the presentation clear and objective?

Look for

- Personal relevance of the topic
- Sound rationale for investigation of the problem
- Broad societal context for the problem
- Clear portrayal of the general intent of the study
- Evidence of bias in language

Review of Relevant Literature

Consider

1. To what extent is the viewpoint balanced and appropriately comprehensive?
2. How has attention been given to both historical precedent and more recent work?
3. How coherent is the theme of the review of relevant literature?
4. Where did the researchers appear to emphasize primary, rather than secondary sources?

Look for

- Objectivity with previous research findings
- Accumulation of knowledge reported in the literature with explanations for any gaps in time
- Evidence that previous literature guided the objectives for the study
- Reliance on citation of primary sources

Objective Statements/Research Questions/Hypotheses

Consider

1. To what extent were the objective statements/research questions/hypotheses clearly stated?
2. How has the review of relevant literature supported development of the objective statements/research questions/hypotheses?

Look for

- Clear understanding of purpose for study
- Researchers' predictions

Qualitative Study

Context and Significance

Consider

1. How important is the topic?
2. To what extent is the presentation clear and objective?

Look for

- Exploration of new phenomena, as well as how people experience them
- Personalized style of writing
- Continuing interactions among data gathering, literature reviews, and research questioning
- Personal relevance of the topic
- Sound rationale for investigation of the problem
- Broad societal context for the problem
- Clear portrayal of the general intent of the study

Review of Relevant Literature

Consider

1. To what extent is the viewpoint balanced and appropriately comprehensive?
2. How has attention been given to both historical precedent and more recent work?
3. How coherent is the theme of the review of relevant literature?
4. Where did the researchers appear to emphasize primary, rather than secondary sources?

Look for

- Preliminary review of relevant literature
- Balanced and sufficiently comprehensive review of relevant literature
- Includes contemporary and historical studies, with outcomes from these studies synthesized
- Reliance on citation of primary sources

Objective Statements/Research Questions

Consider

1. To what extent were the objective statements/research questions clearly stated?
2. How has the review of relevant literature supported development of the objective statements/research questions?

Look for

- Preliminary identification of a guiding research question(s)
- Guiding research question(s) served as general framework that guided the study initially
- Sufficiently open-ended to facilitate exploration of themes that emerge during the study

CHAPTER 4

Who Answered the Question? Evaluating the Methods Section— Part I: Participants

CHAPTER CONCEPTS

Cluster sampling

Convenience sampling

Generalizability

Higher-risk sampling
procedures

Lower-risk sampling
procedures

Participants

Purposive sampling

Quota sampling

Random

Representative sample

Research sample

Simple randomization

Strata

Stratified randomization

Systematic sampling

Target population

Introduction

You have now learned to make some preliminary critical assessments about a published research study based on perusing the Introduction section of a research article. Essentially, you are asking yourself the main question: Is it worth my time to read this article, and if I do, what can I hope to gain from doing so?

Assuming this initial evaluation persuaded you to continue reading, you would next proceed to a description of what actually was done and the procedures that were followed. This is called the Methods section, and it provides you with a systematic and logical structure for determining how the researchers designed their research plan, as well as put those procedures into action.

The three primary topics usually included in the Methods section are participants, procedures, and data collection tools and analyses. Each of these may be identified, though not always, with separate subheadings in the article. The first topic provides information about the individuals who participated in the study. The researchers may refer to these individuals as subjects or participants. Next, the researchers explain the research design of the study, as well as what they did and their rationale for such decisions. The final topic describes the data collection tools that the researchers used to gather data and the techniques used to analyze information about the phenomenon or variables being investigated. Essentially, the Methods section should provide enough detail for the reader to determine whether the study was well designed, as well as replicate the study with a different group of participants if so desired.

Although the Methods section of an article may include additional information, these three topics are central components. Our focus in this chapter is to address the evaluation of the researchers' choice of participants for their study. In the next chapter, we will cover appraisal of the procedures and data collection tools, as well as the completeness with which they were presented.

Participants

To illustrate the first step in the evaluation of the Methods section, consider the following scenario. A professor in a prestigious law school begins each first-year class by writing the following on the board:

> 2
> 2
> equals = ?

The professor then turns to the new students and demands, "What's the answer?" Anxious to please, several students quickly respond, "The answer is four."

The outcome for these students is a lengthy and not especially positive prognosis for their future in law school, punctuated by the professor's words, "But, how can you possibly know the answer, when you don't even know what the question is?" This scenario illustrates a simple and key point in evaluation of the methods employed during a research study. The first step in evaluating the participants, as well as the procedures and data collection tools, is that the appraisal must be in reference to the hypotheses, research questions, or objective statements that guided the research study.

You must know what the question is to ascertain whether the participants used were adequate and appropriate. This information, which we described in Chapter 3, should be provided in the Introduction, just before the Methods section begins. Regardless of format, the hypotheses, research questions, or objective statements are the primary templates that you will use in a critical evaluation of how participants were selected. In essence, evaluating the participants in a research study begins with, and is focused on, a single question: Do the participants identified in the research report appear appropriate and sufficient to address the objectives of the study?

Some Definitions

Researchers often describe the process used to select participants in a research study with specific terminology. Although these terms may be unfamiliar to you, we believe you will find them fairly self-descriptive.

Target Population

When research studies are conducted, there is always some group about which the results are supposed to provide information. There are times in qualitative studies when that group is comprised only of the participants in the study and generalizations are not made beyond that group. More often, however, the participants serve a surrogate role and represent a wider target group. In some research reports, this target group is explicitly identified. In others, you may have to infer the target group from information provided in the Introduction. The target group, which is called the target population, represents individuals about whom the researchers want to be able to make reasonable inferences.

Research Sample

With the vast majority of quantitative research studies, and some qualitative studies, the actual data comes from a research sample that the researchers selected to represent the target population. Researchers must proceed in this way because often it is impossible to work with all individuals from the target population. Researchers instead use a representative sample of them and then attempt to generalize their reported findings to the target population. Ultimately, as the consumer of the study, you will have to decide the extent to which you believe that the research sample accurately reflects the target population.

In most research studies in the education, health, helping, and social sciences professions, participants are comprised of people, which may be children, adolescents, or adults. For simplicity and clarity in our descriptions and examples, we will assume a human sample of participants. However, keep in mind that there are instances in which the research sample is inanimate. One example would be a certain type of research endeavor, referred to as reviews of literature, where the researchers' objectives are to provide a comprehensive and thorough summary of a specific topic area. Another example would be another type of research endeavor called a meta-analysis, where researchers identify a specific topic and locate previously published studies related to this topic. The researchers then establish criteria to select articles to include as "subjects" in their meta-analysis. In essence, a meta-analysis is a study of studies.

 Exercise 4.1

The following excerpt is from an article that was published in a scholarly journal. As you read the excerpt, try to identify the target population and

research sample. Discuss your ideas with a small group of peers. Then, compare your findings with the explanation we provide at the end of the chapter.

"Talking Across Worlds": Classist Microaggressions and Higher Education

The microaggressions perspective has been used to frame the interpersonal discrimination and exclusion experienced by people in marginalized social groups (Sue et al., 2007). Originally explored with respect to racism, the term microaggressions refers to the daily indignities, invalidations, and slights that are experienced by people of color (even when the perpetrators are not aware of having done so). Given that classism can be understood as a form of oppression on the order of racism, it is possible that this framework can be applied analogously to the experiences of poor and working-class individuals—and institutions of higher education represent a promising site for the exploration of this question. When they attain admission to these institutions, students enter a setting that has historically been the province of more privileged social groups—not only with regard to class, but in terms of race and gender as well. Moreover, campus diversity initiatives often provide little attention to issues of social class and classism. What messages do poor and working-class students receive from faculty, administrators, and peers about members of their social groups? What are the experiences, needs, and challenges that characterize the experiences of these students? What do these messages and experiences suggest about the existence of classist microaggressions? To address these questions, we conducted a qualitative analysis of narrative data gathered from interviews with graduate students who identified as coming from poor or working-class backgrounds. The findings have implications for the scholarly exploration of manifestations of classism as well as the development of enhanced programming, services, and support structures for students from poor and working-class backgrounds. ...

Method

Participants

Fifteen participants were interviewed for this study, including three participants who identified as male and 12 who identified as female. This number corresponds to the number of cases identified as being appropriate for consensual qualitative analysis, which is understood to range from roughly 8 to 15 (Hill et al., 1997). The average age of participants was 26.8 years (range = 23–39). One participant identified as Asian/Asian American, six as Black/African American, two as Latino/a, and six as White/Euro-American. With regard to religious affiliation, eight participants identified

as Christian, one as spiritual, and one as agnostic. Four participants reported that they held no religious or spiritual affiliation, and one participant did
not complete this item. Two participants identified their sexual orientation
as gay, 10 participants as heterosexual, one participant as "fluid," and one
participant as bisexual; one remaining participant did not complete the
item. All interviewees identified themselves as having grown up in poor
or working-class families, and all were matriculated graduate students at
a large urban northeastern American university. …

Reference

Smith, L., Mao, S., & Deshpande, A. (2016). "Talking across worlds": Classist microaggressions and higher education. *Journal of Poverty, 20*(2), 127–151. doi:10.1080/10875549.201
5.1094764

Evaluating the Participants

Journalism students are taught that a news story should include the five W's and
H: What? Who? Where? When? Why? How? You will use these same questions
to evaluate information provided about participants in the Methods section of a
published research report.

What Is the Target Population?

In many qualitative studies, and some quantitative studies, the target population
is the only relevant group. For example, if the objective of a survey research
study is to describe characteristics of students enrolled in a specific course at a
particular university during a given semester, the researchers might choose to
gather data from all those who meet these criteria. In that case, there would be
no separate research sample because everyone is already included in the target
population.

We want to point out that it's not the gathering of data from all participants
that defines the target population. Instead, the target population is defined by
the research objective, which in the example above includes all students who are
enrolled in a specific university course. However, if the researchers plan to use
these data to make inferences about characteristics of students in similar courses
at different universities, or even at that same university during other semesters,
the participants now become a research sample for a different target population.
That new target population could be all students in similar courses at different
universities or students at that same university over a period of time.

As you evaluate the "what" question regarding participants, you need to
also consider to what extent the objectives of the study will provide information
appropriate to the identified target population.

Who Participated in the Study?

Your next question for evaluation of the participants involves who actually provided data for the study. This question is important whether the participants are the target population or a representative sample of the target population. Answering this question depends on the amount of information provided to you by the researchers. The general rule is that the more information given, the better you will be able to judge the extent to which the results can be generalized. What you are particularly looking for is any information about characteristics of participants that might have some impact on findings reported in the study.

For example, a research study that explores persistence among students might involve a research design that explores the effect on persistence with use of different student support strategies. If there is some reason to suspect differences on persistence, such as with academic standing, age, disability, ethnicity, gender, socioeconomic status, and so on, then the researchers should certainly reveal all relevant characteristics among those who participated in the study.

As you evaluate the "who" question regarding participants, you need to look for sufficient information and characteristics, as well as the language used to describe the participants.

Where Were the Participants?

The information from this question extends the description of the participants by examining the setting in which the research study took place. If the participants were university students, where was the university located? Were there any special characteristics of the university itself—private or public, large or small, main campus or satellite campus, urban or rural, research institution or regional institution? In what specific settings were data collected—large lecture halls or small labs? Essentially, you are looking for descriptions about the setting that appear likely to have influenced reported findings from the study.

As you evaluate the "where" question regarding participants, you must decide if the researchers provided adequate information about the setting, as well as whether it was conducive to achieve the objectives of the study.

When Were the Data Collected?

When you answer this question, two pieces of information are needed: (1) the date when the data were gathered, and (2) the date when the article was actually published. It is extremely likely that there will be some time lag between these two dates. A period of up to two years is not unusual, however, the gap could be longer and may therefore contribute to results that have an expired shelf life.

As you evaluate the "when" question regarding participants, keep in mind that timing is an important factor and may limit the extent to which the findings could be generalized. Events may occur in the time between conducting a research study and its publication that could dramatically impact the relevance of reported findings.

Why Was This Sample Selected?

With this question, you are evaluating the rationale that underlies the researchers' selection of participants for the research sample. A researcher cannot draw a research sample from a group made up only of one segment of a population and then make that segment representative of the whole population. Consider, for example, that a group of researchers who work at an elite private university want to determine whether academic performance among undergraduate students would be improved with greater use of technology tools. Out of convenience, they formed their research sample among undergraduate students at their institution, which consists of mostly White, middle-class, and relatively privileged individuals. Would the findings from their study be generalizable to all undergraduate students? The obvious answer is "No" because their research sample would exclude undergraduate students who are ethnically and socioeconomically diverse.

As you evaluate the "why" question regarding participants, the burden of proof is on the researchers who prepared the report. It is their responsibility to provide a sound rationale for the selection of their research sample.

How Was the Sample Selected?

With this final question, you are evaluating the procedures used by the researchers to form their research sample. Researchers use a variety of sampling techniques to ensure that the sample seems likely to provide adequate representation of the target population. Some sampling procedures increase the odds that the sample will actually be representative of the target population. In the material that follows, we categorize these as lower-risk sampling procedures. However, researchers may instead, for a variety of reasons, choose procedures in which the odds are only neutral at best that a representative sample will be selected. We have identified these as the higher-risk sampling procedures. Remember, though, that neither the lower-risk or higher-risk sampling procedures guarantee a representative, or atypical, sample.

What all this means is that researchers often have some difficult decisions to make in how they do things. Each choice may have some benefit, as well as a cost. Researchers must take into account their resources, such as the amount of available time, the cost of some procedures over others, and the accessibility of various groups of people. Unfortunately, all too often researchers may rely on samples of convenience, such as university students attending their classes or current clients or patients, which greatly limit the generalizability of their results.

In the following section, we provide an overview of some of the common sampling procedures and discuss their relative advantages and risks. For the purpose of evaluating the "how" question regarding participants, keep a focus on the bigger picture as you read about each procedure. Ultimately, the primary concern is the extent to which the selected sampling procedure is likely to produce participants who accurately represent the target population.

Lower-risk sampling procedures. One or more of the following lower-risk sampling procedures might be evident in the researchers' description of how they selected the research sample:

- Simple randomization
- Stratified randomization
- Cluster sampling
- Systematic sampling

Simple randomization. Selecting a sample through simple randomization is the easiest sampling procedure to describe but may be the most difficult to implement in actual research studies and thus seldom will be evident in the studies you read. The concept is straightforward—a condition is created in which every member of the target population has an equal chance of being selected for the research sample. If, for example, you were planning to conduct a study of characteristics of the graduate students in a university, you might begin with a list of all graduate students currently enrolled. This comprehensive list represents your target population. Then, using a computer-based randomization tool, a research sample of predetermined size would be generated. A significant drawback to this procedure is you would have to begin with a listing of all possible participants in a target population. Such a listing could be available, but in real life studies that rarely occurs.

Stratified randomization. Researchers who use stratified randomization take steps before selecting the sample to ensure that relevant characteristics for their study are adequately represented in the sample selected. The process of stratification is again quite straightforward. The researchers ensure representation by randomly sampling participants within strata that appear relevant, such as age, ethnicity, gender, race, or socioeconomic status. Let's assume that a researcher wants to explore gender differences among graduate students and technology use and desires an equal number of participants for each stratum (50% males and 50% females). The researcher would first need a list of the total population and divide it into two groups—male students and female students. Then, the researcher would randomly select the desired number of participants from each group. Similar to simple randomization, stratified randomization requires a comprehensive listing of all possible participants in a target population. Each possible participant must be clearly marked to only one stratum—participants cannot fit into both categories.

Cluster sampling. This method entails the selection of groups, or clusters, within a target population. Researchers find this sampling procedure particularly useful when conducting studies among large populations. With cluster sampling, a researcher simply needs to identify a characteristic in the target population that enables the division of discrete clusters, such as cities, classrooms, hospitals, or regions. Formed clusters should be homogenous among each other, yet heterogeneous within themselves. The researcher then either randomly or systematically selects clusters for their research sample. Although this sampling procedure is time- and cost-efficient, it is less precise than other sampling procedures.

Systematic sampling. The final sampling procedure in the lower-risk category to be considered here is the use of systematic sampling. We're including it for completeness in our presentation, but the need for using it has decreased dramatically with the availability of computer tools to generate randomized samples from target population lists.

In essence, the systematic sampling procedure approximates randomization and is much simpler to do if it's being done by hand. Assume that a researcher has the target population list. The first name in the list would be selected at random. The rest of the sample would be selected using some system, such as every tenth name or every seventh city. This approach nearly simulates a situation where everyone had an equal chance of being selected for the research sample. The primary risk with this sampling procedure would be the presence of patterns within the target population list. Let's assume that a target population list containing the names of all students enrolled at a university organized student names by alternating gender (student no. 1 = male, student no. 2 = female, student no. 3 = male, student no. 4 = female, etc.). If a researcher wanted to create a research sample where males and females had an equal chance of being selected, they would not be able to use systematic sampling. In this case, every fourth student would produce a research sample that consists of only female students.

Higher-risk sampling procedures. Common sense might suggest that studies using higher-risk sampling procedures would be automatically suspect. But for many important areas of inquiry in the education, health, helping, and social sciences professions, the lower-risk procedures simply cannot be applied. Using any one of the lower-risk procedures assumes that a researcher has or can obtain access to a master list of all members in the target population.

Because a comprehensive master list of the target population may not be available to a researcher or may not even exist anywhere, there has to be another option. In actual fact, the majority of research studies you read will seldom include research samples selected by truly random procedures. Instead, the samples in those research studies will have been chosen using one, or some combination of the following procedures:

- Convenience sampling
- Quota sampling
- Purposive sampling

Convenience sampling. The use of convenience sampling is so pervasive that it is tempting here to define it simply as "this what researchers actually do." Essentially, as its name implies, it is a procedure in which researchers choose the research sample among participants who are a convenient, easily accessible group. Examples include classes of students, a current client or patient base, individuals associated with an organization, employees in a workplace, or social media connections.

Convenience sampling is a higher-risk procedure because the chances of underrepresenting or overrepresenting groups within the target population are higher than with true randomization. The key in evaluating the adequacy of a convenience sample is determining whether the participants seem likely to be representative of the target population. To make this judgment, it is especially important for the researchers to provide extensive information about the individuals who participated in the study.

Quota sampling. This is an interesting derivative of the stratified randomization procedure. The main difference is quota sampling is not random. To use quota sampling, researchers typically begin with some desired total number of participants and a goal related to some specific demographic characteristics of the sample, such as equal gender representation.

For example, assume that you have a series of questions you'd like to have answered from a certain number of respondents from various types of communities. You're going to obtain the information through interviews, so you've decided to limit the size of the sample to 100 participants with equal representation for three types of communities: rural, urban, and suburban. At a well-attended community event, you approach individuals who are willing to answer your questions. You keep at it until you've obtained responses from 34 rural dwellers, 32 urban dwellers, and 34 suburban dwellers.

Obviously this is a higher-risk sampling procedure because you are meeting the strata criteria with a limited group from whom to choose. In our example, if you went to the actual communities to elicit participation, you might get a far different response pattern compared with those who voluntarily attended the community event.

Purposive sampling. The last of the higher-risk procedures that we will cover is purposive sampling. These samples are chosen because the researchers know, or at least think they know, things about the characteristics of participants in the research sample that would probably make them reflective of the target population. In a study where a researcher wants to know what factors impact educational attainment among underrepresented graduate students, the only individuals who can provide this information are current or former graduate students who are underrepresented. Thus, the adequacy of this sampling procedure rests on the judgment of the researchers, which greatly limits the generalizability of findings.

Purposive sampling is the sampling procedure most widely used in qualitative studies. Keep in mind that many qualitative studies may not use sampling procedures at all because the research sample may also be the target population. Such studies are also careful to note the limitations of their ability to generalize its findings because the research was based on a small sample that was deliberately selected precisely because they were perceived to be in the best position as informants to reveal relevant data.

In this section, we addressed some of the common sampling procedures used in research studies. This section was not intended to be comprehensive, but its purpose was to provide you with enough information to evaluate the "how" question regarding participants.

 ## Exercise 4.2

Now that you have a basic understanding of common sampling procedures, you now have an opportunity to apply these understandings. Read the two journal article excerpts below and try to identify the sampling procedures that the researchers used. Be sure and support your responses with information provided in the journal article excerpts. Discuss your findings with a small group of peers. Then, compare your responses with the explanations we provide at the end of the chapter.

EXCERPT 1

Persistence Factors Among Online Graduate Students With Disabilities

The U.S. Government Accountability Office (2009) indicated that 11% of students enrolled in postsecondary institutions in the United States are persons with disabilities. However, students with disabilities encounter many barriers to secondary education: lack of academic readiness, financial difficulties associated with disability expenses in addition to educational expenses, stigma and potential discriminatory reactions, and lack of appropriate accommodations and support at school (DaDeppo, 2009). Due to these obstacles, students with disabilities enroll and complete secondary studies at lower rates than nondisabled persons. ...

This study provided a conceptual framework of persistence grounded in field data to address the following questions: (a) What reasons lead students with disabilities to choose an online program? and (b) What factors contribute or hinder persistence among graduate students with disabilities enrolled in online programs?

Method

This qualitative study employed principles and procedures based on grounded theory methods (Charmaz, 2006). A qualitative approach was selected due to a lack of research on the topic of persistence among graduate students with disabilities enrolled in online programs.

Participants

Thirty-five graduate students with disabilities (27 women, 8 men) participated in this study, ranging in age from 23 to 62 ($M = 39.60$, $SD = 11.03$). The minimum selection criteria encompassed participants reporting having successfully completed at least one class in a graduate online program and having a disability prior to enrollment. Three participants enrolled in blended programs in which more than 50% of classes were studied online; remaining participants enrolled fully online. Eighteen participants enrolled in online programs within online universities, whereas the other 17 participants enrolled in online or blended programs within traditional brick and mortar institutes. Programs were located in 14 universities across the United States. The Americans with Disabilities Act (ADA) of 1990 (ADA, 1990) and subsequent amendments provided a three-part definition of disability. A person with a disability is someone who: (a) has a physical or mental impairment that substantially limits one or more major life activities, (b) has a record of such impairment, and (c) is regarded as having such impairment. The range of possible conditions included as disabilities is broad. For the purpose of this study, participants' self- reported disabilities were grouped into seven categories: (a) attention deficit/hyperactivity disorder (ADD/ ADHD), (b) developmental conditions (autism), (c) emotional conditions (e.g., depression, obsessive-compulsive disorder, posttraumatic stress disorder, (d) health impairments (e.g., diabetes, asthma, lupus), (e) learning disabilities (e.g., reading, processing information, remembering), (f) physical disabilities that interfere with daily life tasks (e.g., mobility, manual dexterity), and (g) sensory conditions (e.g., blindness, deafness, or severe vision/hearing impairment). Twenty-one participants reported having a single disability, and the rest reported multiple disabilities across groups. The range of education varied from one class completed to completion of all coursework. Table 1 summarizes the participants' demographic information. Students were invited to participate through forums and listservs frequented by online learners or persons with disabilities; professional associations who distributed research invitations to members; and through the participant pool at the first researcher's institution. The participant pool is a virtual bulletin board that links researchers to potential participants. Information regarding this study was distributed via multiple listservs, such as: ACPA (American College Personnel Association), DSSHE (Disabled Student Services in Higher Education), DREAM (Disability Rights, Education, Activism, and Mentoring), and NABS (National Association of Blind Students). Information on these listservs was obtained through the researchers' disability office, colleagues, and the Internet. Interested students contacted the first author and were then e-mailed to explain details of the study. Participants completed both the demographic and consent form and submitted via e-mail; phone interviews were arranged at their convenience. Participants were offered a financial incentive of $50 for participation. The study obtained institutional review board approval from the first author's institution. ...

Reference

Verdinelli, S., & Kutner, D. (2016). Persistence factors among online graduate students with disabilities. *Journal of Diversity in Higher Education, 9*(4), 353–368. doi:10.1037/a0039791

EXCERPT 2

Toward a Successful Vocational Rehabilitation in Adults With Disabilities: Does Residential Arrangement Matter?

Approximately 19% (56.7 million) of the total U.S. population have some form of disability (U.S. Census Bureau, 2011) (Note: Persons with a disability are those who have a physical, mental, or emotional condition that causes serious difficulty with their daily activities.) One major problem that people with disabilities constantly face is unemployment. Of about 35% of the working-age individuals with disabilities eager to participate in the labor force, only 30.2% are actually working (U.S. Department of Labor, Bureau of Labor Statistics, 2013, April). Individuals with disabilities tend to remain unemployed for longer periods of time than their counterparts without disability, and when they are employed, they typically earn less money (U.S. Census Bureau, American Community Survey, 2013). The results of these large-scale population studies, unfortunately, exclude institutionalized people such as those living in adult correctional facilities and nursing homes (Note: All previously mentioned statistics are based on only civilian noninstitutionalized population 16 years old and over.). In the United States, nearly 1.5 million people live in nursing homes (Jones, Dwyer, Bercovitz, & Strahan, 2009), and about 1 in 13 males and 1 in 33 females with disabilities reside in correctional facilities (Stapleton, Honeycutt, & Schechter, 2012).

In part to mitigate the unemployment problem of people with disabilities, the federal government started the vocational rehabilitation (VR) program. This program provides—among many others—individualized and supportive services to assist persons with disabilities obtain jobs that match their skills and abilities (U.S. Department of Education, n.d.). ...

We designed this study to assess the relationship between residential arrangement and vocational rehabilitation outcomes among adults with disabilities. The interest was in finding out whether the types of residence would stand as a significant risk factor in the presence of other preservice factors, such as demographic backgrounds, type of impairment, functional limitations, and other referral factors, which were more intuitively related to vocational rehabilitation outcomes. In addition, we aimed at evaluating whether the relationship of interest was mediated by service factors such as the types of service people with disabilities received.

Methods

Data Source

Our analysis was based on the data from a VR program in a Midwestern state. Information from each VR consumer was originally collected as a part of the agencies' service record and was maintained in an integrated database by the state-level agency. We were granted access to retrieve the de-identified records spanning from 2004 to 2013. For the purpose of analysis, we restricted data extraction to consumers aged 18–65 at referral, who were not involved in transition services for youth with disabilities after their acceptance in the VR program, and whose cases had been closed following a period of participating in a VR service plan. The purpose of the selected age range was to avoid homogeneity with respect to residential arrangement (in younger and older populations) and to guarantee that the individuals were in productive ages (such that assessing employment outcomes of vocational training would be relevant). We excluded consumers receiving transition services due to the different nature of that program. We also selected only those individuals whose cases were closed after receiving a VR service plan in order to ensure the availability of outcome measures. Of the 210,112 persons in the database, 46,570 met our criteria and were selected for analyses.

Reference

Langi, F. G., Oberoi, A., & Balcazar, F. E. (2017). Toward a successful vocational rehabilitation in adults with disabilities: Does residential arrangement matter? *Journal of Prevention & Intervention in the Community, 45*(2), 124–137. doi:10.1080/10852352.2017.1281053

Summary and Closing Thoughts

This chapter addresses the first task involved in evaluating the Methods section in a research article—the researchers' choice of participants for their study. Evaluation of this aspect is partly dependent on information that the researchers provided in the Introduction section. During this recursive process, you must first determine whether the individuals selected to participate in the study were appropriate and sufficient to address the hypotheses, research questions, or objective statements identified by the researchers.

We also provided you with six evaluation tools to establish a framework with which to determine appropriateness and adequacy with the researchers' selection of participants. The first two evaluation tools offer guidelines to identify and assess the target population and research sample for the study. The following two evaluation tools consider the location of participants and time frame of data collection in relation to the publication of findings from the study. The remaining two evaluation tools examine the research sample more closely by gauging the researchers' rationale for its selection, as well as the procedures used to obtain the sample.

With respect to sampling procedures, we provided an overview of the most common procedures, which we categorized as lower-risk sampling procedures and higher-risk sampling procedures. The purpose for this overview was not intended to be a complete and comprehensive description of social research sampling procedures. Rather, our goal was to provide you with enough information to recognize frequently used sampling procedures, judge their suitability to achieve the research objectives, and determine sufficiency with the researchers' explanations.

EXAMPLE 4.1 EXPLANATION

The authors of this study sought to explore issues of social class and classism among poor and working-class students in higher education environments. Thus, the target population was students from poor and working-class backgrounds. The research sample consisted of graduate students enrolled at a large urban northeastern American university who identified as coming from poor or working-class backgrounds. Specifically there were 15 participants, of which the average age was 26.8 years, and the following demographic characteristics:

- *Gender: Three identified as male and 12 as female.*
- *Race/ethnicity: One identified as Asian/Asian American, six as Black/ African American, two as Latino/a, and six as White/Euro-American.*
- *Religious/spiritual affiliation: Eight identified as Christian, one as spiritual, one as agnostic, four reported that they held no affiliation, and one made no indication.*
- *Sexual orientation: Two identified as gay, 10 as heterosexual, one as "fluid," one as bisexual, one made no indication, and one did not provide a response.*

EXAMPLE 4.2 EXPLANATION

In Excerpt 1, the researchers set the following research questions for this study:

- *What reasons lead students with disabilities to choose an online program?*
- *What factors contribute or hinder persistence among graduate students with disabilities enrolled in online programs?*

With this in mind, the target population was graduate students with disabilities who were enrolled in online programs. The research sample consisted of 35 graduate students: 27 women and eight men who ranged in age from 23 to 62 years old. The researchers used convenience sampling procedures, as they sought participation among individuals that seemed likely to be representative of the target population. Specifically, participants were recruited via forums and listservs frequented by online learners or persons with disabilities, professional associations, and a virtual bulletin board that links researchers to potential participants at one of the researcher's institutions. Thus, selection of participants was not random because no comprehensive list of all possible participants was available.

The objective for the research study in Excerpt 2 was to assess whether successful vocational rehabilitation (i.e., obtaining employment) among adults with disabilities was affected by residential arrangement. The target population was adults with disabilities who live in different types of residential arrangements. The researchers conducted this study in a midwestern state and were provided access to a database maintained by a state-level agency that contained information for every vocational rehabilitation consumer in the state. The researchers set specific selection criteria with which to select individuals from the database to include in data analyses. Because all individuals that met the selection criteria were included, no sampling procedures were used. Therefore, the research sample in this study was also the target population.

Evaluation Tools for the Methods Section—Part I: Participants

Quantitative and Qualitative Studies

Target Population

Consider
What was the target population?

Look for
- Whether the target population is also the sample
- Alignment to research objectives

Research Sample

Consider
Who participated in the study?

Look for
- Enough information so that results can be generalized
- Characteristics that may influence responses
- Unusual characteristics
- Language used to describe characteristics

Location

Consider
Where were the participants?

Look for
- Specific information about the setting
- Appropriateness of setting for research objective
- Aspects of setting that may influence findings

Time Frame

Consider
When were the data collected?

Look for
- Specific information about the timeframe for data collection
- Significant lapses in time or subsequent events that may influence relevance with findings

Rationale for Sampling Technique

Consider
Why was this sample collected?

Look for
- Utilization of sampling techniques to accurately represent the target population
- Appropriateness of sampling techniques to achieve research objective

Sampling Techniques

Consider
How was this sample collected?

Look for
- The manner in which participants were selected
- Descriptions of advantages and risks associated with selected sampling technique

CHAPTER 5

How Did They Answer the Question?

Evaluating the Methods Section—Part II: Procedures and Data Collection Tools

CHAPTER CONCEPTS

Audit trail

Case studies

Coefficient alpha

Constant data comparisons

Controlled variable

Data collection tools

Deductive analysis

Dependent variable

Equivalent forms

Ethnography

Experimental designs

Expert reviews

Factor analysis

Grounded theory

Independent variable

Inductive analysis

Instruments

Item-to-item correlation

Inter-rater reliability

Internal consistency

Member checking

Narrative research

Natural settings

Nonexperimental designs

Quasi-experimental designs

Peer debriefing

Phenomenology

Pilot testing

Procedures

Qualitative designs

Quantitative designs

Reflexivity

Reliability

Replicate

Role of researcher

Test-retest

Triangulation

Validity

Variable

Introduction

After you figure out what you want to do, the next step is to determine exactly how you are going to do it. You need a plan, of course—one that could be followed by others should they wish to repeat the task that you completed. To illustrate the importance of this plan, consider the following scenario:

> You meet a new group of friends who each have different cultural backgrounds. To learn about one another's culture, you invite your friends to participate in an around-the-world dinner party. To prepare for the dinner party, each person first selects a popular ethnic dish from their culture of which no one else would be familiar. Next, each person writes out precise, detailed instructions for how to make their selected ethnic dish and sends their written instructions to you. Then, you distribute the collected cooking recipes among the group, making sure that everyone receives an unfamiliar ethnic dish. Finally, each person creates their "assigned" dish using only the written directions they were provided and brings the dish to the dinner party.

In this scenario, how important are the written directions for the cooking plan? To what extent are detail and precision valuable with the steps, or procedures, especially among cooks who are new to their assigned recipe?

Whether the scenario is a cooking recipe or an investigation into whether yoga reduces stress levels, you would still need to design a set of procedures that fully describe how to complete the task. Before anyone else could decide if the results you obtained were useful (or if the cooking creation was a success), they would need to evaluate whether the route you described was appropriate. Of course, your cooking creation might taste delicious, or the data you collected on those who participated in yoga might be quite interesting, but it would still be important to know just how you arrived at your conclusions. Maybe it was sheer luck. Or, perhaps the result is impressive, but it cannot be duplicated by anyone else. We want to emphasize that empirical investigations require a plan, and for the outcome to be meaningful, the plan must have complete information.

In this chapter we continue evaluation of the Methods section of published research studies. You will recall in the previous chapter we explored evaluation of participants—our focus now shifts to the appropriateness of the selected procedures and tools used to collect data, as well as the completeness with which they were described. It is important to recognize that these two elements work together in your evaluation of whether they could legitimately address the objectives identified by the researchers.

There is no one best way to conduct research. In fact, there are a large number of different research designs available in both quantitative and qualitative approaches. However, there are necessary parameters, and some designs simply cannot provide the information needed to achieve the objective identified by the researchers. The good news is that your evaluation of the procedures and data collection tools used by the researchers does not require you to identify, by name, the specific design used. In the Introduction section of the research report, the researchers have identified what they were trying to learn. In the Methods section, we only have to inspect how they went about the task and decide if the procedures and data collection tools they chose were likely to provide information relevant to achieve their objective.

In Chapter 3, you learned that the intent of a research study is typically provided by the researchers near the end of the Introduction, just before the Methods section. The format may include hypotheses, research questions, or objective statements. For clarity and simplicity in the material that follows, we will consistently use "research objective" as a generic identifier for the researchers' goals within a specific study.

Evaluating the Procedures

In the previous chapter, we emphasized that when determining whether the participants included in the study were appropriate, you must take into consideration exactly what the researchers' objective was for the study. "Appropriate" is a conditional term that must be defined with a reference—appropriate for what? The "what" is always defined by the research objective.

This same idea continues with the following key question: To what extent do the procedures appear appropriate and sufficient to address the research objective? Answering this question involves two steps, with each step using information provided in the Methods section of the research report.

Descriptions of the Procedures in Sufficient Detail

Evaluating the procedures in a research report begins with a simple criterion: Was sufficient detail provided in the report? The description of the procedures must include enough detail so that another researcher may replicate the study as it was originally conducted.

Consider, for example, a study in which the research objective was about the effects of an instructional approach on student learning. Participants in the study were graduate students who were seeking a master's degree in the same program at the same university. During a designated semester, the researchers established three different sections of the same course required for all program majors, such as Research Methods, and delivered each section using a different instructional approach:

- Face-to-face: all course content was delivered in a classroom setting
- Hybrid: half of the course content was delivered in a classroom setting, and the other half was delivered online
- Online: all course content was delivered online

Participants were randomly assigned to one of these three course sections. Throughout the semester, the researchers collected samples of students' work as artifacts that represented student learning.

In the Methods section, the researchers described each of the instructional approaches at length, but they neglected to specifically describe the course requirements, such as lectures, assignments, and assessments. Could you replicate this study without that information? The answer, we think, is clearly, "No." A myriad of possible ways to teach a course on research methods are available, and without knowing exactly what types of learning activities and exercises were used, it is essentially impossible to make a reasonable interpretation of any comparative results.

How much information is enough information? At some point during the evaluation of completeness, a value judgment on your part will be required. A research report, obviously, cannot include every single detail about what was done during the study. The task is to be sure that all information essential to replicate the study was provided. It is also keep in mind that each publication has space and length requirements, which sometimes limits the amount of detail that can be included.

Relevance of the Procedures to Achieve the Research Objective

In your assessment about whether procedures were relevant to the research objective of the study, the logical first step is to identify whether the research design was primarily quantitative or qualitative. This may not be difficult because the researchers may have included this information in the Introduction section. As a reminder, this information may also be obtained by glancing through the Results section of the article. When the research design is quantitative, findings are reported with numerical descriptors and comparisons. By contrast, qualitative research designs use verbal narratives.

In the two following sections, we describe procedures that researchers commonly address in studies that use quantitative and qualitative research designs. These descriptions should guide your evaluation of the procedures to determine whether they are relevant to the research objective. When a study uses a mixed methods research design, you will want to identify where the researchers placed an emphasis—on either the quantitative or qualitative aspect—and use the corresponding set of procedures to guide your evaluation. However, you may occasionally encounter an article in which the mixed methods design has a roughly equal balance of quantitative and qualitative procedures. In these cases, it is best to conduct your appraisal using both sets of procedures.

Procedures in Quantitative Research Designs

As you'd expect there are many different types of research designs available for the quantitative researcher. The particular choice might depend on the type of data collected, the timing of data collection, and the amount of control needed for variables in the investigation. The various quantitative designs typically involve gathering information to describe phenomena, identify relationships, or compare outcomes.

Describe Phenomena

The primary focus of descriptive research designs is to provide a general overview of a variable or phenomenon and discover "what is." These nonexperimental studies are descriptive in nature and give summaries of basic, descriptive data, which may lead to the identification of patterns. For example, the following research question may lend itself to this type of quantitative design: How has social media use changed over the past 5 years?

Identify Relationships

Another type of nonexperimental research design investigates relationships among two or more variables (see Table 5.1) to explore whether they tend to go together. These correlational designs are usually conceptualized with a metaphor of prediction. An example would be if researchers surmised a possible relationship between physical activity levels (independent variable) and self-esteem (dependent variable). After measuring these two variables, they would compute a statistical measure to determine the extent to which the variables are related to one another.

Compare Outcomes

Experimental research designs are used to test hypotheses or theories and make outcome comparisons. These types of research designs test for causality between independent and dependent variables. Let's say a researcher wanted to compare the effectiveness of two different types of therapy for anxiety. They assigned clients to receive either cognitive therapy (Group 1) or narrative therapy (Group 2). To compare outcomes for the two types of therapy, the researcher would measure and compare levels of anxiety among clients from both groups after a period of time.

Table 5.1

Types of Variables	
Variable	An element or factor in an investigation that is likely to change.
Independent Variable	The element or factor that the researcher manipulates.
Dependent Variable	The element or factor that may change in response to changes made to the independent variable.
Controlled Variables	All other elements or factors in an investigation that must be kept the same.

Experimental research designs may be categorized as quasi-experimental or true experimental designs. They are similar in that both types of designs involve manipulation of the independent variable. The difference, however, is that quasi-experimental designs do not utilize randomization among participants, whereas true experimental designs do. Quasi-experimental designs are frequently used in the education, health, helping, and social sciences professions because researchers often have to employ convenience sampling techniques due to the presence of naturally formed groups, such as classes of students, family units, neighborhoods, organizations, or volunteers.

Reflective Exercise 5.1

With quantitative studies, researchers may explicitly identify the specific type of design, or they may refer to it implicitly. Regardless, you must be able to identify the type of design used by the researchers to conduct a thorough evaluation of the Methods section of an article. Read the three article excerpts below and identify (1) the type of quantitative research design used, and (2) specific aspects of the design. Discuss your initial ideas with a small group of peers and arrive at a consensus. Then, compare your findings with the answers provided at the end of the chapter.

ARTICLE 1

Methods

Overview of Cooking Matters

Cooking Matters was designed for low-income adults and uses hands-on meal preparation, facilitated discussion, and an interactive grocery store tour to teach participants how to shop economically and prepare healthy meals. *Cooking Matters* participants meet for 6 weeks, once each week for 2 hours, to learn basic cooking skills and nutrition concepts, and to prepare and share a meal together under the guidance of a nutrition and culinary educator. ...

Study Design and Data Collection

The *Cooking Matters* impact evaluation used a quasi-experimental design to examine intermediate and long-term outcomes at 3- and 6-month follow-up. ...

Cooking Matters partner agencies in six states (CA, CO, ME, MA, MI, and OR) agreed to participate in the study. Designated points of contact at

Jennifer A. Pooler, et al., "Cooking Matters for Adults Improves Food Resource Management Skills and Self-Confidence Among Low-Income Participants," *Journal of Nutrition Education and Behavior*, vol. 49, no. 7. Copyright © 2017 by Elsevier B.V.

each partner agency coordinated with the study team regarding logistics and training for course coordinators to administer the study materials. ...

Reference

Pooler, J. A., Morgan, R. E., Wong, K., Wilkin, M. K., & Blitstein, J. L. (2017). *Cooking Matters for Adults* improves food resource management skills and self-confidence among low-income participants. *Journal of Nutrition Education & Behavior, 49*(7), 545–553. doi:10.1016/j.jneb.2017.04.008

ARTICLE 2

This paper reports the findings from an experimental study of consumer perceptions and behavior in response to nutrient content claims (NCCs) on a vitamin-fortified snack food, a food type that has not previously been studied in this context. We hypothesized that the presence of an NCC for added nutrients on a fortified snack food (1) reduces the likelihood of looking at the Nutrition Facts label, (2) increases product purchase desirability, and (3) positively influences perceptions of product healthfulness.

Methods

Participant Recruitment

Data for this study were collected online. The questionnaire was administered over a 17-day period in October and November 2014. Study participants were recruited from Research Now's e-Rewards online panel, which, at the time the study was administered, had more than 3.2 million active members enrolled in the United States. ...

Randomly selected e-Rewards panel members were sent an e-mail invitation to participate in the study. After clicking on the link in the e-mail invitation, panelists were directed to the online instrument. ...

Study Design and Procedures

One of the primary components of the study was a choice experiment in which participants were randomly assigned to study conditions and asked to complete two tasks. ...

Reference

Verrill, L., Wood, D., Cates, S., Lando, A., & Yuanting, Z. (2017). Vitamin-fortified snack food may lead consumers to make poor dietary decisions. *Journal of the Academy of Nutrition & Dietetics, 117*(3), 376–385. doi:10.1016/j.jand.2016.10.008

ARTICLE 3

Objectives

The primary goal of this study was to assess changes in craving for and consumption of chocolate and other sweets in alcohol-dependent patients during and up to six months after outpatient alcohol detoxification. ...

We hypothesized significant correlations, indicating that chocolate consumption might be a strategy for coping with alcohol craving.

Methods

Study Subjects

One hundred and fifty outpatients aged 18–75 years who met the criteria for alcohol dependence according to the Diagnostic and Statistical Manual of Mental Disorders (DSM-IV; American Psychiatric Association, 1994) and International Classification of Diseases (ICD-10; Dilling, Mombour, Schmidt, & Schulte-Markwort, 1994), and who were starting a one-week detoxification treatment within the next four days, were enrolled in this study. …

Study Design

This questionnaire-based survey had a prospective, observational design with four points of measurement. …

Reference

Stickel, A., Rohdemann, M., Landes, T., Engel, K., Banas, R., Heinz, A., & Müller, C. A. (2016). Changes in nutrition-related behaviors in alcohol-dependent patients after outpatient detoxification: The role of chocolate. *Substance Use & Misuse, 51*(5), 545–552. doi:10.3109/10826084.2015.1117107

Considerations for Evaluating Quantitative Procedures

In the Introduction section, the researchers have identified what they wanted to find out—the research objective. In the Methods section, the researchers shift their focus to tell you how they went about doing it. Don't allow yourself to be overwhelmed by terminology, numbers, or formulas. Your task is to simply evaluate whether what they did would be likely to provide the information they were seeking.

First, consider how the researchers conducted the entire study from start to finish. In other words, look at the procedures holistically to gain an initial understanding of what the researchers did. Then, examine each aspect of the procedures separately. During this examination, some questions you may consider include: What permissions to conduct the study, if any, were sought and obtained? How did the researchers inform participants about the study? How did participants provide consent? What was the time frame for data collection? Within this time frame, what specific steps did the researchers follow to collect data? Once data were collected, what specific techniques and methods did the researchers use to analyze data?

As you consider these and other questions relevant to the researchers' descriptions of procedures in the study, remember our cooking and yoga analogies we presented at the beginning of this chapter. For the outcome of an investigation to be meaningful, the researchers must provide sufficient information about their procedures. In other words, you must determine whether you could replicate the study based on the information that the researchers provided about its procedures.

Procedures in Qualitative Research Designs

There are several key points to keep in mind with qualitative studies. First of all, they place more emphasis on verbal narratives than numerical data. Secondly, the objectives in qualitative studies are more open-ended and flexible, evolving over time. For instance, there are no hypotheses and, in fact, researchers are discouraged from making predictions lest they influence and bias the results. Thirdly, participants, often conceptualized as informants or respondents, are more likely to be selected using higher-risk sampling techniques.

Qualitative research methodology has been described as a phenomenon with a short history but a long past. It has only been within the last several decades that this methodology has been accepted into the mainstream of research in the education, health, helping, and social sciences professions. But the perspectives and techniques used in contemporary qualitative research have well-established roots in the research methodology long favored in anthropology, as well as in some elements of the case studies that provided the early foundations for counseling and psychotherapy.

Five elements are especially characteristic of qualitative research designs:

- They are usually conducted in natural settings.
- The researcher is often personally involved and makes no apology for that.
- Multiple forms of data are collected and may include interviews, observations, and artifacts.
- The emphasis is on process as much as any product.
- The search for meaning is evident through inductive and deductive analyses.

The Setting

It would be very unusual to find a qualitative study in the education, health, helping, and social sciences professions conducted in a controlled, laboratory setting. Natural settings, which are often referred to as research sites, are the overwhelming preference for such studies. The belief supporting qualitative, field-based research is that separating the phenomena being investigated from the site in which they naturally occur diminishes the quality of the information provided. In effect, there is no substitute for being there.

The Researcher

With qualitative studies, researchers themselves are often directly involved with the study. For example, they may conduct interviews, complete observations, or collect public or private documents. With this in mind, researchers must describe their role in the study and disclose any background information, beliefs, or biases that could potentially influence their interpretations.

The Data

Rather than relying on a single source of data, qualitative studies generally use triangulation, which involves collecting and validating data from multiple sources. Because qualitative studies rely on interpretations during data analyses, triangulation provides researchers with a comprehensive and robust technique with which to examine and interpret data. Sometimes researchers will ask several different evaluators to assist with coding and interpreting data in order to check for some degree of consistency among the themes identified.

The Process

Although quantitative studies primarily focus on outcomes, the emphasis in qualitative research is on process. A qualitative researcher, for example, could have little interest in whether a student arrived at the correct answer and a great deal of interest in the steps that were followed along the way. Unlike quantitative research designs, which are fixed frameworks, qualitative research designs are flexible and unfold as researchers collect data in the field. This allows for maximum flexibility as the process unfolds, especially when exploring relatively new phenomena.

The Search for Meaning

The focus of qualitative research is the deliberate attempt to learn how people attempt to make sense of their lives. Qualitative researchers arrive at these understandings by using inductive reasoning and analysis, whereas quantitative researchers are more likely to begin with an established theory, make predictions of specific outcomes based on that theory, and then test the accuracy of the predictions. In contrast, qualitative researchers will often be traveling in the opposite direction, using extensive and detailed analyses collected in a specific setting to then construct a theory explaining what was found (which can then be tested afterward using quantitative methodologies).

The keys that we gave you earlier—emphasis on words, rather than numbers—are only tools to quickly differentiate between the two types of studies. The true differences between the quantitative and qualitative research designs go far beyond which data type is preferred. Qualitative research is not just another way of performing a quantitative study. It is instead a uniquely different way of thinking about the purposes and objectives of research.

Although qualitative studies typically share the elements listed above, it would be a mistake to assume that all qualitative studies include these features. There are five basic subtypes of qualitative research designs: case studies, ethnography, grounded theory, narrative research, and phenomenology research, plus several newer, evolving methods, such as feminist and critical race theory. Each subtype and the corresponding procedures might or might not be relevant for a particular research objective. Thus, your job is to assess the appropriateness of the procedures described by the researchers in the Methods section in relation to the research objective identified in the Introduction section.

Table 5.2 Common Qualitative Research Designs

Type	Features	Focus
Case studies	• Provides a detailed investigation of one or more cases.	• To provide a complete description for each case.
Ethnography	• Provides a detailed investigation of the culture of a group of people from the perspective of group members.	• To cultivate holistic descriptions of the group and targeted characteristics.
Grounded theory	• Develops and generates a theory based on data that has been systematically collected and analyzed.	• To develop an explanation of the "how" and "why" of a phenomenon under study.
Narrative	• Depicts the experiences and lives of individuals as voiced through their own stories.	• To discern the essence of storied events and consider contexts that potentially influence the individual's experiences culturally, historically, or socially.
Phenomenology	• Describes how individuals experience events subjectively through feelings, judgements, or perceptions.	• To portray how others understand and view a phenomenon under study.

Considerations for Evaluating Qualitative Procedures

With qualitative studies, you want to first identify the role of the researchers. To what extent were the researchers personally involved with the procedures? If the researchers played a significant role among participants, how did the researchers identify factors, such as biases, ethical issues, personal and professional background understandings, and values, that may influence their interpretations? What previous experiences do the researchers have with the problem under study, participants, or research site? How might these experiences influence their interpretations?

 Reflective Exercise 5.2

In qualitative studies, it is important to understand the exact role of the researchers. Read the excerpts below and consider how the researchers described their role in their studies. Reflect on the researchers' involvement with the participants, study procedures, and interpretations. Share your reflections with a peer. Compare your reflections with the answers provided at the end of the chapter.

ARTICLE 1

Menstruation is a process that women experience throughout most of their lives and is an embodied symbol of womanhood, fertility, and health. ...

To better understand how young women view and uptake these messages from menstrual suppression advertisements today, we turned to a feminist critical discourse lens to identify, name, and unpack the embedded discourses around online menstrual suppression commercials. The goal of this study was to understand the meanings young women attach to menstrual suppression and how these messages might inform their decision-making regarding their use. We define menstrual suppression in our article as the use of oral contraceptives to prevent menstruation from occurring either in its normal frequency or interrupting the process for extended periods of time (Society for Menstrual Cycle Research, 2011).

As academics in Psychology and Social Work and clinical practitioners, we approach this topic making our individual standpoints transparent to reflect our feminist values and paradigm of practice. We are a mother and daughter and menstruating women. The differences in our age bookmark two diverse experiences of using oral contraceptives: 35 years ago as a

Colleen McMillan and Amanda Jenkins, "'A Magical Little Pill That Will Relieve You of Your Womanly Issues': What Young Women Say about Menstrual Suppression," *International Journal of Qualitative Studies on Health and Well-Being*, vol. 11, no. 1. Copyright © 2016 by Taylor & Francis Group.

birth control method for the mother and currently as a lifestyle option for the daughter.

Reference

McMillan, C., & Jenkins, A. (2016). "A magical little pill that will relieve you of your womanly issues": What young women say about menstrual suppression. *International Journal of Qualitative Studies on Health & Well-Being, 11*(1), 1–12. doi:10.3402/qhw.v11.32932

ARTICLE 2

This article is an interpretative phenomenological analysis exploring what it is like to experience the world synesthetically, and how synesthesia can inform our understanding of exceptional experiences (ExE) including subjective paranormal experiences.

Synesthesia

Synesthetic experiences occur when there is an involuntary sensory or conceptual response (or responses) to an inducing stimulus. ...

Methods

Aims and Design

This study adopted a case study design and employed interpretative phenomenological analysis (IPA) to explore the following research questions: What it is like to experience the world synesthetically and how can synesthesia inform our understanding of exceptional experiences?

Reflexivity

The interview was conducted by the author, who had previously met the participant when he had come to volunteer for the research study. Some topics had previously been explored in the context of this earlier conversation but were revisited more formally during the interview process. The author has an academic background in the psychology of exceptional experiences and some personal experiences with synesthesia (time-space synesthesia). This may have facilitated the rapport between the interviewer and interviewee and enabled a deeper conversation. The author was aware of the research literature (which is mostly quantitative) and had also met and had conversations with several other synesthetes prior to this interview. As such, she had an emerging sense of the benefits and difficulties surrounding these types of experience in addition to a desire to help to normalize experiences which tend to be marginalized. Despite these biases, the interview and analysis were approached as a conversation whereby the researcher attempted to be present, nonjudgmental, and nonleading with a view to deeply exploring Harry's subjective experiences and encouraging him to reflect on and explore his experiences.

Christine A. Simmonds-Moore, "An Interpretive Phenomenoogical Anlysis Exploring Synesthesia as an Exceptional Experience: Insights for Consciousness and Cognition," *Qualitative Research in Psychology*, vol. 13, no. 4. Copyright © 2016 by Taylor & Francis Group.

Reference

Simmonds-Moore, C. A. (2016). An interpretative phenomenological analysis exploring synesthesia as an exceptional experience: Insights for consciousness and cognition. *Qualitative Research in Psychology, 13*(4), 303–327. doi:10.1080/14780887.2016.1205693

After you have identified and evaluated the role of the researchers, you will want to examine the procedures they implemented closely. Keep in mind that the design of qualitative studies often unfolds during the investigation, so we recommend that you evaluate each step in succession, rather than holistically. This way, you may better understand why the researchers chose to implement specific procedures over others. Questions to consider during this part of your evaluation include: How did the researchers gain entry to the research site? What steps were taken to secure any required permissions? How were participants informed about the study? How did participants provide consent? How were data collected? What protocols were established for documenting or recording data? What strategies did the researchers use to analyze data? How did the researchers make interpretations?

Again, keep our cooking and yoga analogies in mind when you examine the researchers' descriptions of qualitative procedures and compare them to the research objective. It is critical that the researchers provide complete information so that another researcher could replicate their study. Therefore, your task in evaluating the procedures is simply to make your best judgment about whether you believe the researchers provided sufficient information about the procedures and if they were appropriate for the research objective.

Evaluating the Data Collection Tools

In addition to providing complete descriptions of appropriate procedures, researchers must also provide complete descriptions of appropriate data collection tools in the Methods section of a research report. Data collection tools, also referred to as instruments, set absolute limits for the ultimate value of a study. Unless appropriate tools were used to collect and gather the data, the results of the study are inconsequential and the researchers have essentially wasted their time.

Descriptions of the Data Collection Tools in Sufficient Detail

In both quantitative and qualitative studies, it is the obligation of the researchers to provide sufficient information for a reader to evaluate the appropriateness of the data collection tools. If this information is not complete, or if the tools used do not seem appropriate, we strongly advise you to be cautious regarding any definitive conclusions you draw from this study.

Relevance of the Data Collection Tools to Achieve the Research Objective

Which data collection tools do researchers use to gather information? It should come as no surprise that researchers tend to use different types of data collection tools in quantitative and qualitative studies. When the procedures indicate the use of quantitative research designs, the data collection tools are likely to be tests, questionnaires, surveys, and other instruments that describe or measure the outcome with numbers. On the other hand, qualitative research designs use data collection tools that better describe outcomes with words, such as documents, interviews, and observations. The tools may differ, but the good news is that the two primary quality concerns are essentially identical. Are the data reliable, and are the data valid?

The simplest definition of reliability is that it involves consistency. In a qualitative study of patient care in the outpatient setting, if a researcher finds evidence of trust between patients and nurses, would another researcher observing at the same time reach the same conclusion? Let's say the same topic was explored quantitatively, and 100 patients completed surveys consisting of closed-ended questions with which to report their perceived levels of trust with their nurses. Would a different sample of participants produce different results?

In either of the above examples, the question is not whether the results would have been identical. Most likely, they will not. The question with these examples is how much difference might be evident with another observer, a different research sample, or perhaps if the observational or survey data had been gathered at a different place or time?

On the other hand, the concept of validity, sometimes interpreted as truthfulness, is better defined as relevance. An observation or a survey, for example, could very well be valid for one purpose while not providing relevant information for another. Norm-referenced achievement tests, such as the Scholastic Aptitude Test (SAT) or Graduate Record Exam (GRE), are two examples. Such tests can provide information about how well an individual is performing in comparison with a peer group while providing essentially little useful information about exactly what an individual has or has not mastered. In addition, such standardized tests may be biased against more culturally diverse test takers, as well as those whose brains don't process knowledge in this rather structured format of choosing a single correct response among four options.

In the strictest sense, evaluating reliability and validity involves some complex issues with both quantitative and qualitative research designs. Most notably, each is situation-specific to a degree. For example, estimates of the reliability of a specific data collection tool may come from a particular group of participants and may (or may not) apply when used elsewhere. In this same manner, information about validity always requires a qualifier—valid for what use? These nuances and the various ways they are obtained are important especially when developing the data collection tools, but they are not so crucial in the task of evaluation. You will only need to review the information provided by the researchers about their data collection tools and make your best informed judgment about whether the tools used in the study appear to be consistent and truthful for which they were employed.

Table 5.3 Common Ways to Establish Reliability and Validity

Quantitative Research: Reliability	
The following methods use a statistical calculation called a reliability coefficient to serve as an index of reliability:	
Equivalent forms	Determines the consistency of a group of individuals' test scores on alternative forms that measure the same concept.
Inter-rater reliability	Ascertains the degree of consistency between two or more raters.
Internal consistency	Reveals how consistently test items measure a concept.
Test-retest	Evaluates consistency of test scores over time.
Quantitative Research: Validity	
Coefficient alpha	Checks for internal consistency among tests with multiple dimensions.
Expert reviews	A group of experts review a data collection tool and provide feedback regarding its breadth, clarity, and usefulness.
Factor analysis	Employs a statistical technique to determine how many dimensions are measured with a test.
Item-to-item correlation	Checks for internal consistency among tests with one dimension.
Pilot testing	Field-testing of a data collection tool to assess its accuracy.
Qualitative Research: Reliability and Validity	
Audit trail	Includes all raw data collected so that another reader can verify interpretations.
Constant data comparisons	Comparing one data source with another data source rather than considering each singularly.
Member checking	Researchers ask participants to check and confirm accuracy with interpretations.

Peer debriefing or review	Researchers ask a peer to review and provide feedback on the methods, findings, and conclusions of their study.
Reflexivity	Researchers share any potential biases or inclinations that may influence interpretations.
Triangulation	Multiple data sources and procedures are used to cross-check information and interpretations.

Quantitative Data Collection Tools

When new data collection tools have been developed for use in a quantitative study, researchers are expected to provide not only the information about the reliability and validity of the tools, but also some detail about how each was established. If instead they used existing tools and made no adaptations, you are more likely to find citations to support reliability and validity.

In either case, you can anticipate finding: (1) an identification of which of the several types of reliability and validity is being reported, (2) some numerical data, and (3) a verbal appraisal of reliability and validity of the data collection tools as they were used in the study. You do not necessarily need to pay particular attention to the numerical values or to the subtle differences among the various types of reliability and validity. Instead, you will want to be sure that the researchers did in fact provide some information about the data collection tools used, and that the information provided was consistent with the manner in which each data collection tool was used in the study.

Qualitative Data Collection Tools

The quality of data collection tools is equally important in qualitative studies. A major influence on reliability is the amount of information gathered, such as the length of time the researchers spent with participants to gather information about the consistency of the participants' initial responses. In other words, conducting one 30-minute interview with a participant in a study probably elicits less useful data than three 60-minute interviews spaced out over the course of several months.

In a like manner, increasing the number of participants is likely to provide more reliability in the data. Would you give more credence to a study where the researcher interviewed 11 children in one school about their experiences being bullied, or double that number from a wider variety of schools, ages, and settings?

Much of qualitative research rests on observational data. Of particular interest in regard to validity are things done by the researchers to minimize the impact of observer bias and observer effect. Observer bias reflects our tendency to see what we expect to see, and observer effect is the extent to which being observed changes the nature of what is observed. As you know, we often act differently when others are watching compared to when we are alone.

Qualitative researchers have often been leaders in recognizing the need to corroborate their findings through the convergence of data. This process, which is referred to as triangulation, may entail the use of different data sources, multiple methods to collect data, two or more investigators who collect and/or review data, or various theories with which to interpret the phenomenon under study.

What you look for when evaluating the quality of the data collection tools in a qualitative study is twofold. Did the researchers recognize that there could be some limitations in the data being used for their interpretations? What, if any, steps did the researchers take to minimize the impact of these limitations?

Summary and Closing Thoughts

Our belief is that the best way for you to approach evaluation of the procedures and data collection tools described in the Methods section of a research report is through simple logic and common sense. The authors have identified the research objective for their study in the Introduction section, and you have already determined whether the people they studied are likely to be able to provide the desired information. Now, your evaluation considers the following questions: What did the researchers do with participants? Were the researchers clear enough with how they went about conducting the study so that another researcher could replicate it? Do the procedures and data collection tools appear to be sufficient and appropriate for what they wanted to accomplish?

This is really not a difficult process, and we think that the greatest risk you face in making this evaluation is the possibility of getting sidetracked by terminology. Remember, all you need to do here is make your best judgment about whether the researchers used procedures and tools for gathering data that would appear to have a reasonable chance of providing relevant information related to what they were trying to find out by doing the study.

REFLECTIVE EXERCISE 5.1 EXPLANATION

In the study in Article 1, the researchers employed a quasi-experimental research design to compare outcomes. Because the Cooking Matter classes were formed by student enrollment, random sampling techniques were not used.

In the study in Article 2, the researchers used a true experimental research design to test their hypotheses. Individuals were randomly selected to participate from a specific group.

In the study in Article 3, the researchers used a correlational research design to explore the relationship between the craving for and consumption of chocolate and other sweets in alcohol-dependent patients.

REFLECTIVE EXERCISE 5.2 EXPLANATION

The researchers in the study in Article 1 examined the messages that young women encounter regarding menstrual suppression in contemporary advertisements. The researchers were menstruating women, a mother and her daughter, who represent two distinct experiences with menstrual suppression. Therefore, the similarities and differences of the researchers provide a balanced perspective with which to address any potential bias that may arise with interpretations.

This researcher in Article 2 conducted a case study to explore how one participant, Harry, experienced the world synesthetically. The researcher has an academic background in this area and was familiar with available research literature, which they disclosed may be potential biases. The researcher had a previous encounter with the participant, which along with the researcher's personal experiences with synesthesia, likely established a level of comfort and familiarity. The researcher conducted in-depth interviews with Harry akin to a conversation, which enabled the researcher to abandon judgment and provide an open forum for Harry to reflect on and explore his experiences.

Evaluation Tools for the Methods Section— Part II: Procedures and the Tools

Quantitative Study

Procedures: Sufficient Detail	
Consider	*Look for*
To what extent did the researchers provide sufficient detail about the procedures implemented in the study?	• Complete information and sufficient detail for each step in the procedures • How permissions to conduct the study were sought and obtained • How participants were informed about the study • How participants provided consent • The time frame for data collection • How data were collected and analyzed • Enough information was provided to replicate the study

Procedures: Relevant to the Researchers' Objective for the Study

Consider

How are the procedures relevant to achieve the research objective of the study?

Look for
- Type of research design
- Appropriateness of research design
- Relevance of procedures to the research objective

Data Collection Tools: Sufficient Detail

Consider

To what extent did the researchers provide sufficient detail about the data collection tools used in the study?

Look for
- Complete information
- Sufficient detail for each data collection tool
- Focus is on measurement

Data Collection Tools: Relevant to the Researchers' Objective for the Study

Consider

How are the data collection tools relevant to achieve the research objective of the study?

Look for
- Reported metric or technique to establish consistency (reliability) with findings
- Reported metric or technique to establish truthfulness (validity) with findings

Qualitative Study

Procedures: Sufficient Detail

Consider

To what extent did the researchers provide sufficient detail about the procedures implemented in the study?

Look for
- Complete information and sufficient detail for each step in the procedures
- Description for positionality and the role of the researchers
- How the researchers gained entry to the research site
- Steps taken to secure any required permissions
- How participants were informed about the study
- How participants provided consent
- How data were collected
- Established protocols for documenting and/or recording data
- Transcription methods used for nontextual data
- Data analysis strategies
- Explicit descriptions of coding procedures, including the codebook and analytic memoing
- How interpretations were made
- Information about data saturation
- Enough information was provided to replicate the study

Procedures: Relevant to the Researchers' Objective for the Study

Consider

How are the procedures relevant to achieve the research objective of the study?

Look for

- Type of research design
- Appropriateness of research design
- Relevance of procedures to the research objective

Data Collection Tools: Sufficient Detail

Consider

To what extent did the researchers provide sufficient detail about the data collection tools used in the study?

Look for

- Complete information
- Sufficient detail for each data collection tool
- Focus is on description

Data Collection Tools: Relevant to the Researchers' Objective for the Study

Consider

How are the data collection tools relevant to achieve the research objective of the study?

Look for

- Reported technique to establish consistency (reliability) with findings
- Reported technique to establish truthfulness (validity) with findings

CHAPTER 6

What Was the Answer (in English, Please)? Evaluating the Results Section

CHAPTER CONCEPTS

Categorical variables

Coding

Data saturation

Descriptive statistics

Effect size

Empirical findings

Inferential statistics

Measures of central tendency

Measures of variability

Nonparametric tests

Numerical variables

Objective findings

Parametric tests

Probability value

Raw data

Statistical significance

Theory

Theoretical perspectives

Introduction

Thus far you have somewhat of an idea about what the researchers were investigating, including a justifiable rationale that is directly connected to similar studies that have preceded it. The methods and procedures that followed were described in such a way that, if the opportunity presented itself, you could replicate this study to determine whether the results were an anomaly or part of meaningful pattern. In other words, the authors have described their plan, as well as the reasons as to why they proceeded in a particular way. Now your curiosity takes hold and you wonder what they discovered, or at least what they say resulted, from their efforts.

Before you get too excited, keep in mind that the reported results are often presented in a form and language that may seem inscrutable. You finally get to the point of all this and realize that you can't make sense of what was included. If it's a quantitative study, there may be all kinds of statistical descriptions, graphs, tables, symbols, and a certain language with its own vocabulary, grammar, and syntax. In qualitative studies, there is also a particular way of speaking and writing about the phenomena that was under investigation. We urge you not to get too caught up in the nuances of vernacular at this point and instead to concentrate on the basic ideas. After all, your main task is to have a general sense of what is being reported in the Results section before you read what the authors had to say about their findings. That way you can make your own semi-informed decisions about the value of what was reported.

The Results section includes a summary of what the researchers discovered, measured, manipulated, or treated based on the methods used to collect and analyze data. Hopefully, this was something meaningful. In the best possible circumstances, the reported results may persuade you to change the ways you think about your professional practices and lead you to modify the ways in which you operate in the future. For example, imagine that all these years you have been exercising at moderate intensity, hoping to stay in shape and manage weight control. You read a study that presents groundbreaking research, based on large-scale samples, that claim interval training (high-intensity, short-term sprints designed to pump up heart rate close to maximum) is far more efficient, burns more calories throughout the day, and increases overall fitness.

Without minimizing the importance of the results, though, sometimes the greatest value comes even before you get to this section of the report. Reading about the identified problem and review of relevant literature has already educated you about aspects of the profession and provided valuable information that can better inform your practice. However, the findings reported in the Results section provide evidence for the research base in which you ground your professional practices.

At this point, we want to emphasize that the Results section does not interpret findings from the study. In the case of quantitative studies, the results are often described as numerical representations in tables, graphs, or figures. With respect to qualitative studies, that may be direct quotes from the informants that relate to identified themes in the data. It is only in the following Discussion section that researchers would attempt to analyze and make sense of the results.

For quantitative research studies, the process of deciphering the results requires a basic level of proficiency with statistical concepts. Unfortunately, many math phobic readers lose the thread of the presentation with the Results section, either just skipping it and moving on to the conclusions, or just giving up on the article altogether.

With qualitative studies, the data are mostly presented as verbal narratives. Although many readers often find understanding this presentation of data much easier, it is important to recognize it is not without flaw. Sometimes the reporting of results is outstanding, most often it is at least adequate, and sometimes it is poor. Our goal in this chapter is address the special challenges associated with deciphering both empirical and objective findings and provide you with evaluation tools that guide your judgments regarding the quality of reporting.

Example 6.1 Contrast Between Reporting Quantitative and Qualitative Results

The following are excerpts from the Results section of a journal article that described a mixed methods study. As you read each excerpt, note distinguishing characteristics associated with the reporting of empirical and objective findings. Also, consider how each type of finding supports the research objectives of this particular study.

A Mixed-Methods Inquiry Into Trans* Environmental Microaggressions on College Campuses: Experiences and Outcomes

Transgender or trans* students experience interpersonal discrimination, including blatant violence and microaggressions on campus (Rankin, Weber, Blumenfeld, & Frazer, 2010). They also face macro-level environmental microaggressions (Sue, 2010) through institutional policies and practices, and social norms that maintain the male/man and female/woman sex/gender binary (Bilodeau, 2009; McKinney, 2005; Seelman, 2014). Environmental microaggressions are apparent on the systemic level and convey exclusionary messages toward marginalized groups (Sue, 2010). The message that trans* collegians often receive about their most basic needs is that these needs are not an institutional priority.

… In this mixed-methods study, we address these gaps by using quantitative data to explore the relationship between macro-level microaggressions and psychological distress and academic performance and engagement among trans* collegians. …

Methods

This concurrent mixed-methods study uses data from the National Study of LGBTQ Student Success (http://www.lgbtqsuccess.net/). The larger study utilized an anonymous online survey and semi-structured interviews to examine the experiences, well-being, and academic success of lesbian, gay, bisexual, transgender, and queer (LGBTQ) collegians. …

Results

Quantitative Survey Component

Encountering gender-binary forms was the most common environmental microaggression reported by survey participants ($M = 3.91$, $SD = 1.62$). Approximately 80% of the participants reported either frequently or very frequently experiencing this microaggression, while about 45% reported experiencing gender-binary sexual health information at these frequency levels ($M = 2.76$, $SD = 1.92$). Considerably lower than the other microaggressions, fewer participants (44.8%) reported experiencing inaccurate assumptions about health needs from health care workers more than occasionally ($M = 1.41$, $SD = 1.79$)…

Qualitative Interview Component

As the quantitative results suggest, not having access to safe restrooms can interfere with trans* students' academic performance and development and engagement. Several students discussed the barriers they faced in terms of availability, as well as locating and accessing gender-inclusive restrooms, when available. For instance, James explained that convincing the administration to get such restrooms was quite a challenge, which reflects the barriers trans* students face having their needs addressed:

I think it was last year, we're still working on gender-inclusive bathrooms, and it was such a headache. We brought it up, and we were waiting for them [administration] to talk about it or do something and, of course, nothing happened. It took one of my friends going on a hunger strike for them to actually start talking about it again. Then. … We got back word from the main campus about bathroom codes or some stupid stuff saying that we couldn't do it because we needed a certain number of fixtures [by gender binary] per building and all this bullshit, and it stopped and that was it.

Like James, Toby's efforts to advocate for gender-inclusive bathrooms were similarly stalled by the administration, although apparently support existed: "We [LGBTQ club] got a few gender-neutral restrooms erected. The rest didn't end up getting finished because we wound up in weird conflicts with maintenance over who was paying for the [restroom] signs." …

Reference

Woodford, M. R., Joslin, J. Y., Pitcher, E. N., & Renn, K. A. (2017). A mixed-methods inquiry into trans* environmental microaggressions on college campuses: Experiences and outcomes. *Journal of Ethnic & Cultural Diversity in Social Work, 26*(1–2), 95–111. doi:10.1080/1 5313204.2016.1263817

 ## Reflective Exercise 6.1

In small groups of two to four individuals, pool your collective knowledge, skills, and guessing abilities, to decipher the results presented in Example 6.1. Also share your assumptions about what the researchers might talk about in the Discussion section of this article. As the reader, what are some things you might tentatively conclude based on your reading of this data?

Basic Concepts and Terminology in Quantitative Studies

Understanding some basic concepts and terminology in descriptive and inferential statistics is a prerequisite for evaluating the results presented in essentially all quantitative research studies. If you already possess a moderate or mastery level understanding of statistical concepts, then this part of the chapter will be a good review. If not, the content may take some time and reflection, but we believe you'll be pleased with the outcome of your efforts. Even if you might characterize yourself as math phobic or not good with numbers, you may be able to forever banish these self-labels in regard to basic statistics with a little effort and patience.

We do have a disclaimer. If you were not a statistician when you began this chapter, you will not be one when it is done. We have a much more limited agenda, which entails simply being able to quickly interpret the numerical information typically reported as results in quantitative studies.

While traveling in a foreign country, a complete grasp of the language makes worldwide traveling much easier. However, it is often possible to get around quite well with just a few key phrases, such as, "Thank you," "Where is the bathroom?," and "How much does this cost?" In a similar manner, a complete grasp of statistical concepts would make it much easier to interpret the findings of most quantitative studies, but it is often sufficient to understand just a few key concepts and terms.

Keep in mind that the content in this part of the chapter will not teach you how to handle statistics. There are no standardized formulas, hand calculations, or explanations for how to use statistical software programs. The good news is that if and when you conduct your own studies there are always "stat geeks" with whom you can consult (unless you decide to become one yourself!). Our goal is much narrower—to help you to understand the results reported in quantitative studies. When evaluating a research report, the aim is to know what it means even if you remain uncertain about exactly how it was calculated.

Descriptive and Inferential Statistics

The numbers used to present results of a study come in two distinct "flavors." Some, the descriptive statistics, as the name suggests, simply describe an outcome with a summary number. There is no risk involved. It's like reporting the score or stats of an athletic sport (batting average, on base percentage, assists, free throw percentage). The other flavor, inferential statistics, does include some risk. Their purpose, going beyond what was found in the study, is to draw generalizations using a known outcome to predict one that is not known for sure. Using inferential statistics is like making a wager on the outcome of a game before it even begins.

Descriptive Statistics

There are two primary categories of descriptive statistics. Each may or may not be used to present results in a qualitative study, but one or more will be found when the focus is quantitative. They are used to report typical performance, as well as differences in performance.

Measures of central tendency. The descriptive statistic you will see most often is the one with which you are already likely familiar. It is the average performance of some group on some measure, identified as the mean and labeled with an M. This statistic presents no particular challenge in interpretation. When you see that label you know that the researchers just added some values and divided the sum by the number of values included. If several groups were used in a study and identified as groups X, Y, and Z, their respective mean scores are usually labeled by just adding a subscript with their group identifier, such as M_x, M_y, and M_z.

Given the purpose of its calculation, it is not surprising that the mean, along with two other statistics, median and mode, are defined as measures of central tendency and intend to show how a number fits compared with others in the group. The intent is to use a single numeral to identify what is typical. The median (the value in the middle after values have been placed in rank order) and the mode (the value that occurs most often) are less often reported in research studies.

Measures of variability. Another descriptive statistic likely to be reported in the results of quantitative studies is the standard deviation, which is labeled as SD. This statistic is used to describe how different the values in the group were from one another. It is closely allied with the mean and, in fact, represents the average difference between each value and the mean.

Calculating a standard deviation is a bit complex because of a feature that requires us to say that it *represents* the average instead of it *is* the average. Actual calculations involve first finding the mean of a group of values and then finding the difference between the mean and each value. Next, further calculations entail squaring these differences, adding the squared differences, dividing that sum by the number of values, and then calculating the square root. You only need this information if you are hand calculating standard deviations, which we hope you never have to do. For evaluation purposes, all you need to know is that the standard deviation is a descriptive statistic that represents the average difference and tells you how close the values were to each other (see Figure 6.1).

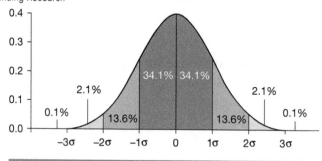

Figure 6.1 Standard Deviation

Fig. 6.1: Copyright © M. W. Toews (CC by 2.5) at https://commons.wikimedia.
org/wiki/File:Standard_deviation_diagram.svg.

To illustrate, let's pretend you have been offered a position at an organization. During the interview process, you were informed that starting annual salaries averaged around $60,000. Employee salaries for this organization are posted publically, so you dig a little deeper to investigate the accuracy of their claim. The results of your salary search did, indeed, confirm their claim—the average starting salary was $60,000. However, you also discovered that the variance among starting salaries was approximately $15,000. In this case, having information about the standard deviation would be more helpful than only having information about the mean, especially in regard to salary negotiation.

The standard deviation and some related descriptive statistics, including the quartile deviation and the range, are defined as measures of variability. The intent is to use a single numeral to identify the typical extent of differences within a set of values. The quartile deviation is associated with the median and may be reported in the situations described above where the median is deemed a more appropriate tool to identify central tendency. The range, as you might guess, is simply the difference between the highest value and the lowest value.

Inferential Statistics

Both quantitative and qualitative studies may use descriptive statistics in the Results section of a research report. Both types of studies describe and summarize the immediate group of data in the study. On the other hand, inferential statistics are generally used in studies when there is a quantitative focus. The goal of inferential statistics to go beyond the immediate data set and, as the name suggests, make inferences. In other words, researchers use information from a sample (the immediate data set) to estimate, generalize, predict, or make a decision about an entire population. Recall from Chapter 4 the various types of sampling procedures researchers may use to create a sample of participants representative of the total population.

There are several tests researchers use to make inferences, test hypotheses, or reach their conclusions. Although we will focus on the most commonly used methods, the underlying question is much the same: Can the findings from the samples be generalized to the entire population? To answer this question, researchers calculate a *p*-value, or probability value, to determine the level of significance with their findings. In the education, health, helping, and social sciences professions, *p*-values that are .05 or less are desired because they indicate that there was a probability of less than five percent of the reported findings occurring by chance. Thus, reported findings where $p \leq .05$ suggests statistical significance.

Quantitative researchers are expected to begin their studies with some prior belief about the probable outcome. You may remember from Chapter 3 that the prior belief can be classified as a

- directional hypothesis, identifying which treatment will be more effective;
- nondirectional hypothesis, considering one of the treatments as more effective; or
- null hypothesis, expecting no difference between the two treatments.

Regardless of the prior belief, it is typical for the inferential statistical analysis to be conducted in the form of a null hypothesis.

Once data has been collected, researchers must first ensure that their data set meets four assumptions before they analyze it with statistical testing:

1. Data must be normally distributed (variables represent a bell-shaped curve when plotted on a graph).
2. Data must have a linear and sequential relationship (data creates a linear line on a graph).
3. Data must be homoscedastic (data from multiple groups have the same variance).
4. Data are independent and not connected in any way.

If the data meets all of these assumptions, then researchers use a parametric test. There may, though, be times when data violates one or more of these assumptions. When this occurs, researchers simply use a nonparametric test. Nonparametric tests are also used when studies involve small sample sizes.

Time Out

Take a deep breath. Those of you who are arithmophobic (fear of numbers)—and yes, that is a real fear—can remind yourselves that all of these statistical terms are simply names for the language that quantitative researchers use to describe their work. You already use some of them in your daily lives when you say things like, "I'd say the average amount of time it takes to drive to my house is a half hour." Or, "I somehow think this humid weather is correlated with the storms we had earlier in the week."

Correlation. A single numeral, the correlation coefficient, is used to describe the relationship between the two values in a sample and provide an estimate for this relationship in the population from which the paired sample was taken. This relationship is typically labeled as an *r* if there are only two measures (admission test score and graduate school grade point average) or as an *R* if there are more than two measures (admission test score and undergraduate grade point average for predicting graduate school grade point average). If there is no relationship between the values, the correlation coefficient is zero. If there is a perfect relationship between them, the correlation coefficient is 1.0.

The primary caution in interpreting this statistic is that a correlation coefficient looks like a decimal fraction but is interpreted quite differently. With correlation coefficients, the size of the relationship is expressed by the numeral itself. The positive or negative sign that precedes the numeral indicates the direction, not the strength of the relationship. When the sign is positive, this suggests that as one score goes up, the other tends to go up, too. A negative sign indicates instead that as one measure goes down, the other also tends to go down, such as with the relationship between the number of hours students worked each week and earned scores on exams.

For example, in a correlation study you might encounter a finding reported as $r = .20$, $p > .05$. The interpretation would be that the probability is greater than 5 in 100 that a correlation this high (.20) would have been found with this sample if the correlation between these variables in the population was zero. In other words, there does not appear to be a statistically significant relationship between these two variables.

 Example 6.2 Bizarre (and Bogus) Correlations

A salient point with correlations is that they do not suggest causation. In other words, when two variables demonstrate a significant correlation, this does not mean that a change in one variable caused a change in the other variable. Below, we have provided a couple of examples that demonstrates this fallacy.

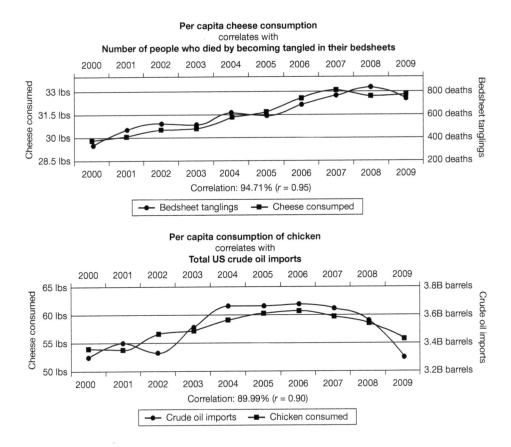

Figure 6.2a,b Per Captia Cheese Consumption Correlates with Number of People Who Died By Becoming Tangled in Their Bedsheets, Per Captia Consumption of Chicken Correlates with Total US Crude Oil Imports

Ex. 6.2a: Source: http://www.tylervigen.com/spurious-correlations.
Ex. 6.2b: Source: http://www.tylervigen.com/spurious-correlations.

Most of the correlation coefficients you will find reported in quantitative studies are *Pearson product-moment coefficients*, commonly referred to as Pearson's *r*, and is calculated with reference to the means and standard deviations. Pearson's *r* is a parametric test, and the nonparametric tests include Spearman rank order correlation coefficient (Spearman's rho) and Kendall rank correlation coefficient (Kendall's tau).

The *t*-test. The *t*-tests are parametric tests that compare the means of one or two groups. There are three types of *t*-tests that are used in specific situations:

- One-sample *t*-tests compare the sample mean to a known or hypothesized population mean. Suppose a clinic implemented a new prenatal care program for women who qualify for government assistance to reduce low birth weight babies. A one-sample *t*-test would be appropriate in a situation where a researcher examines the weight of babies born to 50 women who participated in the program. This group of women would be the research sample mean. The known mean could be the reported national statistic for average birth weight. A nonparametric test for this situation is the Wilcoxon signed-rank test.

- Two sample *t*-tests compare the means of two independent samples that are not related with each other. These are also known as unpaired or independent samples *t*-tests. To extend the scenario described above, a researcher could compare the birth weight of babies born to 50 women who participated in the program (Independent Sample A) to the birth weight of babies born to 50 women who did not participate in the program (Independent Sample B). A nonparametric test for this situation is the Mann-Whitney U test.

- Paired samples *t*-tests compare two means that are from the same sample. These are also known as dependent or related measures *t*-tests. To continue with the current example, a researcher could compare the birth weight of first- and second-born babies born to women who participated in the program during both of their pregnancies. In this example, the research sample consisted of the same women and took two different measures for birth weight. A nonparametric test for this situation is the Wilcoxon signed-rank test.

Analysis of variance. The name of this test may seem a bit off-putting, but it actually is very descriptive and quite useful in a number of ways. When things differ from one another, they could be said to vary a little or a lot. The total amount that they vary could be called the variance. Studying something in detail is analysis. Therefore, studying in detail the differences between things would be an analysis of variance (ANOVA). In everyday life, conducting an ANOVA would be valuable to compare the effectiveness of several different medications in treating Alzheimer's disease, multiple teaching methods for enhancing student learning in mathematics, the impact of a social program for families who live in poverty administered in a number of locations, and so on.

Researchers use ANOVAs to compare means from two or more different groups. This parametric test explores variances due to differences between each group, as well as variances due to differences between individuals within each group. There are several types of ANOVAs that are used in specific situations:

- One-way ANOVAs use one independent variable that has two or more levels, or groups, to assess differences in one dependent variable. For example, this test would be appropriate in a study that explores patient satisfaction levels as perceived quality of care (dependent variable) between racial groups (Native American, Asian, Black/African American, Hispanic/

Latino, White/Non-Hispanic, two or more races). A nonparametric test for this situation is the Kruskal–Wallis H test.

- Factorial ANOVAs use multiple independent variables that each has two or more groups to assess differences in one dependent variable. To extend the previous example, this test would be appropriate in a study that explores patient satisfaction levels as perceived quality of care between racial groups and the highest level of education obtained (less than high school, high school/GED, Associate's degree, Bachelor's degree, Master's degree, Doctoral degree). A nonparametric test for this situation is the Aligned Rank Transform procedure.

- Repeated Measures ANOVAs are used to examine changes or differences in the mean over time by taking three or more measurements from the same sample. For example, this test would be appropriate in a study that explores patient satisfaction levels as perceived quality of care among a group of patients at three different points in time (initial visit, 3-month follow-up visit, 6-month follow-up visit). A nonparametric test for this situation is the Friedman test.

- Multivariate analysis of variance (MANOVA) extends ANOVA tests by investigating differences between independent groups on two or more dependent variables. Using the same example, this test would be appropriate in a study that explores patient satisfaction levels as perceived quality of care and perceived involvement in decision making (dependent variables) between racial groups and the highest level of education obtained.

Analysis of covariance. The ANCOVA is a special type of ANOVA that can be used when there is some question about whether participants in the groups being investigated were sufficiently alike when the study began. When you see an ANCOVA was used in the study, you know that the values being compared are not the ones actually made by the participants, such as with posttest scores. Instead, the values have been statistically adjusted to account for differences on another variable, such as pretest scores, before the analysis is conducted.

Suppose that researchers began with a belief that in a distance learning environment, full-time students would have greater gains in course performance than part-time students. On the posttest, the mean score for full-time students was 88 and 84 for part-time students. The difference was statistically significant ($r = .02$), suggesting that full-time students performed better. But, there's more. A pretest was administered at the beginning of the class to identify what students already knew about the content. On the pretest, the mean score of full-time students was 55 and 53 for part-time students.

An ANCOVA creates new scores to compare, taking into account the actual differences on both pretests and posttests and the correlation coefficients among the scores. The outcome produces "new" posttest scores that have been statistically adjusted for differences between the groups with the pretest scores. With a set of sample data for the example above, this adjustment came out with a new mean score of 86.9 for the full-time students and 87.8 for the part-time students. According to these findings, the part-time students actually have the higher score. Furthermore, the difference was not statistically significant (p = .07), suggesting that neither full-time nor part-time students outperformed the other based purely upon enrollment status. Notice that without the adjustment the researchers would have made an erroneous conclusion.

Also notice that this adjustment is not the same as simply subtracting the pretest from the posttest to produce a gain score. The latter is not a recommended procedure because of issues associated with measurement error. The ANCOVA is an often recommended procedure when there is reason to believe that groups were not equivalent before the intervention began. A nonparametric test for this situation is Quade's rank analysis of covariance.

Chi-square. The Chi-square is a nonparametric test that investigates differences with categorical variables. Categorical variables yield data in categories (gender, race, religion, political preference), whereas numerical variables yield numerical data (GPA, IQ, blood pressure, weight). There are two types of Chi-square tests that are used in specific situations:

- Chi-square test of independence determines if a relationship exists between categorical variables by calculating a statistic that compares the data counts of categorical responses between two or more independent groups. An example of a research question that might use this test would be: What is the relationship between age and how people vote?

- Chi-square goodness of fit test determines whether random categorical variables follow an expected probability distribution. An example of a research question that might use this test would be: Are different socioeconomic groups equally represented among members of a specific church congregation?

The statistical tests presented in this chapter were selected because they are the ones most likely to be found in the studies you read. They also provide the foundation for most of the other statistical tests you might encounter. Remember also that finding a statistically significant difference, $p < .05$, doesn't alone provide direct information about what caused that difference. Even if the observed difference is quite large, identifying the cause of a difference is more a function of how the research was designed than how the data were analyzed.

To compensate for this interpretive limitation with statistical significance, most journals now recommend that researchers provide an additional statistic called the effect size in the results. The effect size gives you some additional information about how important any observed differences may be. A common measure for effect sizes is Cohen's *d*, which calculates the sizes of observed differences. Depending on the type of statistical test, effect sizes are interpreted as small, medium, or large.

Reflective Exercise 6.2

Okay, we have overloaded you with so many terms, concepts, names, and statistical devices that all sort of blends together. You may also be asking yourself the legitimate question, "Why do I have to bother to learn all this stuff? I just want to help people." Good question.

Brainstorm on your own, or in small groups of three to four individuals, as many reasons you can think of for why learning (not mastering) statistical language and procedures could enhance your work and life. Some of your reasons may be silly, as well as practical. Keep in mind the purpose of any brainstorming exercise is to be spontaneous and open-minded while going for quantity of ideas, as well as quality.

Evaluating the Quantitative Results

There are two primary factors for you to consider in evaluating the content in the Results section in both quantitative and qualitative research reports. We begin evaluating the content in the Results section of quantitative research reports with what by now is a familiar theme—the presentation of results should use sufficient detail and reflect the research objective of the study. The researchers should also present their results in a logical sequence and organized manner, avoiding any discussion, explanations, or interpretations. Also, keep in mind that quantitative findings do not definitively prove anything or establish causality. Rather, they provide empirical evidence to confirm or reject a hypothesis, recognize trends and patterns, or demonstrate associations between variables.

Presentation of the Findings in Sufficient Detail

When conducting an evaluation of the Results section for a quantitative study, you will look for systematic, textual descriptions of findings. Researchers may also present findings using visual displays, such as tables and graphs. Tables use columns and rows to present large amounts of numerical values and textual information, and figures refer to all other types of visuals, such as graphs, charts, and photographs. Visual displays should be self-explanatory, have clear titles, and extend—not repeat—key points addressed in textual descriptions. Unfortunately, both textual descriptions and visual displays can be highly misleading, so caution is warranted when you form impressions from them.

 Example 6.3

"There are three types of lies—lies, damn lies, and statistics."

When evaluating published research reports, you must be as critical of the visual elements as you are with what the researchers have written. Look at the examples below and see if you can identify the most appropriate visual display. For the three remaining graphs, see if you can identify the misleading elements.

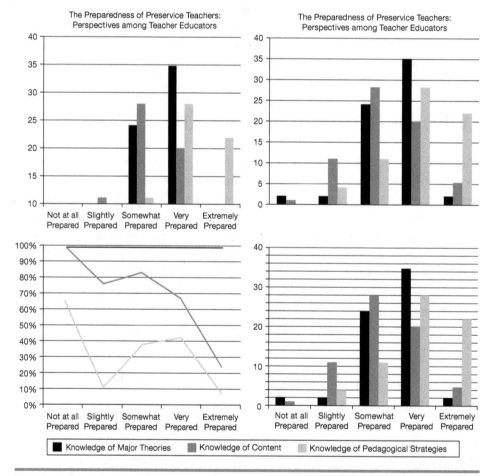

Figure 6.3a-d The Preparedness of Preservice Teachers: Perspectives among Teacher Educators

During your evaluation of the Results section in a quantitative research report, consider the following questions:

- Were any unanticipated events that occurred during data collection reported?
- Was detailed and sufficient information provided that described the raw data collected?
- Did the raw data fit the assumptions underlying statistical testing? If not, were appropriate adjustments or modifications made?
- Was detailed and sufficient information provided that described all findings resulting from analytic techniques?
- If descriptive statistics were reported, were sample sizes (n), measures of central tendency (M), and measures of variability (SD) reported?
- If inferential statistics were reported, did the researchers report the test statistic (t-value, F-value, r-value), along with a p-value?
- Were effect sizes reported for statistically significant p-values?
- Were visual displays used appropriately? You can judge appropriate use by examining whether the visual display: (1) is clearly labeled; (2) has proper scaling; (3) uses font, ruling, typeface, and spacing to enhance readability, (4) summarizes and supports key findings, and (5) includes all relevant information so that they may be "read" independent of text explanations.

Relevance of the Findings to Achieve the Research Objective

Reported results should clearly address the research objective of the study. If the researchers choose to provide information not directly related to their research objective, it should be clearly identified as such and include some explanation for its inclusion. During your evaluation, consider the following questions: Are the results relevant to the research problem under investigation? Have the researchers refrained from interpreting results? Was an explanation provided for any information included that was not relevant to the research objective?

Basic Concepts and Terminology in Qualitative Studies

Understanding some basic concepts and terminology used in qualitative research is also essential to evaluate the results effectively. Similar to the previous section in this chapter that addressed basic concepts and terminology for quantitative studies, our goal is to provide you with a sufficient understanding of fundamental notions and verbiage used in qualitative studies. Again, keep in mind that the content in this part of the chapter will not teach you how to perform qualitative analyses. Rather, it will help you understand the results reported in qualitative studies.

There are several qualitative designs that are somewhat familiar to use, such as case studies (an in-depth analysis of an individual, event, organization, or group) or ethnography (the method favored by anthropologists, often by observing how people behave, communicate, and interact within their natural environment). In addition, narrative research seeks to make sense of people's stories about their lives. Similarly, phenomenology explores the experiences of individuals who experience the same phenomenon.

Because qualitative designs rely heavily on the interpretation of subjective data, qualitative researchers may use theory as an orienting lens with which to explore issues among marginalized or underrepresented populations. Using such theoretical perspectives guides researchers to examine issues of importance among underserved groups and present findings that inspire action for social change. For example, researchers may use critical theory to capture the reality among a particular group who experience societal constraints attributable to a shared characteristic, such as class, disabilities, ethnicity, gender, race, religion, or sexual orientation. More specifically, use of feminist theory provides a lens for researchers to understand issues related to gender discrimination, whereas queer theory provides the necessary framework to focus on individuals who identify as lesbian, gay, bisexual, transgender, questioning, or queer.

Qualitative Analysis Techniques

Prior to beginning data analysis, researchers usually first transcribe their data. In Chapter 5, we referenced types of qualitative data collection tools, which include nontextual data, such as audio-recorded or videoed interview files. Researchers must determine the best way to transform this data for analyses, such as word-for-word dictations, written anecdotal notations, or frequency counts. In many cases, researchers choose to transcribe their own data, not just to save money but also so they can more fully immerse themselves in the material. It is, therefore, important to know the positionality of the researchers to determine how their beliefs, characteristics, and viewpoints may have influenced ways in which data were interpreted and represented.

Qualitative data analysis is an iterative process where researchers engage with data, identifying significant concepts and conceptualizing interpretations. After an initial reading of all data, researchers use coding to assign excerpts of data to categories. Researchers may begin coding with a predetermined list of a priori codes, which generally consists of about 10 to 40 codes that derive from the study's research objective, conceptual or theoretical framework, previously conducted studies, or existing knowledge among the researchers. Researchers may also use emergent codes, which are concepts, ideas, or meanings that materialize from the data. While coding, researchers maintain a codebook, where they keep a record of all codes assigned, along with definitions, guidelines, and examples.

The process of coding data varies slightly, depending on the specific analysis technique that researchers use. With most techniques, coding occurs at two levels: (1) open coding, where researchers label chunks of text with provisional codes; and (2) axial coding, where researchers confirm the accuracy of provisional codes, identify possible relationships, and refine their coding scheme by adding, deleting, revising, and merging coding categories. Throughout the coding process, qualitative researchers write notes to themselves through analytic memoing, which documents reflective insights about what they learn about the data.

Example 6.4 An Example of Coding in Qualitative Research

Below is an example of how a researcher coded qualitative data that were collected during a study that explored experiences of therapists who treat clients coping with fatherhood issues. The data below is an excerpt from an interview where the researcher posed a question and the participant (the therapist) provided a response. Note how, after transcription, the researcher first highlighted what he considered to be meaningful material, and then initially coded the data by descriptively labeling it in the margin. He ended up with hundreds of these provisional codes, which were eventually classified into a half dozen broad themes that described how therapists conceptualize and experience their clinical work with these clients.

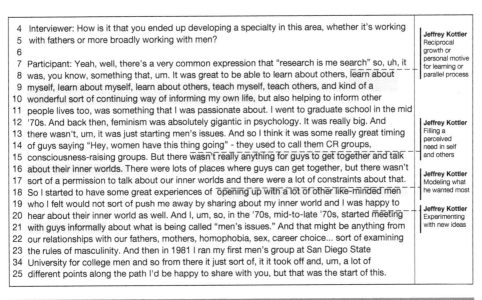

Figure 6.4 An Example of Coding in Qualitative Research

There are several ways in which qualitative researchers analyze their data. We will focus on the most commonly used methods, which may be conducted manually by hand, with the assistance of technology, or with qualitative software. No matter which process researchers use, their goal during data analysis is to achieve data saturation, or the point at which no new themes or insights emerge.

Grounded theory analysis. Grounded theory analysis is one of the most widely used data analysis techniques in qualitative studies. The primary goal of this technique is to generate a theory (or at least a conceptual framework) from data. Researchers who use grounded theory analysis first explore the data inductively using open and axial coding. While coding, researchers apply the constant comparison method, where they continuously compare concepts present in the data to arrive at deeper conceptual understandings. After axial coding, researchers then use selective coding to analytically identify the main phenomenon in the data. During this phase of coding, researchers consider all of their entries in the codebook, analytic memos, and identified categories to select one category as the core category that best described the main phenomenon. Once the core category is identified, researchers characterize its properties and then systematically determine its relationship to other relevant categories.

Content analysis. Content analysis is a qualitative analysis technique used exclusively for analyzing text data. Essentially, researchers who use content analysis rigorously examine the language within large amounts of text to organize and deduce meaning. With content analysis, researchers must first decide whether they will employ a manifest analysis (refrain from interpretations and limit analyses to explicit descriptions visible in the text), a latent analysis (search for underlying meanings that are inferred from the text), or a combination of the two. Once the level of analysis has been determined, researchers explore the data using open and axial coding to identify categories and any possible subcategories. The final step involves drawing conclusions based upon identified categories and subcategories, relationships between categories, and the presence of any patterns.

Researchers attempt to break down data with grounded theory and content analysis techniques. On the contrary, researchers approach data analysis more holistically with certain types of qualitative studies, such as case studies, ethnography, phenomenology, and narrative research. In addition to analyzing content, researchers also analyze form with these types of studies. Analyzing content and form together enables researchers to look for patterns and themes in the data, as well as ways in which spoken and written language were used to convey meanings.

Evaluating the Qualitative Results

The criteria for evaluating qualitative studies are essentially the same as those used when the report described a quantitative study. The information provided in the Results section of a qualitative study is typically much longer than in a quantitative study. This occurs, in part, because much of the data consists of direct quotations or excerpts from the data to provide rich detail about what the researchers found.

Presentation of the Findings in Sufficient Detail

When conducting an evaluation of the Results section for a qualitative study, you will look for descriptions and analyses that are presented clearly and in sufficient detail. Rather than summarizing what was learned with a statement like, "Many participants were apparently angry," specificity is expected. What exactly was said or done? Who specifically said or did it? Precisely, what was the context? Typically, there are representative quotations from the participants that illustrate the identified themes that were evident in the data. For instance, the following block quotation might be included that relates directly to a theme in a study about student uncertainty, confusion, and anxiety related to studying statistical concepts in a research course:

> It's not that I don't see the value in this stuff [sighs and shakes his head], it's just that I feel so stupid because it all gets muddled in my head. I pretend to understand things that I really don't get at all because I guess I don't want others to know that this all seems beyond me. I've just never been good at this stuff. When I was younger in math classes, I would just zone out. And my grades were pretty pitiful so I just gave up and lost interest. I think in another world, I wish I could start over again and maybe concentrate and study harder when I was younger so I had a better grasp of the basics. But I think for me, now, it's too damn late.

 Reflective Exercise 6.3

In the block quotation above, carefully read and highlight or underline anything that seems to stand out to you as being meaningful or significant. One example, to get you started, might be: "I feel so stupid."

After identifying important data through open coding, try to assign a label to each piece with axial coding. For example, you might assign the label "Feelings of Inadequacy" to the code "I feel so stupid."

Finally, what central theme do you see as represented in this block quotation that may have led the researcher to include it as a key feature of the study?

In evaluating the presentation of qualitative results, you should look for balance. On the one hand, you want enough information to assess the adequacy of the findings. On the other hand, you don't want to be overwhelmed by extraneous information. That is generally not too much of an issue considering the space limitations of professional journals.

During your evaluation of the Results section in a qualitative research report, consider the following questions:

- Was detailed and sufficient information provided that described the type of data collected?
- For nontextual data, were descriptions regarding transcription methods provided?
- Did the researchers address their positionality?
- Was explicit information about coding procedures provided, including maintenance of the codebook and engagement with analytic memoing?
- Did the researchers provide information regarding data saturation?
- Was detailed and sufficient information provided that described all findings resulting from analytic techniques?
- Were direct quotations and data excerpts used appropriately?

When you are done reviewing the results, you should have a sense of what transpired, what was gleaned from the data collection, and tentative confidence that the results presented appear representative of what was initially planned. As a bonus, you should also find the descriptive data somewhat interesting and your curiosity piqued regarding what the researchers have to say about it in their discussion of results.

Relevance of the Findings to Achieve the Research Objective

Similar to quantitative studies, reported results in qualitative studies should clearly address the research objective of the study. After evaluating the sufficiency of detail with the presentation of findings, consider the following question: Are the results relevant to the research problem under investigation?

Summary and Closing Thoughts

Evaluating a research report means thinking critically about what is presented, not just accepting as factual truth whatever the researchers say. Before you look at their interpretations and conclusions, you want to digest and understand enough of the results so that you can form your own impressions and opinions. One of the gifts of learning to critically read research reports and interpret results is that it makes you a far more intelligent and informed thinker in any context of your life when you are presented with information that may be suspect or unreliable.

Although we certainly believe that researchers are responsible professionals, they have invested a lot of time in conducting the study, analyzing the results, and preparing the report. Their own biases and blind spots may have influenced what they perceived and reported in the results. Therefore, a tendency to overstate or selectively report their findings would not be surprising. Your control for this tendency is to read the results yourself and form your own conclusions before you read what the researchers have to say about their findings. Otherwise, you may find it difficult to fully evaluate how researchers discuss the results and significance of their study in the last section of their research report—the Discussion section.

We won't pretend that it is an easy task to make one's way through the results reported in research studies. Feeling a bit overwhelmed by the amount of information presented is not an unusual response. Although the journey may at times be difficult, the destination can be important.

Evaluation Tools for the Results Section

Quantitative Study

Sufficient Detail	
Consider	*Look for*
How did the researchers present the findings with sufficient detail?	• Explanations for unanticipated events
	• Detailed descriptions of collected data
	• Complete information for findings
	• Proper reporting for descriptive and/or inferential statistics
	• Appropriate use of visual displays

Relevant to the Researchers' Objective for the Study

Consider

To what extent are the results relevant to achieve the research objective of the study?

Look for

- Relevance with results to the research objective
- Absence of interpretations
- Explanations for information that is not relevant to the research objective

Qualitative Study

Sufficient Detail

Consider

How did the researchers present the findings with sufficient detail?

Look for

- Detailed descriptions of collected data
- Complete information for findings
- Appropriate use of direct quotations and data excerpts

Relevant to the Researchers' Objective for the Study

Consider

To what extent are the results relevant to achieve the research objective of the study?

Look for

- Relevance with results to the research objective
- Absence of interpretations
- Explanations for information that is not relevant to the research objective

Glossary of Terms

Term	Definition
Analysis of covariance (ANCOVA)	A special type of ANOVA that statistically adjusts values prior to conducting the analysis to account for differences on another variable.
Analysis of variance (ANOVA)	A quantitative parametric test that (1) compares means from two or more different groups, (2) explores variances due to differences between each group, and (3) explores variances due to differences between individuals within each group.
analytic memoing	Reflective insights that a researcher writes to themselves while coding qualitative data.
axial coding	The second level of coding during qualitative data analyses.

case study	An in-depth qualitative analysis of an individual, event, organization, or group.
Chi-square	A nonparametric quantitative test that investigates differences with categorical variables.
coding	A qualitative analysis technique that assigns excerpts of data to categories.
Cohen's d	A common measure for effect sizes that calculates the sizes of observed differences.
constant comparison method	Continuously comparing concepts present in qualitative data to arrive at deeper conceptual understandings.
content analysis	A qualitative analysis technique used exclusively for analyzing text data.
correlation coefficient	A quantitative statistic that describes the relationship between two values in a sample and provides an estimate for this relationship in the population from which the paired sample was taken.
data saturation	The point at which no new themes or insights emerge during qualitative analyses.
descriptive statistics	Quantitative measures that report typical performance, as well as differences in performance.
effect size	A quantitative measure that determines the strength of a statistically significant finding.
emergent codes	Concepts, ideas, or meanings that materialize from qualitative data.
ethnography	A qualitative research design where researchers observe how people behave, communicate, and interact within their natural environment.
grounded theory analysis	A qualitative data analysis technique that seeks to generate a theory from data.
inferential statistics	Quantitative measures that draw generalizations using a known outcome to predict one that is not known for sure.
latent analysis	A qualitative data analysis technique where underlying meanings are inferred from the text.
manifest analysis	A qualitative data analysis technique that refrains from interpretations and limits analyses to explicit descriptions visible in the text.

mean	A measure of central tendency that reports typical performance.
measures of central tendency	Quantitative measures that report how a number fits when compared to others in the group.
measures of variability	Quantitative measures that report differences in performance.
median	A measure of central tendency that reports the value in the middle after values have been placed in rank order.
mode	A measure of central tendency that reports the value that occurs most often.
narrative research	A qualitative research design that seeks to make sense of people's stories about their lives.
nonparametric test	Quantitative tests used when data violates one or more of the four assumptions.
open coding	The first level of coding during qualitative data analyses.
p-value	A probability value that determines the level of significance with quantitative findings.
parametric test	Quantitative tests used when data meets all four of the assumptions.
Pearson product-moment coefficient	A parametric quantitative test that is the most common measure of correlation.
phenomenology	A qualitative research design that explores the experiences of individuals who experience the same phenomenon.
quartile deviation	A measure of variability that reports the semi-variation of the difference between the third quartile and first quartile in a frequency distribution.
range	A measure of variability that reports the difference between the highest value and the lowest value.
raw data	All collected data that has not been subject to any analyses or manipulation.
selective coding	The third level of coding used during grounded theory data analyses in qualitative studies.
standard deviation	A measure of variability that represents the average difference between each value and the mean.
t-test	A parametric quantitative test that compares the means of one or two groups.

CHAPTER 7

So, Now What? Evaluating the Discussion Section

CHAPTER CONCEPTS

Conclusions	Limitations	Summary
Further research	Practical significance	Theoretical significance
Implications	Statistical significance	

Introduction

It is the nature of human experience that first we do something, and then we talk about it. So it is with research reports that researchers follow a logical process of providing background for the topic under study and saying what they intend to do (Introduction section), how they intend to do it (Methods section), what they discovered (Results section), and then what they think it all means. This chapter focuses on the last stage of this process, the Discussion section.

The last section of a research report is significantly different in style and content from the sections that preceded it. Ideally, the information in the Results section should be independent of any preconceived notions of the researchers—they are expected to simply report what they found. In contrast, the Discussion section provides the researchers the opportunity to go beyond their actual findings and speculate about the implications of their results. Hopefully, this is where it all comes together and starts to make sense.

We know that it is tempting to read the abstract of an article, and then, if it seems interesting, skip right to the Discussion section to find out the bottom line and its implications. We've done this more than a few times ourselves. We have pointed out some dangers in doing this because it would reflect a level of trust and uncritical judgment that is often not warranted. Besides, now that you have some basic skills to decipher the various components of a research report, we hope you will find it both interesting and actually kind of fun to critically evaluate the things you read.

Although guided and informed by the data generated in a study, a research report also has room for speculation, inference, and reflection. If, for example, a study found that students who present issues with academic performance tend to be enrolled in online courses and programs, this could mean any number of things. The researchers may interpret their data to suggest that issues with academic performance stem from balancing multiple responsibilities (family, school, work) and low levels of self-regulation. The Discussion section is the place in the report where the authors have a chance to tell the story of what they believe the results of their study mean. Thus, the prose thus tends to be more familiar and accessible.

As we have mentioned previously, each scholarly journal has its own requirements for headings in articles. With the Discussion section, you may see a variety of headings used in different journals, such as Summary, Conclusions, Implications, Discussion and Implications, and so forth. You might also see multiple headings used to address each requirement separately. Regardless of how the Discussion section is addressed, it encompasses the last part of the research report, and there should be a clear demarcation between it and the results of the study. This boundary signals that a different narrative voice will be employed to discuss, rather than to merely present, information.

Before we look at some of the specific tools you can use to evaluate the Discussion section, think about the context from the viewpoint of a critical reader. The researchers have just finished telling and showing you what they found, convincing you that the topic was important, they had sufficient understanding of the topic, and they possessed sufficient skill to design an appropriate study. Now they are about to tell you what they think it means. To what extent will you agree with them?

Obviously, your first response to the question would probably be that the answer depends on what the researchers say in the Discussion section. Remember, though, that you don't come to the table, so to speak, with empty hands. Something about this article caught your attention, so you decided to take the time to read it. In most cases, you already have some interest and knowledge about the topic. (We're ignoring for the moment the fact that some things are assigned by instructors rather than selected by readers.) Because you are likely to have some prior knowledge, our caution is that what you already know or believe may often predispose you to be overly critical or overly accepting of the conclusions drawn by the researchers.

For example, suppose today that you picked up an article in which the primary hypothesis was that spending one's time in graduate school does not improve the quality of a person's life or even advance one's career. In fact, the article contended that graduate school harms relationships, creates long-term stress disorders, and wastes money. It's likely that just the act of reading those words elicits some emotional response from you. And, most important in this example, that response can make it difficult to read the Results and Discussion sections with an objective eye. Instead, you will likely be looking for evidence to support your existing beliefs—that the money and time you have spent in graduate school are not wasted.

To further illustrate the concern, assume that you have just finished reading a report in which the results were in sharp contrast to a belief that you, and perhaps most practitioners in your field, hold quite sacred. For example, in the field of counseling, the results of the study may have found that the therapeutic relationship between the client and the counselor had no effect whatsoever on whether a positive treatment outcome was obtained. Or, a study in leadership and administration showed that an authoritarian style was far more effective than a democratic one. Or, perhaps the results in a study of the factors that are most important in weight loss programs indicated that diet was the only component that produced positive results. In each case, the results are quite at odds with current standards of practice. In what ways would your prior beliefs impact what these researchers have to say?

 Reflective Exercise 7.1

Consider the scenarios above or something comparable from another field. Either individually or in small groups of three to four individuals, reflect on the following questions:

1. *How strong would those results have to be for you to consider changing your existing beliefs?*
2. *Would any evidence be sufficient to keep you from simply discounting the findings?*
3. *In what ways would you be more likely to be critical of the study than you would if the findings had supported the common beliefs in your field? If so, could you justify such a response?*

To be critical of findings counter to prior beliefs is, of course, quite a common response. That's one reason new advances in science and technology takes so long to be accepted and adopted. People tend to resist innovations that contradict their most familiar and comfortable assumptions and practices. Take, for example, Hungarian physician Ignaz Semmelweis who proposed that bacteria from the unsterilized hands of surgeons were the reason one in eight patients died from infections after undergoing surgery. He was the first to introduce handwashing in chlorinated water before attempting any surgical procedure, after which he cut patient mortality dramatically. Rather than being appreciated for his discovery, the medical profession was appalled by his insinuation that they were the ones who were killing their patients out of neglect. He ended up being committed to a mental hospital where he later died in despair.

Assuming that the prior belief was supported by a foundation of previous research, drastically modifying that belief on the basis of just one study would be foolhardy. But, it's not hard to picture the outcome if all results inconsistent with earlier beliefs were simply ignored or were subject to intense criticism simply because they didn't agree with an earlier notion. So, when you begin to read what the researchers present in the Discussion section, we urge you to be aware of the following caveats:

1. We are tempted to approach with disdain anything inconsistent with what we already believe and think we know.

2. Our prior beliefs may have been based on studies with even more design flaws than the one now being read.

With these two caveats in mind, there are several features you should expect to find specifically addressed in the Discussion section of the report: a summary of findings that were reported in the Results section, implications of findings, limitations of the study, areas for further research, and conclusions of the study.

Summary of Findings

Not surprisingly, the final part of this section of the report will often include a brief summary of the findings presented in the previous section. Be very cautious as you read this summary because it is more than just a little tempting for the researchers to stretch a bit in this presentation.

There should be clear differentiation in style between text in which the outcomes are presented and writing that expounds on those findings. Elaboration is allowed, in fact, expected in this section, but they should be clearly identified as going beyond the actual findings. Example 7.1 illustrates how the words selected by the researchers to summarize their findings may overstate the actual outcomes.

Example 7.1

The Actual Data	Summary of Findings
Participants used a scale to rate their level of satisfaction with the types of interactions experienced with their therapist. For each type of interaction, the following mean scores were reported: • 32.4 Face-to-face interactions • 31.2 Online interactions • 33.1 Online interactions with video	**A Satisfactory Summary** Although the mean scores were quite similar among all three types of interactions, a slightly higher satisfaction score was reported among group members who experienced online interactions with video. **A Summary That Goes Too Far** The results clearly support the belief that online interactions with video are superior to both face-to-face interactions and online interactions.

The content identified in Example 7.1 as a satisfactory summary is consistent with the data in the left-hand column. Notice that the exaggerated summary, though factually accurate, misrepresents the data through omission, failing to note how close the scores were to one another, and by use of the value-laden terms "clearly" and "superior."

Implications of Findings

Although there obviously should be some connection between the results of the study and subsequent implications that are described, researchers have extensive latitude to speculate about how far the results can be extended. Researchers must be very careful to avoid both timidity and exaggeration when speculating about the implications of their findings.

Researchers must first establish significance with their findings and discuss how the findings contribute to the research objective of the study, as well as a broader societal perspective. Significance may be described in statistical, practical, or theoretical terms (see Table 7.1).

Statistical Significance

Statistical significance was our focus in the preceding chapter for quantitative studies. Researchers find a difference between two groups after one receives a treatment not offered to the other. That difference is evaluated as statistically significant if it appears unlikely to have occurred by chance alone.

Whether the difference between the groups after the treatment is large or small is not necessarily the primary factor in determining statistical significance (remembering that the size of the sample also plays a major role). A probability

Table 7.1

Statistical significance	Were the results beyond what might be expected as outcomes from chance alone?
Practical significance	Were any differences large enough to make a difference in real-life applications?
Theoretical significance	Were the findings consistent with predicted outcomes from a theory?

value is calculated to estimate the likelihood of finding the observed difference in the samples if the entire population had been included. If that probability value is less than 5 in 100 ($p \leq .05$), by tradition the outcome is identified as statistically significant.

Practical Significance

In contrast, there is no universally agreed procedure for calculating the practical significance of a research finding. It is used in both quantitative and qualitative studies and will usually be a function of personal or societal standards. Practical significance answers the question, "So what?" when findings have practical or meaningful implications. To illustrate, consider the hypothetical mean satisfaction scores for the types of interactions we presented in Example 7.1. The data showed a difference of 0.7 in favor of online interactions with video when compared to face-to-face interactions. If the number of participants in the study was quite large, this difference could have been big enough to be identified as statistically significant, meaning it was unlikely to have occurred by chance. But, simply stating statistical significance with this finding tells the reader nothing about its importance and begs the question: What exactly does this mean for professional practice? With this example, the researchers could establish practical significance by describing implications for practitioners related to the addition of video to online interactions with their clients.

Depending on the context of the study, terms such as clinical significance or social validation may be used instead of practical significance for discussion of whether the study reported findings were large enough to have a significant impact in real life. Whichever term is used, remember that practical significance is not identical to a finding of statistical significance. Example 7.2 shows how a qualitative researcher established practical significance with the implications of findings.

Example 7.2 Excerpt From Discussion Section of a Published Journal Article

---

Discussion

This qualitative study used four focus groups *(n = 30)* to answer the research question: What is the experience of male graduate students at a female-concentrated university? Participants described experiences of discrimination and a lack of university connection, but they did not indicate an urgent need for additional supports or university changes (Davies et al., 2000). Why might this be the case? To answer that question, we developed an emergent theory that is grounded in the study's data and integrated with related theory and research (see Figure 1). At the individual level, participants exhibited a high degree of academic motivation that was developmentally congruent with graduate students and indicative of positive characteristics of traditional masculinity. Those individual factors worked in unison with supportive relationships with faculty and peers which, together, functioned as protective factors against perceived discrimination and concerns about the female-concentrated culture. Those factors appeared to not only protect against negative experiences but to facilitate participants' path toward the positive outcomes of retention, academic success, and graduation.

The emergent theory sheds light on factors that support and impede male graduate students' academic success at a female-concentrated university. . .

— Summary

— Implications

"It's Not Like Undergrad:" A Qualitative Study of Male Graduate Students at an "All-Women's College"

Example 7.2: Anthony Isacco and Mary Beth Mannarino, from "'It's Not Like Undergrad:' A Qualitative Study of Male Graduate Students at an 'All-Women's College,'" *Psychology of Men & Masculinity*, vol. 17, no. 3, p. 290. Copyright © 2015 by American Psychological Association.

Reference

Isacco, A., & Mannarino, M. B. (2015). "It's not like undergrad:" A qualitative study of male graduate students at an "all-woman's college." *Psychology of Men & Masculinity*, *17*(3), 285—296. doi:10.1037/men0000021

Theoretical Significance

There's one more area of significance that may be presented somewhere in the Discussion section, the theoretical significance of the results. Whether this will be included depends on the specific research objectives of the study, but when relevant, this provides a quite different frame of reference for conclusions and implications of the findings.

To illustrate, assume that we propose a new recovery model to promote positive changes in people's addictive behaviors. The theory underlying this model might be that there are two distinct stages necessary for such a recovery to occur. In the first stage, it is proposed that supportive relationships are key. In the second stage, there are some advisable strategies to follow to prevent relapses. Our theory assumes that both stages are essential.

We seek evidence that either supports or refutes this model. (We actually prefer evidence that supports it, but we have to consider the possibility of the latter.). We then complete a study that includes a control group receiving a traditional form of addiction treatment, and an experimental group that employs the principles of our proposed model. The participants are then assessed after each weekly session.

When analyzing the results, we find both good and bad news related to statistical, practical, and theoretical significance. When the study began, it appeared that our random assignment to treatment and control groups had worked well. The average level of symptoms of distress was essentially the same between the two groups. After just two weeks, those in our new treatment group displayed longer-lasting recovery and reduction of corresponding symptoms than their peers in the other group. For the purposes of this hypothetical study, let's assume that the difference between the two groups was dramatic. Thus, in the Results section, we could report a statistically significant difference in favor of the experimental group. As implications in the Discussion section, we could suggest that this finding in favor of our model was sufficiently strong enough to indicate a practical or clinical significance, as well. So, there was good news, especially for the participants in the experimental group.

Let's assume, however, that in the first stage that included supportive relationships, this was a process that lasted only two weeks. Our proposed theory suggested that both stages of the treatment plan were essential to lead to lasting changes in the reduction of addictive behavior. Therefore, in the Discussion, we would also have to report that these results did not have theoretical significance. The positive change took place after just one of what we thought were two required stages, and there was no evidence in the results to indicate that the second stage was even necessary.

Limitations of the Study

Somewhere in the Discussion section your attention should be directed to what could not have been found in the study because of the way it was designed. Nobody (as far we know) has ever designed and completed the perfect study that controlled every possible variable, covered every conceivable limitation, and resulted in absolutely flawless data that could not be challenged. Even though your critical analysis of the report may have identified some possible problems (perhaps even more than the researchers would want to admit), these are supposed to be acknowledged in the Discussion section.

We think you'll agree that this is quite a lovely tradition in which researchers are expected to identify, label, and own the things they may have missed or didn't address in their study. It's sort of like asking someone who is trying to make an important point to take an opposing view of things and invalidate their own case. There are even some qualitative strategies, such as theoretical sampling, in which researchers will deliberately seek participants with perspectives that directly contradict the emerging model. You can appreciate this would lead to a far more robust conceptual framework that takes into consideration exceptions to the rule.

Limitations are often focused on the specific research sample used for the study. For example, researchers who conducted a qualitative research study might note that all of the participants came from a location where they might have attitudes specific to that setting. Or, quite often in quantitative studies, the researchers remind the reader that the research sample was drawn from a group of individuals who may not reflect the general population.

Possible concerns about the research sample are easy for researchers to identify and thus are frequently included as limitations. But, there are other limitations with the methods of the study that may be mentioned, as well. In the report itself the researchers won't dwell at length on the limitations because they don't wish to completely undermine all their effort and work. But, if no limitations are included, you are left with the possibility that the researchers were either unaware of them or thought that they were so well masked that they could be ignored. In either case, bad idea! Example 7.3 provides several examples of how different researchers addressed the limitations present in their studies.

 ## Example 7.3 Excerpts of Limitations

Example 1

However, some limitations should be acknowledged. First, participants were recruited from two non-fee paying, single-sex schools in the same postal code area of Dublin, neither of which was considered to be disadvantaged. Thus, generalisability of the results may be limited across location and socio-economic status. Furthermore, the opt-in method of obtaining consent may have resulted in the recruitment of adolescents who are more motivated to engage with activities and interventions related to mental health. ...

Rachel Kenny, Barbara Dooley and Amanda Fitzgerald, "Developing Mental Health Mobile Apps: Exploring Adolescents' Perspectives," *Health Informatics Journal*, vol. 22, no. 2. Copyright © 2014 by SAGE Publications.

Reference

Kenny, R., Dooley, B., & Fitzgerald, A. (2016). Developing mental health mobile apps: Exploring adolescents' perspectives. *Health Informatics Journal, 22*(2), 265–275. doi:10.1177/1460458214555041

Example 2

There were several limitations to the study design, which must be considered when interpreting the findings. First, the present study was an exploratory study that included a relatively small sample of participants. The small sample size may have limited the ability to detect significant changes in the study variables. In addition, it prevented generalizability, in particular of the quantitative findings. ...

Reference

Chiu, C., Hu, Y., Lin, D., Chang, F., Chang, C., & Lai, C. (2016). The attitudes, impact, and learning needs of older adults using apps on touchscreen mobile devices: Results from a pilot study. *Computers in Human Behavior, 63*, 189–197. doi:10.1016/j.chb.2016.05.020

Example 3

The current study has a number of limitations. First, we only examined the Apple iTunes App Store and did not investigate the Google Play apps store. Although many of the apps have both versions, there may be unique apps in the Google Play store that this study did not cover. Second, we followed the 2010 USDA Dietary Guidelines for Americans to code whether the diet-related apps enabled self-regulation of calories and balanced food groups/nutrients. However, we did not break down the nutrients into smaller categories. ...

Reference

Zahry, N. R., Cheng, Y., & Peng, W. (2016). Content analysis of diet-related mobile apps: A self-regulation perspective. *Health Communication, 31*(10), 1301–1310. doi:10.1080/104102 36.2015.1072123

Areas for Further Research

This is another quite interesting part of the Discussion section because it requires the researchers to think deeply, not only about the results of their work, but how others might follow the line of inquiry in the future. Researchers suggest ways that their discoveries might be pursued in subsequent studies, either to validate, replicate, or perhaps take the results to the next level. Regardless, you can expect the researchers to say, in one form or another, "More research is needed on this topic." More than just a strategy to ensure future employment for researchers, noting areas for further research stands as a universal truth. No study or series of studies will be sufficient to provide the ultimate answer.

One of the beautiful things about the research process is that all of the scholars in the world—past, present, and future—stand together as collaborators, each of us building on the work that has been completed previously. Consider, for example, the academic journal *Philosophical Transactions* has been in continuous publication for more than 350 years! This means that scholars and researchers have been citing one another and building their ideas and propositions as a community on research projects over centuries.

Each researcher experiments with new practices, or tests the ones already in use, notes the outcomes, and then shares what they discovered with the wider community. Other researchers are then able to use these efforts to continue advancing the knowledge base a small step forward. Each researcher is, in effect, a collaborator with the giants of the past, building on the ideas of previous researchers with their own work. No matter how significant their contributions, researchers want to always end the Discussion section of a research report with a statement that others need to follow up with what was found, apply thwe concepts to other settings, replicate reported efforts to see if similar results were obtained, or take the ideas to the next level.

Look for more than just the simple statement that more research is needed—this is like saying you could use a little more money. There should be specific suggestions about how those studies could be designed to complement the currently reported findings. Example 7.4 shows several ways in which researchers have identified areas for further research.

 ## Example 7.4   Excerpts of Areas for Further Research

Example 1

Through this theoretical lens it is clear that couples develop expectations for each other concerning mobile phone use in the relationship, but it is not clear as to how such expectations are formed. Studies that investigate whether couples should or do explicitly discuss rules surrounding mobile phone use in the relationship and how the discussion, or lack thereof, of mobile phone expectations relates to relationship satisfaction are needed. The successful negotiation of expectations might allow partners to mitigate the potentially stressful and annoying aspects of mobile phone use in a romantic relationship.

Reference

Juhasz, A., & Bradford, K. (2016). Mobile phone use in romantic relationships. *Marriage & Family Review, 52*(8), 707–721. doi:10.1080/01494929.2016.1157123

Example 2

Researchers should collect data across different samples, including both post-college participants as they develop romantic relationships that lead to marriage or cohabitation and individuals in their 40s to 60s who may experience cell phones differently due to generational differences or the more established, longer-term nature of their relationships. Unlike young adults, older adults did not have cell phones during adolescence or their early adulthood and thus may be more likely to engage in practices such as turning phones off or putting them away during romantic interactions. Questions also remain about cultural differences in the experience of dating partners' cell-phone use to non-present others. For instance, individuals in collectivist cultures may not voice discursive struggles around community and romance as well as control and freedom due to a greater emphasis on the needs and desires of the collective rather than the individual. Future research should address these questions. ...

Reference
Miller-Ott, A. E., & Kelly, L. (2016). Competing discourses and meaning making in talk about romantic partners' cell-phone contact with non-present others. *Communication Studies, 67*(1), 58–76. doi:10.1080/10510974.2015.1088876

Example 3

We studied college students' get-acquainted interactions in a design that involved a structured self-disclosure task conducted over Skype, and that included the manipulation of whether one member of the dyad had access to his or her social network through communication devices. Each of these aspects of our design offered strengths for the specific issue we were examining (isolating the actor effects of being hyperconnected in a social interaction). However, future research could further examine these issues in a variety of additional contexts, with different samples, with different types of relationships, and varying the type and degree of hyperconnection.

Reference
Sprecher, S., Hampton, A. J., Heinzel, H. J., & Felmlee, D. (2016). Can I connect with both you and my social network? Access to network-salient communication technology and get-acquainted interactions. *Computers in Human Behavior, 62*, 423–432. doi:10.1016/j.chb.2016.03.090

Conclusions of the Study

Although often presented together in the Discussion section of the research report, conclusions and implications are not identical. The researchers had initial ideas, assumptions, and hypotheses that were initially established and articulated before the investigation began (quantitative studies) or developed as the research progressed (qualitative studies). These may have been stated in the form of research questions or objectives, but underlying hypotheses were implicit. Were these predictions supported by the results they found?

The primary caution for you in evaluating conclusions of the study is to be sure that they flow logically from the results and that they don't overreach beyond what may be derived from the reported findings. The researchers do have some freedom to speculate about the ultimate meaning of their results, but you will want to assess whether there are lines of separation evident between what was found (results), what was restated as the findings (summary), what the findings might mean (implications), and what the findings do mean (conclusions).

 ## Reflective Exercise 7.2

Below are two excerpts of conclusions that were included in the Discussion section of published articles. Read each excerpt and consider how the researchers presented the conclusions. Reflect upon your ideas either individually or in small groups of three to four individuals.

Excerpt 1

This study provides qualitative evidence for leisure education courses as a form of complementary health programming to support adaptive coping and positive well-being in college-attending emerging adults. Leisure education does merit consideration as student affairs leaders seek to develop complementary and/or integrative opportunities to encourage health and well-being among their students. College campuses already possess the facilities and the equipment to begin leisure education courses, but the establishment of this form of complementary health programming will ultimately depend on student affairs leaders to make this vision a reality.

Reference

Hartman, C. L., Evans, K. E., & Anderson, D. M. (2017). Promoting adaptive coping skills and subjective well-being through credit-based leisure education courses. *Journal of Student Affairs Research and Practice, 54*(3), 303–315. doi:10.1080/19496591.2017.1331852

Excerpt 2

Retaining college students of all backgrounds, but particularly those students who could benefit from extra support, is of concern to student affairs professionals. Identifying effective ways to enhance these students' academic success and persistence in college is critical. The current study suggests individual counseling delivered by graduate students can positively impact these domains. Serving as a model, CRISP [Counselors providing Resources, Integration, Skill development and Psychosocial support] offers a low-cost approach for addressing the growing concern of undergraduate retention. Implementation of CRISP provides the opportunity to expand student services while training future counselors to work with undergraduate populations.

Reference

Cholewa, B., Schulthes, G., Hull, M. F., Bailey, B. J., & Brown, J. (2017). Building on what works: Supporting underprepared students through a low-cost counseling intervention. *Journal of Student Affairs Research and Practice, 54*(3), 261–274. doi:10.1080/19496591.2017.1331445

Summary and Closing Thoughts

There are no hard and fast rules about the order in which information should be provided in the Discussion section, and you will often find information about implications, limitations, future areas of research, and conclusions interspersed throughout this section. The Discussion section should, however, open with a clear statement about how the findings relate to the overall research objective of the study. For example, if stated in the form of hypotheses, did the results indicate support or nonsupport for the beliefs that guided the study? Regardless of form, a brief summary statement about the findings reported in the Results section can be expected to begin the Discussion.

Evaluation Tools for the Discussion Section

Quantitative and Qualitative Studies

Clear Presentation	
Consider	*Look for*
How did the researchers present the discussion with clarity?	• Clear demarcation between the summary of findings, implications, limitations, future areas of research, and conclusions • Logical flow and coherence with ideas
Relationship to Study Objectives	
Consider	*Look for*
To what extent does the discussion relate to the objectives of the study?	• Relevance with discussion to the research objective
Summary of Findings	

Consider

How did the researchers present a summary of findings?

Look for

- Logically follows the Results section
- Elaboration beyond the actual findings
- Consistency with reported findings (i.e., no exaggerations, omissions of data, avoidance of value-laden terms)

Implications of Findings

Consider

How did the researchers address implications of findings?

Look for

- Establishment of statistical, practical, or theoretical significance
- Detailed descriptions of how the findings contribute to the purpose of the study, as well as a broader societal perspective

Limitations of the Study

Consider

How did the researchers acknowledge limitations of the study?

Look for

- Identification of possible problems with the design of the study

Areas for Further Research

Consider

How did the researchers suggest specific areas for further research?

Look for

- Specific suggestions about how future studies could be designed to complement the findings of the current study

Conclusions of the Study

Consider

How did the researchers present conclusions of the study?

Look for

- Clear statements regarding how the research questions or objectives were supported by the results

Practice Evaluation Exercises

It's been a long journey, but we've reached our first destination. This chapter has covered the elements needed to evaluate the final section of the research report. The only thing left in the report is the References section and perhaps some Appendices. We know you don't need guidance from us about evaluating these (although you might be surprised, if not dismayed, about the number of errors in citations that slip by the editing process and can be a real pain when you try to look up one of the references).

To conclude this section of the book, we'd like you to try to evaluate a quantitative and qualitative research report in their entirety. So you won't have to thumb back through the chapters, we present complete evaluation tools for each type of research report on the pages that follow. In order to make the experience the most meaningful, try to evaluate each type of research report on your own before reading the examples we present in Appendix A and Appendix B.

Evaluation Tools for a Quantitative Research Report

Introduction Section

Context and Significance

Consider

1. How important is the topic?
2. To what extent is the presentation clear and objective?

Look for

- Personal relevance of the topic
- Sound rationale for investigation of the problem
- Broad societal context for the problem
- Clear portrayal of the general intent of the study
- Evidence of bias in language

Review of Relevant Literature

Consider

1. To what extent is the viewpoint balanced and appropriately comprehensive?
2. How has attention been given to both historical precedent and more recent work?
3. How coherent is the theme of the review of relevant literature?
4. Where did the researchers appear to emphasize primary, rather than secondary sources?

Look for

- Objectivity with previous research findings
- Accumulation of knowledge reported in the literature with explanations for any gaps in time
- Evidence that previous literature guided the objectives for the study
- Reliance on citation of primary sources

Objective Statements/Research Questions/Hypotheses

Consider

1. To what extent were the objective statements/research questions/ hypotheses clearly stated?
2. How has the review of relevant literature supported development of the objective statements/ research questions/hypotheses?

Look for

- Clear understanding of purpose for study
- Researchers' predictions

Methods Section Part I: Participants

Target Population

Consider

What was the target population?

Look for

- Whether the target population is also the sample
- Alignment to research objectives

Research Sample

Consider

Who participated in the study?

Look for

- Enough information so that results can be generalized
- Characteristics that may influence responses
- Unusual characteristics
- Language used to describe characteristics

Location

Consider

Where were the participants?

Look for

- Specific information about the setting
- Appropriateness of setting for research objective
- Aspects of setting that may influence findings

Time Frame

Consider

When were the data collected?

Look for

- Specific information about the time frame for data collection
- Significant lapses in time or subsequent events that may influence relevance with findings

Rationale for Sampling Technique

Consider	*Look for*
Why was this sample collected?	• Utilization of sampling techniques to accurately represent the target population
	• Appropriateness of sampling techniques to achieve research objective

Sampling Techniques

Consider	*Look for*
How was this sample collected?	• The manner in which participants were selected
	• Descriptions of advantages and risks associated with selected sampling technique

Methods Section Part II: Procedures and the Tools

Procedures: Sufficient Detail

Consider	*Look for*
To what extent did the researchers provide sufficient detail about the procedures implemented in the study?	• Complete information and sufficient detail for each step in the procedures
	• How permissions to conduct the study were sought and obtained
	• How participants were informed about the study
	• How participants provided consent
	• The time frame for data collection
	• How data were collected and analyzed
	• Enough information was provided to replicate the study

Procedures: Relevant to the Researchers' Objective for the Study

Consider	*Look for*
How are the procedures relevant to achieve the research objective of the study?	• Type of research design
	• Appropriateness of research design
	• Relevance of procedures to the research objective

Data Collection Tools: Sufficient Detail

Consider	*Look for*
To what extent did the researchers provide sufficient detail about the data collection tools used in the study?	• Complete information
	• Sufficient detail for each data collection tool
	• Focus is on measurement

Data Collection Tools: Relevant to the Researchers' Objective for the Study

Consider

How are the data collection tools relevant to achieve the research objective of the study?

Look for

- Reported metric or technique to establish consistency (reliability) with findings
- Reported metric or technique to establish truthfulness (validity) with findings

Results Section

Sufficient Detail

Consider

How did the researchers present the findings with sufficient detail?

Look for

- Explanations for unanticipated events
- Detailed descriptions of collected data
- Complete information for findings
- Proper reporting for descriptive and/or inferential statistics
- Appropriate use of visual displays

Relevant to the Researchers' Objective for the Study

Consider

To what extent are the results relevant to achieve the research objective of the study?

Look for

- Relevance with results to the research objective
- Absence of interpretations
- Explanations for information that is not relevant to the research objective

Discussion Section

Clear Presentation

Consider

How did the researchers present the discussion with clarity?

Look for

- Clear demarcation between the summary of findings, implications, limitations, future areas of research, and conclusions
- Logical flow and coherence with ideas

Relationship to Study Objectives

Consider

To what extent does the discussion relate to the objectives of the study?

Look for

• Relevance with discussion to the research objective

Summary of Findings

Consider

How did the researchers present a summary of findings?

Look for

• Logically follows the Results section
• Elaboration beyond the actual findings
• Consistency with reported findings (i.e., no exaggerations, omissions of data, avoidance of value-laden terms)

Implications of Findings

Consider

How did the researchers address implications of findings?

Look for

• Establishment of statistical, practical, or theoretical significance
• Detailed descriptions of how the findings contribute to the purpose of the study, as well as a broader societal perspective

Limitations of the Study

Consider

How did the researchers acknowledge limitations of the study?

Look for

• Identification of possible problems with the design of the study

Areas for Further Research

Consider

How did the researchers suggest specific areas for further research?

Look for

• Specific suggestions about how future studies could be designed to complement the findings of the current study

Conclusions of the Study

Consider

How did the researchers present conclusions of the study?

Look for

• Clear statements regarding how the research questions or objectives were supported by the results

Evaluation Tools for a Qualitative Research Report

Introduction Section

Context and Significance

Consider

1. How important is the topic?
2. To what extent is the presentation clear and objective?

Look for

- Exploration of new phenomena, as well as how people experience them
- Personalized style of writing
- Continuing interactions among data gathering, literature reviews, and research questioning
- Personal relevance of the topic
- Sound rationale for investigation of the problem
- Broad societal context for the problem
- Clear portrayal of the general intent of the study

Review of Relevant Literature

Consider

1. To what extent is the viewpoint balanced and appropriately comprehensive?
2. How has attention been given to both historical precedent and more recent work?
3. How coherent is the theme of the review of relevant literature?
4. Where did the researchers appear to emphasize primary, rather than secondary sources?

Look for

- Preliminary review of relevant literature
- Balanced and sufficiently comprehensive review of relevant literature
- Includes contemporary and historical studies, with outcomes from these studies synthesized
- Reliance on citation of primary sources

Objective Statements/ Research Questions

Consider

1. To what extent were the objective statements/research questions clearly stated?
2. How has the review of relevant literature supported development of the objective statements/research questions?

Look for

- Preliminary identification of a guiding research question(s)
- Guiding research question(s) served as general framework that guided the study initially
- Sufficiently open-ended to facilitate exploration of themes that emerge during the study

Methods Section Part I: Participants

Target Population

Consider
What was the target population?

Look for
- Whether the target population is also the sample
- Alignment to research objectives

Research Sample

Consider
Who participated in the study?

Look for
- Enough information so that results can be generalized
- Characteristics that may influence responses
- Unusual characteristics
- Language used to describe characteristics

Location

Consider
Where were the participants?

Look for
- Specific information about the setting
- Appropriateness of setting for research objective
- Aspects of setting that may influence findings

Time Frame

Consider
When were the data collected?

Look for
- Specific information about the time frame for data collection
- Significant lapses in time or subsequent events that may influence relevance with findings

Rationale for Sampling Technique

Consider
Why was this sample collected?

Look for
- Utilization of sampling techniques to accurately represent the target population
- Appropriateness of sampling techniques to achieve research objective

Sampling Techniques

Consider
How was this sample collected?

Look for
- The manner in which participants were selected
- Descriptions of advantages and risks associated with selected sampling technique

Methods Section Part II: Procedures and the Tools

Procedures: Sufficient Detail

Consider

To what extent did the researchers provide sufficient detail about the procedures implemented in the study?

Look for

- Complete information and sufficient detail for each step in the procedures
- Description for positionality and the role of the researchers
- How the researchers gained entry to the research site
- Steps taken to secure any required permissions
- How participants were informed about the study
- How participants provided consent

- How data were collected
- Established protocols for documenting and/or recording data
- Transcription methods used for nontextual data
- Data analysis strategies
- Explicit descriptions of coding procedures, including the codebook and analytic memoing
- How interpretations were made
- Information about data saturation
- Enough information was provided to replicate the study

Procedures: Relevant to the Researchers' Objective for the Study

Consider

How are the procedures relevant to achieve the research objective of the study?

Look for

- Type of research design
- Appropriateness of research design
- Relevance of procedures to the research objective

Data Collection Tools: Sufficient Detail

Consider

To what extent did the researchers provide sufficient detail about the data collection tools used in the study?

Look for

- Complete information
- Sufficient detail for each data collection tool
- Focus is on description

Data Collection Tools: Relevant to the Researchers' Objective for the Study	
Consider	*Look for*
How are the data collection tools relevant to achieve the research objective of the study?	• Reported technique to establish consistency (reliability) with findings • Reported technique to establish truthfulness (validity) with findings

Results Section

Sufficient Detail	
Consider	*Look for*
How did the researchers present the findings with sufficient detail?	• Detailed descriptions of collected data • Complete information for findings • Appropriate use of direct quotations and data excerpts

Relevant to the Researchers' Objective for the Study	
Consider	*Look for*
To what extent are the results relevant to achieve the research objective of the study?	• Relevance with results to the research objective • Absence of interpretations • Explanations for information that is not relevant to the research objective

Discussion Section

Clear Presentation	
Consider	*Look for*
How did the researchers present the discussion with clarity?	• Clear demarcation between the summary of findings, implications, limitations, future areas of research, and conclusions • Logical flow and coherence with ideas

Relationship to Study Objectives	
Consider	*Look for*
To what extent does the discussion relate to the objectives of the study?	• Relevance with discussion to the research objective

Summary of Findings

Consider

How did the researchers present a summary of findings?

Look for

- Logically follows the Results section
- Elaboration beyond the actual findings
- Consistency with reported findings (i.e., no exaggerations, omissions of data, avoidance of value-laden terms)

Implications of Findings

Consider

How did the researchers address implications of findings?

Look for

- Establishment of statistical, practical, or theoretical significance
- Detailed descriptions of how the findings contribute to the purpose of the study, as well as a broader societal perspective

Limitations of the Study

Consider

How did the researchers acknowledge limitations of the study?

Look for

- Identification of possible problems with the design of the study

Areas for Further Research

Consider

How did the researchers suggest specific areas for further research?

Look for

- Specific suggestions about how future studies could be designed to complement the findings of the current study

Conclusions of the Study

Consider

How did the researchers present conclusions of the study?

Look for

- Clear statements regarding how the research questions or objectives were supported by the results

CHAPTER 8

Doing Research: Accountant, Explorer, or Both?

CHAPTER CONCEPTS

Advisor	Creativity	Intrinsic motivation
Closed-ended questions	Curiosity	Open-ended questions
Conscientiousness	Divergent thinking	
Convergent thinking	Extrinsic motivation	

Introduction

T hus far, we have covered the basics of how to make sense of research studies that other professionals have conceived, implemented, and described. The reality is that practitioners are too busy serving others to take the time to conduct formal research studies and publish their findings. Most practitioners, however, are concerned with increasing their effectiveness and promoting successful outcomes. As such, it turns out that practitioners engage with research any time they attempt to answer questions that concern their professional practice. It's just that most of these endeavors are neither very systematic nor well constructed, which produces results that are less than optimal, possibly biased, and often misleading.

If you are an undergraduate or graduate student, you may be expected, quite soon or in the future, to plan and conduct a formal research study. This could be in the form of a course or program project, thesis, dissertation, or a collaborative endeavor with co-researchers. Whereas we aim to provide you with the rudimentary knowledge and skills to take on such an enterprise, we also want to equip you with the knowledge and skills needed to use research in more practical, everyday ways. To illustrate the importance of this goal, consider the following scenarios:

- You are faced with a new challenge on your job—a problem you've never faced previously. Before tackling this novel situation, you want to familiarize yourself with the latest research on what has been demonstrated to be the most and least effective methods. Once you identify appropriate studies, you select the most promising one that presented favorable results and replicate the methods. Then, you collect and review data to evaluate its impact on your situation. Depending on the results, you may have to repeat your replication efforts using methods from other studies. When a viable solution is found, you share your findings with colleagues at a department meeting.

- You have been attempting to help someone and are failing miserably. You have run out of options and can't figure out what is sabotaging the results, even though your strategies have proven so effective in the past. You want to assess precisely where the breakdown occurs that prevents your efforts from being successful. You recognize that the only way to gain this information is by engaging in varied dialogue with this person. Each time you implement a new strategy, you and this person meet twice a week to discuss what is working, what isn't working, and so forth. In between each meeting, you ask this person to keep a journal with daily entries that address the same topics. Using information shared during the meetings and in the journal, you evaluate the effect of each implemented strategy and make any necessary modifications.

- You have a growing interest in trying an innovative lifestyle program that promises improved health through a specialized approach to diet and exercise. This lifestyle has recently become mainstream and is endorsed heavily by well-known celebrities in the media. Before making an initial investment for program services, you decide to send out a survey using various social media platforms to ascertain how real people perceive the program. Using an online poll maker, you pose a handful of closed-ended questions (On a scale of 1 to 5, with 5 being the highest, how satisfied are you with the program?) and open-ended questions (What do you like the most about the program? Least?). When your poll closes, you perform frequency counts, and possibly use descriptive statistics to analyze data collected from responses to the closed-ended questions. With the open-ended questions, you explore the data qualitatively using content analysis techniques, looking for possible themes. Once you complete your analyses, you share your findings, along with your decision to make the program investment or not, on the social media platforms where you originally sent out your poll.

Time to Get Into Action

It is one thing to be able to read and make sense out of what others have researched and reported, but quite another to try it yourself. It is more straightforward to be critical of others' work—to find evidence of biases, holes in their logic, flaws in their methodology, or mistakes in their analyses. Yet, it is even more challenging to construct and implement your own study in such a way that it will stand up to the scrutiny of others, not to mention make a significant contribution to your field.

At this very moment, you may not consider yourself a systematic or skilled researcher, but we want to point out that you already understand and practice the basic ideas of research in your daily life. For example, when you are interested in making a costly purchase, it is likely that you do a "review of relevant literature" of sorts, scanning consumer reports and reviews to inform yourself about what others have previously discovered. As a driver, you have likely established a "control group" of standard routes to work or school, taking into account the time of day, traffic patterns, and perhaps even points of interest along the way. Then you have "experimented" with alternative paths to see if you could improve your performance, measuring the outcomes both quantitatively (drive time) and qualitatively (appeal of the route). You constantly generate "hypotheses" in life based on information you have collected. In your work, you have conducted qualitative "interviews" to explore the experiences of others with a particular phenomenon and then grounded your "data" in some type of theory to explain what you found.

We want to reassure you that in many ways this part of the book about doing research is not nearly as demanding as you might expect. For one thing, you are already familiar with the basic concepts. Secondly, you have also reviewed plenty of examples of what others have done and how they have done it. Thirdly, you have a pretty decent idea of what is considered good research and what is not. Essentially, you will be elaborating on what has become familiar ground. But, a focus on doing also brings a need for some additional knowledge and skills.

In the first part of the book, there was a continuing emphasis on the idea that everything in a research study is—or should be—driven by the research objective. We will begin our description of how to do research with a chapter devoted to identifying and framing the purpose for your study, including how your review of relevant literature contributes to this task.

You will need participants for your study, whether it is a large-scale survey or a case study of one individual or entity, so you'll find a chapter with suggestions for selecting them. Additionally, you'll find information regarding selection of an appropriate research design, procedures, and the data collection tools. This section of the book also includes a chapter that delineates guidelines for securing and analyzing the data you collected. We also include a chapter of the do's and don'ts when establishing significance and noting implications to situate your findings in broader, real-world contexts.

We want to caution you that the descriptions above imply a linear process when the reality of research is much more interactive and cyclical. This is especially the case with qualitative methodologies when the data collection, analyses, and literature review can all take place simultaneously. For example, the way you will go about selecting your participant sample is highly dependent on the research design you select. Qualitative designs often use purposive samples (those deliberately chosen according to some criteria rather than through random selection) and require use of a relatively small sample group. Some quantitative designs may also have relatively small sample groups, whereas other quantitative designs require larger groups of participants. Don't forget that in quantitative studies, the hypotheses, research questions, or objective statements are clearly stated at the beginning of the study. Conversely, the initial research question often only sets the stage for what follows in qualitative studies. In such studies, new research questions emerge while information is being analyzed for the results.

Adopting Dual Perspectives

As suggested by the title of this chapter, there are stereotypical behaviors of both accountants and explorers when doing research. For example, the careful attention to detail that you expect from an accountant is essential when conducting a research study. Sloppy or incomplete work is unacceptable when you are reviewing the literature, implementing the design, or analyzing and reporting the results. Attention to detail is more than just a suggestion—it's a command.

Similarly, research requires bold decisions to explore uncharted territories as one would expect from an explorer. As a matter of fact, the majority of published studies generally make some type of claim to address a gap in the literature where no or little previous research exists. Investigating the unknown is not just a challenge for the courageous—it's essential for progress in every professional discipline.

One of the benefits that could very well result from your study of research is that you will learn habits and procedures that serve you well in other facets of your life. Let's take, for example, the apparently simple task of asking questions. Research training teaches you that the way you ask a question is just as important as the question itself. This is no less true in any other area of your life. As you will learn in the next chapter, questions can be framed in such a way that either limit communication (closed-ended questions), or they can be designed to encourage elaboration (open-ended questions). For example, notice below the very different kinds of responses that are likely to be elicited by asking questions in a closed or open format.

Closed-ended Questions	Open-ended Questions
Did anything interesting happen at school today?	What was the most interesting thing that happened in school today?
That was a pretty good effort you made, wasn't it?	How did you feel about the effort you made just now?
When you say that you learned a lot from the experience, do you mean in terms of your decision-making skills?	What did you learn from the experience?
Should I make rice or pasta for dinner?	What should I make for dinner?
Do you know what I mean?	What did you understand about what I just explained to you?

You will notice that the closed-ended questions are the sort that are often asked by medical professionals, such as, "Does it hurt more in your wrist or your hand?" They tend to elicit the one-word answers "yes" or "no." This might often be helpful to physicians or detectives who want specific answers to questions designed to narrow down clues, but they are absolutely worthless when doing interviews, or for that matter, when trying to have a meaningful conversation with someone. In fact, we can think of few interpersonal skills that are more crucial for building intimacy in relationships than the ability to prompt others with exploratory, open-ended questions that give them freedom to respond in the most authentic way.

Learning research procedures, like formulating good questions, will not only help you find things you want to know, but enhance many of your most important undertakings. The steps in the process of formulating and implementing your own research study will guide you to proceed in a systematic, consistent, logical, and intuitive manner. These steps are not unlike any problem-solving strategy:

1. Become aware there is a problem that needs to be addressed.
2. Collect relevant background information to help you better understand the context of the problem.
3. Define the parameters or variables that are part of the presenting problem.
4. Design an intervention or strategy to solve the problem.
5. Make some predictions about what you think might happen.
6. Assess or measure the results.
7. Discuss what happened, acknowledging implications, possible limitations, and possible areas needing additional research.
8. Communicate what you learned with others.

This process works well as a general scheme for conducting research, and it works equally well in addressing any life concern that you might face. Becoming a skilled researcher teaches you to become a better accountant and a better explorer. These roles might seem like they are contradictory, yet when doing research, it helps to be both divergent and convergent in your thinking. Like an explorer, divergent thinking enables you to search out all possible answers to a problem. Like an accountant, convergent thinking permits you to narrow down all the information collected to identify the best possible explanation.

Like the divergent explorer and convergent accountant, you will begin your journey with the glimmering of an idea about what you hope to discover. This will lead to hypotheses in the case of quantitative studies or the formulation of a guiding question with qualitative studies. You will have access to some "maps" prepared by those who have gone on this journey, or a similar one, before you.

This is what you know as a review of relevant literature. Through conducting your study and sharing the outcome with others, you provide new maps for those who will follow in your footsteps, adding detail to what is already known, correcting errors in previous information, and creating new knowledge.

Sometimes you find exactly what you were looking for. It is more likely that you will stumble onto something even more valuable. Serendipity—finding something good accidentally—has resulted in countless contributions to our understanding of the world in which we live. Ivan Pavlov wasn't looking for psychological explanations of behavior, which later became known as classical conditioning—he was seeking more information about the digestive system in dogs when examining rates of salivation. René Descartes was idly watching a fly on the wall when he invented analytic geometry. Archimedes of Syracuse was enjoying a hot bath when he cried out, "Eureka," and identified the principle of buoyancy. Sir Alexander Fleming developed penicillin after seeing one of his bacterial experiments ruined by the growth of a strange mold. Dynamite, Velcro, antibiotics, welding, matches, X-rays, Teflon, post-it notes, pacemakers, chocolate chip cookies, potato chips, cornflakes, Play-Doh, Coca-Cola, the microwave, and Viagra were all fortuitous discoveries that occurred when the investigators were actually looking for something else.

We are not suggesting that all good things come by accident. Louis Pasteur's statement, "Chance favors the prepared mind," reminds us that prior knowledge may often be the key to being able to recognize something new and valuable. Most important at this point is the obvious reality that you won't find what you are looking for, or something else for that matter, unless you are actively looking. Pushing the image of the explorer just a little further, there were certain elements (food, transportation) that all explorers had to consider before beginning a journey if they wanted to arrive at their destination safely. Unfortunately, countless expeditions on both sea and land have had disastrous outcomes because the explorers did not prepare sufficiently, plan for adequate provisions, or anticipate unforeseen circumstances.

The Three C's

We believe that your success as a researcher relies on three essential characteristics: (1) curiosity, (2) conscientiousness, and (3) creativity.

Curiosity

Curiosity is the first thing that captures your interest, if not your imagination. If you are totally satisfied with your life and the way you do your work, you are not going to be a very motivated to search for anything new or different. If you have already reached a point of saturation in your satisfaction levels, you would not pursue more education, new relationships, or a different career. Therefore, you already have the essential characteristic required of a good researcher. This is what fires up a researcher to discover new ideas, new territory, and new possibilities for the future.

Conscientiousness

Conscientiousness is the "doing-it" characteristic. Talk is not nearly enough, nor is coming up with good ideas, unless you act on them. Akin to the explorers of the past, doing good research requires continuing attention to detail and prudent exercise of due caution. For example, months of your work can be lost if you forget to include a critical element in a questionnaire and don't find the omission until after the data have been gathered. Your study may also be delayed because you didn't have a contingency plan for videotaping scheduled interviews if the power supply fails in your recording equipment.

But, your capability for conscientious effort is already evident. It is not possible to get as far as you have in the academic and professional world without having to demonstrate the capability for sustained effort and complying with rules and regulations imposed by self and by others. Conscientiousness also involves a certain degree of responsibility and follow-through. Like any complex activity in life, research involves solid organization—planning what you are going to do and how you are going to do it. You must have a plan for how you are going to proceed, as well as the time and commitment needed to complete the job.

Creativity

That leaves the last of the characteristics—creativity. You can do research without it, but you can't do good research. You can be an adequate technician by simply following scripted procedures, but you won't make novel contributions. You can follow someone else's recipe, but you will never improve it, much less concoct a dish of your own. Your work won't really make a difference. The problems being confronted by the people you serve will remain as problems.

There are many definitions for creativity, but perhaps the most helpful one in this context was provided by a Hungarian biochemist, Albert Szent-Gyorgyi, who was awarded a Nobel Prize in 1937 for his studies in physiology and medicine. In describing scientific inquiry, he said, "Discovery consists of seeing what everybody has seen and thinking what nobody has thought." Think of the implications of that statement. You needn't be waiting for some kind of epiphany that completely changes the field in which you work. It could happen, but it probably won't.

You can examine old problems and current challenges with the intention of finding a fresh viewpoint that leads to satisfactory solutions. Of course, some of your solutions might create different problems. Our point is that creativity can often be found by looking at an old problem in a new way, seeing things that have never been viewed before. You are more likely to do good research that ultimately brings something new to the table and can contribute fresh solutions for problems.

 Reflective Exercise 8.1

For this task, you will first need to join a small group of three to four individuals who share your interest in a particular specialty area. Then, follow the steps below.

1. *Identify current problems associated with the practice of your specialty area.*
2. *As a group, select one problem on your list as the focus for your discussion.*
3. *Without consideration of factors such as cost and feasibility, generate a list of new ways the problem you've selected might be addressed. As in any brainstorming activity, focus on quantity of ideas and generate as many possible solutions to the problem as you can.*
4. *Among all possible solutions, come to a consensus on just one of them that might be worth investigating further.*
5. *Finally, think about how research studies might be designed to investigate the implementation and efficacy of your selected solution.*

We would be willing to venture that Reflective Exercise 8.1 was not the easiest thing you've ever tried before, although we hope it was fun to let your imagination run free with few limitations. Identifying unresolved problem areas is not particularly difficult. In society at large, there have been problems we have faced for generations—poverty, racism, violence, territoriality—that seem no closer to long-term solutions. In all of our professional specialty areas, there are dilemmas that have also seemed to defy resolution. And, if you are not curious about possible solutions, you should be.

The difficulty in the exercise was more likely with the charge to identify solutions that may not have been tried before. We've probably all heard that we occasionally need to "think outside the box." This is easy to say, but it is not always easy to do. But, this arguably is the litmus test for research. Everyone who understands your specialty area is most likely already aware of the problem. Creativity is when your view of the problem elicits thoughts, ideas, and strategies that apparently have eluded others.

Finally, our guess is that it wasn't especially difficult to see how research could be used to investigate the new ideas. Unless you are curious, nothing significant will happen. Unless you are conscientious in conducting your research study, you won't know if you've helped to solve the problem. Most important of all, the likelihood that your research will really matter is most often a function of how much creative thought was devoted to it.

Why You Do Research

We move now from the abstract to the concrete. What factors might motivate you to conduct a particular research study? The first possibility is that this task is simply a requirement for your academic program or profession. This may be in the form of a presentation, project, or written document, such as a thesis or dissertation. Regardless of the specific format, you'll be designing, conducting, and reporting the results of a study because you have a requirement to satisfy to attain your academic or professional goals.

The other scenario, and the one we want to encourage, is that you are conducting the study to find out stuff that you really want to know. The two motives are hardly mutually exclusive—just because you are required to complete a research project does not mean that you can't enjoy the process, especially if you have the option to pick a topic that is intriguing and actually related to your present or future work. There are, in fact, many things in life that you have been obligated to do and yet discovered afterward that they were, in fact, wonderful experiences. We are not promising that is the case, but we are reminding you that you can choose to make the research journey more interesting and valuable.

Extrinsic Motivation: It's Required

Choosing the topic and advisor. The focus in the next chapter is on identifying and framing your research questions. You will find a variety of suggestions, with emphasis on factors related to the topic itself. Before we get into these details, we first want to consider some human relationship features that can make what you perceive as a requirement to be much more satisfying.

The most formal of the required research studies are those projects that are typically prepared with direct guidance from one faculty member, with possible oversight from others. The individual who is guiding your research endeavor, we'll refer to him or her as an advisor, plays a key role from beginning to end. In some academic programs, you might have some input in the selection of your advisor, and if you have such a choice, it is extremely important that you make the selection carefully.

Regardless of how you ended up with your advisor, there are a number of questions you should consider:

- How comfortable do you feel with this person? To what extent do you feel your questions and concerns are acknowledged and responded to respectfully?
- What are this person's areas of research interests? Do they intersect with what you propose to do?
- How familiar are you with this person's published work?
- What do others say about what it is like to work with this advisor?

In some cases, you may not have the luxury of selecting your advisor, or a switch of advisor assignment is necessary. With either scenario, you will still find it useful to review these questions so that you can work more cooperatively with your research mentor.

If your research project requires you to form a committee, it is a good idea to consult with your advisor about the composition of your committee to make sure everyone gets along. It would be naive and misguided to choose members based solely on their expertise, without considering how the individuals might interact together. It is generally good advice to first pick an advisor whose judgment you trust (assuming you have a choice). Then, consult with him or her to put together a committee that not only provides the sort of guidance you want, but is also composed of individuals who respect and work well with one another.

So, how do you accomplish this compatibility check? Do your homework first. Identify and read some of your potential advisor's publications. Arrange for time to talk with him or her about your research plans. Listen carefully to suggestions about the feasibility of your planned research study. It's one thing to have an advisor with whom you interact with periodically. It's quite another to have an advisor who is charged with providing ongoing guidance and support through the duration of your study.

To a lesser degree, these same concerns apply to your committee members, if required. Again, your advisor will typically play the key role in selecting the other members. At this point in your academic career, he or she knows more about research than you do and can provide invaluable assistance in helping you to shape the focus and scope of your study. We encourage you to seek a degree of compatibility with an individual whose opinions you can respect.

Checklist 8.1 Things to Consider When Choosing an Advisor (If You Have a Choice)

1. Select someone whom you respect and you believe respects you as well.

2. Make sure your research interests are compatible with this individual.

3. Look at the person's track record as an advisor. Do their advisees complete their studies in a reasonable time period?

4. Review the prospective advisor's published research to see if you like the research that they are doing.

5. What is the person's time availability?

6. What is the "scoop" according to others who have worked with the prospective advisor?

7. Does this person have clout and is accomplished enough that they can help you disseminate your work?

Knowing the rules. Required research projects generally serve as a culminating experience of an academic program requirement. They are conducted and reported with strict specifications for each part of the process, including approved formats for the presentation of your findings. Be certain that you are aware of these before you begin your study. Determine whether a handbook or other written resource that delineates the expectations and guidelines is available. If you are unsure, ask your advisor, program chair, or other program personnel. Be wary of asking for this information from other students—they may be misinformed or have outdated information. Under these circumstances, it is always best to seek information from program personnel who are directly involved with the research project requirement.

Before leaving this section, there's one other point we want to emphasize. Earlier we noted that a research study may be required as a culminating activity to demonstrate the mastery of necessary skills that might be helpful in your professional practice. A second goal for you is to advance the knowledge in your field. Keeping your focus on both objectives will make it much easier to accept demands from your advisor or your committee, even when they do not seem congruent with your ideas. Research projects completed as program requirements ultimately result in a product that is not yours alone. You will have plenty of opportunity to do it your way after you successfully complete your program.

Intrinsic Motivation: It's for Me

We introduced the idea earlier that you have been a researcher your whole life, even if you didn't identify yourself as such. Every time you said to yourself that you wanted to try something different in your life or work, you were, in effect, doing research. An instructor may be curious to see whether it makes a difference giving a weekly quiz on Monday rather than Friday, or at the beginning of class as opposed to towards the end. An organizational leader might decide to begin the day informally visiting with employees in the lounge area instead of responding to e-mails. A behavioral health or medical professional might want to try completing notes immediately after each interaction with a client or patient rather than doing all of the paperwork at the end of the day.

There's a common feature in these diverse examples. You've been doing it one way, and then you decide to try another way to note the effects. Whether your motivation was increasing effectiveness or avoiding boredom, some monitoring of the outcome is inevitable. Something in your daily activities was intentionally changed. That's the independent variable. You observed what happened after making the change. Were the scores on the quiz better, worse, or about the same? Did starting the day with the staff help in any way to establish a positive organizational culture? Was it easier to write good case notes when the task wasn't postponed until the end of the day? Those are dependent variables. Where did you get the idea for the change in the first place? This almost had to come from something you had read or heard, and by definition, that's like a review of relevant literature.

 Reflective Exercise 8.2

This exercise has two distinct components. You will engage with an individual component first, and then follow with a small group component.

Individual Component

On a sheet of paper, make two columns. In the first column, list as many examples as you can remember of instances in your life or at work when you have tried something different. It doesn't have to be anything major—just something when you wanted to see what would happen if you changed something you had been doing.

Then, in the second column, put a few words to describe the outcome. Complete sentences are not necessary, just enough words to jog your memory of the event. We've provided an example below to help get you started.

What I Tried	*How It Worked*
• *Stopped checking e-mail on holidays and the weekends*	• *Slept better. Felt more relaxed. Interacted with family and friends more.*
• *Brought my lunch from home instead of buying my lunch.*	• *Saved money. Ate healthier. Felt less rushed.*

Small Group Component

Form small groups of three to four individuals. It may be helpful to have homogenous groups formed according to specialty areas, but this is not essential. Each member of the group should share at least one of their "what I tried" and "how it worked" examples. The task of the group is to suggest what might have contributed to the outcome, other than the change you made, as well as how the change might have been implemented in such a way to obtain the outcome described.

You're Probably Not Doing It Very Well

You may already have the skills to design and conduct research and feel defensive when we suggest otherwise. Your only motivation in trying something different could have been because you were bored out of your mind in your work setting and willing to try anything just to add some spice. In that case, whatever change you made most likely worked very well indeed.

One of the desired outcomes of Reflective Exercise 8.2 was calling attention to the need for caution when you make a change and it appeared to make things better. Why should you be concerned? After all, you did it, it worked, and you'll probably keep doing it. There is that old saying about not looking gift horses in the mouth, though.

The concern is needed because the positive outcome you observed could have been created by something quite different than the change you made. In the language of research, the outcome you observed on the dependent variable may have been a function of one or more extraneous variables and not related at all to the independent variable.

Take, for example, the instructor who adjusted the timing of a weekly quiz. She may have decided to change the quiz date to Monday (independent variable) after reading an article about student success (review of relevant literature). After the first week, she noticed that students achieved higher quiz scores (dependent variable). However, the higher scores could also be a result of easier content, better preparation, charisma of the instructor, and so on (extraneous variables).

In published research studies, there is often concern about the extent to which findings will generalize to other settings and populations. It may not be immediately obvious how this same concept applies when you are doing some-thing primarily to satisfy your own curiosity. For example, the instructor who changes the timing of a quiz might not have thought of sharing her findings with colleagues or publishing the results in a professional journal. Her primary purpose was to simply see if a change in her professional practice had a desired effect on student performance.

With just a little reflection, however, concern about the extraneous variables would be of great concern to the instructor. Higher performance was evident when she adjusted the timing of the weekly quiz. Would that be expected to continue in future weeks? Would it be evident with other students? What about the more high stakes assessments, such as the midterm and final exam?

In fact, these are exactly the same issues confronted when studies are done with the intent to share findings with a wider audience and expand the frontiers of professional knowledge. The only thing different is the scope of the frontier—improvement of one's professional practice or adding to the world of knowledge within one's discipline.

Summary and Closing Thoughts

The title of this chapter asked a question. Is the researcher an accountant, an explorer, or both? We've suggested that the answer to the question is both and identified three essential characteristics required among effective researchers. Curiosity has led you to want to try new and different things. Creativity has pro-vided the new things to try. What's left is the conscientious application, carefully using strategies that will allow you to rule out some of the extraneous influences. With such strategies, you can satisfy your curiosity with knowledge that may go beyond the immediate outcomes and enable a continuous process of enhancing the quality of professional practices.

We've acknowledged that there may be another driving force to conduct and complete a research study, such as a program-imposed requirement. Obviously that is an external source of motivation, which is typically considered less valu-able than an intrinsic motivation. We've found, and believe you will as well, that there is a continuing interaction between the external and the internal sources of motivation. You may begin a research study only because it is required, and the looming requirement may serve to keep you going when things get difficult. But, there is an inherent excitement in discovery, and that excitement is magnified for those who've chosen professions when the discovery holds promise of helping others have better lives.

In this chapter we didn't provide specifics about how to do research quite yet. That comes in the chapters that immediately follow. We did provide suggestions about important preparations, including selection of your advisor if it is required and you are given the choice. Although it is perhaps obvious, the more you know about the specific nature of the requirement, including how the final product is to be prepared, the smoother your path will be.

Whether a research study is required or is not, it is our hope that you will embrace the idea of informing your professional practice with research. Some information may be available in the literature, whereas other information may be awaiting discovery. With this in mind, we concluded this chapter with information intended to persuade you that being a researcher isn't something new for you—it's something you already do and have done on a regular basis. We also suggested that you probably aren't a very good researcher yet, but only because you don't usually frame your investigations in a way to get the best possible information from them.

The remaining chapters in this section are intended to provide the tools to make that happen. In this section of the book, we will be taking a different approach. Rather than providing questions to assist you with evaluating content from others, your task will be to begin preparing your own plan for a research study.

CHAPTER 9

What Do You Want to Know, and What Do Others Already Know?

CHAPTER CONCEPTS

Conducting a review of relevant literature	Hypotheses	Research questions
Consulting the literature	Objective statements	Researchable topic
	Research objective	

Introduction

"I'm not exactly sure what I want to do for my research project," the student said to her advisor at the start of the meeting. They were getting together to make some decisions about which problem she would investigate for her study, as well as some preliminary choices about methodology.

"No idea at all?" the professor asked mildly. He was used to this sort of introduction. In fact, sometimes he was more concerned when a student came in with a very definite idea of what he or she wanted to do because their plan was usually very unrealistic.

"Well, I have some rough ideas, but I'm not sure where to begin."

The professor nodded. "What do you have in mind?"

"I don't know," the student answered. "I guess something, maybe, about new professionals and how they cope with adjusting to their first job in the field."

"Sounds like a big area," the professor replied with a smile. "What specifically do you want to know about that?"

The student shrugged helplessly, yet when she saw the professor waiting patiently, she ventured further. "Depression, maybe? I know when I was a new in the field, I felt so discouraged and depressed initially because my responsibilities were nothing like I had imagined. I felt so unprepared for what was expected and so incompetent."

"I see. What exactly are you most interested in knowing about this area?"

"What do you mean?" the student asked suspiciously. It sounded like a trick question.

"I mean the whole topic of depression, burnout, and adjustment is rather broad. What is the research question that you are most interested in exploring? Depending on what question you ask, and how you ask the question, that will suggest a different methodology."

"I know that," the student said with more force than she had intended. But this whole process was so frustrating and anxiety-provoking for her. She wasn't particularly interested in doing a research study in the first place. Maybe that was not exactly true. Because she now understood what research was all about, she did have some issues she wanted to explore more deeply and systematically, but she also felt flooded with how to work out all the details. There were so many things swimming around in her head: Should she do a quantitative or qualitative study? Then, which particular methodology was most appropriate?

"Okay," the professor reassured her, seeing her discouragement and confusion. "What we need to do initially is find a topic or an issue. If you are going to be spending a lot of time reading and investigating this area, then it better be something that especially interests you. What comes to mind for you?"

The student nodded. "Well, I sort of would like to help prevent the kinds of problems that I experienced when I first entered the profession. I'd like to find out what some of the differences are between professionals who do well and flourish during their first year on the job versus those who struggle and eventually burn out."

"Okay," the professor encouraged her, "now you're getting a bit more focused. You will want to pick a topic that is narrow enough that you can realistically familiarize yourself with the literature in the area. Secondly, you'll want to pick something that has not been done before or has little existing research. In other words, something that is not so well worn that there's very little opportunity to make a significant contribution."

"Are you saying, then, that this topic of adjustment has been done before? Because I guess I could do something else about. . . ."

"Hold on there!" the professor interrupted. "I'm not saying that at all. I'm just saying that just as important as what question you investigate is how you ask the question. The way you frame the question will not only suggest whether your topic is researchable, but also which methodology is best-suited for exploring your specific research question."

From the General to the Specific

The dialogue between this student and professor is quite typical of the sort of discussion that takes place during the exploratory stage of formulating a research study. A researcher may have a general idea about something of interest, but has not yet managed to refine the research questions to frame the research objective and approach in such a way that the study can be adequately planned and implemented. This is just as you would expect in the development of any investigation—you start out with a general idea and then, gradually, become more and more systematic and focused.

The importance of the research objective has been a continuing focus in each chapter of this text. From the review of relevant literature to the discussion of findings, the evaluation criteria always came back to whether there was consistency with the research objective. Did the researcher use appropriate participants? Was the research design appropriate? Every facet of a research study, how it is designed and implemented, is guided by the research objective.

The focus of our discussion now changes dramatically. You will no longer be evaluating whether other researchers asked appropriate questions. You won't be using their research objective as a template for critiquing their review of relevant literature, selection of research sample, choice of research design, analysis of findings, and conclusions. You are ready now to stop being a critic of others' work and join the ranks of creative scholars. It's now your job to construct a research objective that will guide how you proceed with your study.

You can readily see from the dialogue that began this chapter the process of identifying a research objective and refining research questions is a complex business—it involves far more than simply what you want to know. As in any construction project, if the plans are not well developed, if the materials selected are not made wisely, and if the procedures are not intelligently and logically ordered, the structure will never be completed or stand for very long. So it is with research—if you don't ask the question in the best possible way, you'll never find the answers you are looking for.

Questions That Can Be Researched, and Those That Cannot

By definition, a research topic can be any issue in need of investigation. But, to be a researchable topic, it must be something that can be investigated through collecting and analyzing data. For example, "Is there meaning to life?" is certainly an important question, but you are not going to be able to answer that question very easily with a research study. You could, though, do a study to address the alternate question, "How do individuals construct meaning in their lives?" In like manner, the question, "Should the death penalty be abolished?" does not work as a research question nearly as well as, "Do states with the death penalty have lower homicide rates?" In essence, the researchable questions tend to be a specific element of a bigger question.

 Reflective Exercise 9.1

In small groups of three to four individuals, consider the following general questions:

- *What parenting style is the most effective?*
- *Should schools (K-12 or postsecondary institutions) ban the use of social media during instruction?*

- *What makes long-term relationships so successful?*
- *What are benefits associated with pet ownership?*
- *Should laws related to firearms be reevaluated?*

For each question above, discuss why they are not researchable in their present form. Then, generate several alternative questions related to the issue that could be researched. Be prepared to share your findings with the whole group.

Your research study will eventually be evaluated by others. The critics may be faculty members if the study was done as a requirement of your academic program. They could be a group of peer reviewers for a journal if you submit a research report of the study for possible publication. Ultimately, the most important critics might be the evaluators of your research—those who decide whether what you discovered is of any use to their professional practice.

Forming Research Questions

Asking questions is one of the most natural forms of communication. After all, you've been doing this since you first began to speak (May I have a cookie? Why is the sun always smiling at me? How do airplanes fly?). But, asking questions well is something else entirely. In fact, one of the most difficult challenges for new professionals is learning to ask good questions, or at least the kind that produce meaningful answers.

Because the way you form your question is such a crucial element in research studies, before we go any further, we want to review some basic skills with formulating questions that we discussed earlier in the context of open- and closed-ended formats. Consider the following scenario:

A child returns from school at the end of the day to find his mother waiting in the kitchen.

"So, did you have a good day at school today?" the mother asks.

"Uh-huh."

"Did you have a chance to go outside during recess?"

The child nods his head.

"Did you learn anything new and interesting?"

"Yup."

"Do you have any homework?"

The child shrugs.

In this very common interaction between a parent and child, what struck you as most ineffective in terms of the questions that were asked?

As we introduced earlier, the questions were all framed in a closed-ended way, meaning that they could be answered with a single word—yes or no. By contrast, you'll recall open-ended questions are exploratory and encourage the other person to give elaborate, detailed answers. In the scenario above, asking questions such as, "How was school today? What did you learn today? What homework might we work on together?" would be more likely to elicit such answers.

Asking the right question is clearly a critical factor in effective communication. In everyday exchanges, we tend to get what we ask for and this is no less the case in the context of a research investigation. When you are doing a quantitative research study, framing your questions for closed-ended responses is often your objective. But, especially if you want to use a qualitative approach for your research study, framing questions for open-ended responses is essential.

 Reflective Exercise 9.2

Pair off with a partner and interview one another to find out what previous experience the person has had doing research. You will conduct this interview in three rounds. In the first round, ask one another only closed-ended questions. For example, you might ask:

- *So, did you do research before?*
- *Did you like it?*
- *Would you say it was pretty easy for you?*

In the second round, frame your questions as completely open-ended questions. You may ask:

- *When was a time in which you did some research?*
- *How did you feel about it?*
- *What was the easiest part for you?*

In the third round, use open-ended questions that include some structure. Examples include:

- *How have things from research influenced your professional practice?*
- *What do you think keeps professionals in the field from using information reported in research studies?*

The purpose of Reflective Exercise 9.2 was to illustrate that the direction of a process is controlled, at least to some extent, by the form in which it is initiated. Closed-ended questions—those in which yes or no answers are likely—often provide too little information. On the other hand, open-ended questions will usually result in lengthier responses, but they may not produce the information actually being sought. Questions that encourage elaboration and are phrased in such a way to increase the chances for getting the desired information offer researchers the best of both worlds. Such questions make it likely that you will end up with what you wanted to know, but they also leave open the possibility that you will learn important things that you weren't expecting.

For simplicity in presentation, there is an assumption of more than one area of interest within your study, and you will consistently see reference to research questions (plural) rather than a singular question. We will use a three-step model to progress from, "I don't know where to start" to "These are my research questions." Note that, as with most important tasks, there is more than one way to accomplish the goal. Some other research methods may structure the task slightly differently, with fewer or more steps, and sometimes with different labels. But, those differences are in form, rather than in function. The ultimate destination is the same—you want research questions that guide the information gathering and information processing required for your investigation.

As you move through the following steps, you'll find a gradual sharpening of focus with each succeeding stage. The three steps are as follows:

1. Identify a topic for your research study.
2. Refine the topic into a research objective.
3. Reframe the research objective into hypotheses or research questions.

Curiosity drives the research engine, and the information for the first step may come from a variety of sources. To get information for the first step, you must guide your curiosity into finding some potential topics for a research study. The second step is most often the easiest of the three tasks. In it, you simply further reduce the research topic to something manageable, researchable, within the limits of your resources, and hopefully of interest to you. The last step is a little more challenging. In it you are asked to reframe your research objective into much more specific (for most quantitative studies) or somewhat more specific (for most qualitative studies) research questions.

Identify a Topic

Where can you find research topics? The easy answer is everywhere. Look around. The world is full of important and unanswered questions. When should a practitioner intervene in a situation that involves conflict? How can practitioners share information about health-risk behaviors in a way that is meaningful to others? How often should practitioners be supervised? A list such as this could go on forever. Some sorting mechanism is essential, otherwise being overwhelmed by possible choices is inevitable.

In the chapter that preceded this one, we suggested two distinct reasons you might be preparing to conduct a study. One of the motives might be intrinsic motivation—there is some compelling interest to explore a topic of passionate interest For example, perhaps there's a new approach that you've thought about trying in your work. Or, a colleague has suggested that you might get better results with a specific change in your methods. Perhaps, there's something going on in your professional practice that is puzzling you enough to want to find an explanation. Under the best possible circumstances, you will select issues to explore and research questions to answer that may enrich your life, increase your job effectiveness, and add to the pool of meaningful knowledge in your field. Even if you must do some sort of research project as a program requirement (extrinsic motivation), you can still pick something that is useful to you. This process begins through the internal process of reflecting on your own interests.

Introspection and Reflection

One of the first research strategies used in psychology was based on a technique called introspection. As the name implies, this means to search within. It is the first step in selecting a research topic that involves identifying your most cherished interests, values, and passions for learning. You may have already identified a general career path. Within that discipline you may have already found yourself gravitating toward some specialty areas and away from others. You would prefer to work with like-minded professionals or perhaps those who think differently. You enjoy working one-on-one, in small groups, or as part of a larger organization. There are some daily tasks that excite you and others that leave you totally bored.

Regardless of your chosen specialty, there are some aspects associated with it that are more appealing to you than others. Looking within yourself to identify how you feel is sufficient to start narrowing your focus to identify an appropriate research topic. Even when the task is required, it will be much more enjoyable if the topic is something in which you have more than just a glimmer of interest.

When you begin the introspective analysis to reveal your interests, don't worry initially about whether the topic is too broad. Bringing your topic down to a manageable size will come only after you've settled on a general area. The immediate need is to set some preliminary boundaries for this general topic. It's not yet necessary to pinpoint anything specific within the general area of interest, and it is certainly too early to be concerned about whether a qualitative or quantitative design is preferred.

This task is similar to planning a vacation or a trip. First, there's the region itself, somewhere far, far away—that's the more general interest. Now, still in the planning stage, consider places that might both qualify and interest you. Let's say, for example, you've settled on Australia for a visit. It's certainly far, far away unless you live there already. Yet, that still covers a huge territory that is impossible to cover in a lifetime, much less a few weeks. Because your time and funds are limited, you might settle for spending time in Sydney and the rest of New South Wales. Or, you could head north to Queensland and the Great Barrier Reef, or perhaps to Perth and western Australia. No matter the destination, one thing is clear—you would run yourself ragged trying to see it all within a single visit. There is a similar process involved when settling on a research topic. You want to pick a region that seems appealing, but also includes territory that is reasonable and realistic to cover.

Reflective Exercise 9.3

1. *Spend several minutes generating a written list of as many research questions that interest you as possible. Try to generate a dozen or more different research questions, not variations of similar themes.*
2. *When you have completed your list, group the questions or topics together according to at least three or four categories that make sense to you. Make sure that each item in your list fits into a group.*
3. *Give each group a category name that captures the essence of the contained items.*
4. *Examine each group, along with their contained items. Notice where your attention and interest is most drawn toward.*
5. *Meet in small groups of three to four individuals. Each group member should share how they used the introspection process and what they discovered.*
6. *After each small group member shares, help one another generate even more possibilities for research questions to investigate in their area of interest.*

Consulting the Literature

The introspection process is an important step but hardly sufficient to get the job done. Now that you've identified some general parameters, it's time to consult some other sources and see what others have done before you. At this early stage you will not be searching for a single answer. Instead, you are exploring ideas to stimulate your thought processes. Your goal at the end of this step is to have some credible possibilities for research topics. And, we think we have just the place to find such ideas.

In Chapter 7 of this text, we pointed out that essentially all research reports include recommendations for further research, typically within the Discussion section. There is probably no better source for ideas about research topics than the recommendations other researchers have already made. The most frequent suggestion will be for just a simple replication, doing essentially the same study again but with a different participant sample. Often, though, there are additional suggestions for studies to extend or clarify the reported findings.

Getting help from the literature to identify your research topic is another three-step process. You start with the part of your specialization that, through the introspective process, you think will be most interesting to you. This provides the key words to use in your search of the literature. This step ends with a list of published articles that have stirred your curiosity.

In the next step, you begin reviewing the articles you collected, focusing on those which seem most intriguing and, of course, the more recent studies. You are not doing a critical review of the study. Instead, you're doing a quick overview until you get to the Discussion section where you will pay close attention to the recommendations for further study. Look there for ideas about possible topics for your own study.

For example, let's assume that your primary research interest is job satisfaction among professionals within your field. With the introspection task, you identified that you were especially looking forward to learning more about professionals who balance family, personal, and work responsibilities. This information is enough to begin your search in the literature.

For the final step, one of the better search tools for scholarly articles is a library's subscription databases. With the research topic we provided above, you may begin your search using keywords, such as "job satisfaction," "work-life balance," and "work and family life." You may then continue searching the databases using different combinations of keywords and refining criteria, such as resource type (peer-reviewed articles) and publication date. Your search efforts will likely produce a number of articles for you to review and identify at least one, and preferably several, possibilities for your research topic based on the recommendations for future research.

Theories within your discipline also suggest another source for research topic ideas. Remember that in this context, theories are much more than just marginally supported opinions. They represent organized attempts to provide explanations for observed facts or phenomena. One of the functions of a good theory is that it allows you to make predictions. The accuracy of the predictions determines the validity of a theory. A prediction from a theory can define a research topic, providing results that support or dispute the validity of the theory.

Although theories may be a rich source of possible research topics, this route is more often appropriate for experienced researchers. To develop a research project from a theory, you have to understand its intricacies and complexities. Except for the rarest of circumstances, your motivation for conducting research is more likely practical rather than theoretical.

There's no reason to overstress about the challenges and burdens of choosing a topic. Some time will be required for this task. But the outcome clearly warrants the time investment. You will have identified some potential topics that are in your general area of interest. You will also feel validated that this subject has sufficient merit because other researchers who have been working in this field for some time recommend that more work be done. As an extra bonus, you will also have a head start on doing the review of relevant literature for your study.

Considering Katie's case. Katie completed the introspection phrase and decided that she would most enjoy investigating employee relationships, specifically in the area of effective conflict resolution strategies. This was an area in which she hoped to specialize someday.

With her interests clarified, Katie began a search for articles where research had been done in either of these areas. She quickly discovered that it was not quite as easy as it appeared. She tried a search using the keywords "employee" and "relationships," but found this search produced entirely too many results. Katie used several other keyword combinations ("employee," "conflict resolution," "conflict resolution strategies," "effective") and filtered the results to include only peer-reviewed articles published within the past 5 years. This narrowing of the literature search was successful in producing a more manageable number of interesting possibilities.

One of the articles was not available in full-text format, so Katie ordered a copy through the library. The library obtained an electronic copy within a week, and the article was worth the wait. As Katie consulted the recommendations for future research, an idea emerged. Katie decided she would like to investigate the use of listening skills during difficult conversations.

Although Katie's first area of interest (effective conflict resolution strategies for the workplace) sounded promising, she repeated the process with her newly developed area of interest (use of listening strategies during conflict resolution in the workplace). "Listening" was a helpful keyword for the second search, and one of the titles in the list looked especially interesting. The title was for a study using listening strategies as a way to manage and prevent conflict within the workplace. Honing in on a specific conflict resolution strategy had not occurred to Katie during introspection. She obtained the article, read the recommendations for future research, and now had a more viable and interesting research topic.

There are some important lessons contained in Katie's case. The first attempt to use the recommended search process was disappointing and useless. Although things at first appeared to be simple, the reality required some creativity in selection of keywords. Another lesson from the case example is that one of the resources that turned out to be especially helpful wasn't immediately available. Giving yourself a great deal of time before any deadline is a rule that will serve you well throughout the research process. Finally, there was evidence of both convergent and divergent thinking in Katie's case. Remember that convergent thinking is directed toward ultimately finding a single answer, whereas divergent thinking is intended to identify multiple paths. Convergent thinking helped Katie narrow her first area of interest, going from general conflict resolution in the workplace to a specific strategy—listening skills. Divergent thinking helped Katie remain open to recognizing a new possibility, one that didn't come directly from introspection. She hadn't thought about focusing on a specific conflict resolution strategy. That possibility was triggered by what she found while searching the literature.

Getting Help From Others

After spending some time in introspection and searching the literature, you have hopefully selected a topic that will work for you. The next step is to turn to trusted individuals to serve as a sounding board. These individuals may be family members, friends, professional colleagues, or other experts who are knowledgeable about research and can provide you with help in identifying a topic area that is both significant and reasonable in scope. If your research project is a program requirement, this step involves your advisor. For the sake of clarity, we will assume you are working with an advisor.

The steps you've taken thus far should enable you to consult with your advisor in such a way that you are informed and have some kind of preliminary plan. Inevitably, when you are asked if you have thought about what you might like to do, you can respond with something other than a shrug such as, "Here are a couple of topics that I have been exploring. What do you think about them?"

Occasionally, students come up with topics that are too narrow in scope, but much more often your advisor will need to help you reduce your initial idea to something that can be accomplished in a reasonable time frame and with the available resources. To illustrate, here are three topics that a student might bring to her advisor. Which of them appears to be most realistic?

- Topic 1: How enrollment in a government course influences actual participation in local, state, and national political activities.

- Topic 2: The relationship between church attendance and the amount of sexual activity in the surrounding high schools.

- Topic 3: If employment of paraprofessionals as teacher's aides increases feelings of professionalism among teachers.

Let's examine each topic and explore the extent to which they are practical studies. With Topic 1, finding out if there is a relationship between taking a government course and political participation would appear to be an important investigation, particularly because this outcome is often a stated goal of government courses. As described, however, it's much too broad, and it would take several years to complete such a study, perhaps over the length of a whole career. An advisor, however, might suggest reducing the scope of the topic, perhaps to investigate the relationship between grades earned in government courses and participation in school government.

As for the study in Topic 2, both of the variables could be quantified (church attendance and sexual activity), so technically this topic is researchable with a quantitative strategy. But all research with human participants requires their consent, as well as consent from guardians and parents when minors are involved. The odds of obtaining permission from guardians and parents to inquire how often their high-school-aged children attend church are probably low. Likewise, the odds of obtaining permission to ask about their children's level of sexual activity are probably even lower. With the improbability of obtaining permission to investigate either variable, it is unlikely that you could conduct this study at all.

With Topic 3, the study might be doable depending on the setting for the study. If the researcher interested in this topic has an accessible population that includes paraprofessionals and teachers, this topic could be explored using either a quantitative or qualitative design, contingent on how the researcher defined feelings of professionalism.

Considering Katie's case. In Katie's example, she is now at the point where she identified a possibility for her topic related to the application of listening skills to resolve conflicts in the workplace. Her advisor was pleased that she had done some homework prior to their consultation, but he seemed unimpressed with her idea about a study of listening skills. Although the answer was not an absolute "no," the unenthusiastic attitude was crystal clear. Katie's advisor shared, "It would be rather difficult to measure listening, and it could take a really long time to ascertain the effects that the use of listening has on resolving conflict. The methodology for this study could present serious issues."

Katie disagreed with her advisor's assessment, but she decided not to press her case.

The good news was that her advisor seemed genuinely excited about the topic of conflict resolution in the workplace and immediately began asking questions. "Have you thought about how conflict resolution is handled among employees who work on-site compared with employees who work off-site? What if you compared face-to-face conflict resolution with one that is handled through the use of technology tools? Could you make this a study of the management of off-site conflict resolution?" The session ended shortly thereafter with a suggestion that Katie should think about the things discussed and come back in a week.

Katie now had a dilemma. She actually had been leaning toward the listening skills study and was excited about this topic. She knew there was another faculty member in her department who would probably be willing to work with her on this investigation. But, she had worked well with her current advisor, and it seemed obvious that she would have no problem getting helpful guidance.

From Research Topic to Research Objective

Having your topic identified is an important accomplishment and a great relief. Alas, there is much left to do. Your next task is to translate the topic into a short, specific verbal description of your investigation. This is your research objective and will typically be stated in a form something like: "The purpose of this study is to. ... "

The essence of the research objective is a further narrowing of the research topic to a more specific area of focus. At this point, there is an important difference in the expected level of specificity that is contingent on whether your study will have a quantitative or a qualitative focus. In quantitative studies, the research objective is placed either at the very beginning of the research report or close to it. In a qualitative study, the research objective is framed tentatively and does not take final form until the study is well under way.

As one example, an investigator started out interviewing children about their experiences with bullies, both past and present. Yet during the course of these conversations, the original research objective evolved into a study of how adult bystanders react (or don't react) to such incidents. It turned out that many of the children felt as much anger toward the adults who did nothing to intervene as they did toward the bullies themselves. When preparing your research objective for both quantitative and qualitative studies, you will want to be careful to ensure that you have reduced the general topic to a manageable project.

Consider the following research objective: The purpose of this study is to create a bully-free world. This is certainly a noble contribution, but that's a lot to ask from just one study Consider the following as an alternative: The purpose of this study is to investigate the relationship between feelings of safety and efforts to reduce bullying among children. We think you'll agree that this is an objective that it is far easier to address.

In this stage of the process, you can readily see that the major task is to take a more general research topic and then translate it into a more specific research objective, which essentially becomes the major objective of the study. Depending on whether you are doing a quantitative or qualitative project, the level of specificity will vary. Quantitative research objectives are typically more specific, whereas qualitative research objectives are typically broader and more open ended.

It is important to remember that the primary differentiation between quantitative and qualitative research objectives is in the extent of specificity, not necessarily in the specific terminology used. Clearly evident in the literature is that researchers have a great deal of latitude in their choice of words. A quantitative researcher might well use the term "investigation" in their research objective, and the term "exploration" is often found in qualitative studies. Different phrasing choices are completely acceptable so long as they convey the more narrow purpose in a quantitative study or the broader range for a qualitative study.

Considering Katie' case. Let's return once again to Katie who we left earlier with a dilemma. As you will recall, her advisor clearly preferred that her research topic would have something to do with using on-site and off-site conflict resolution in the workplace. After meeting with her adviser, Katie's had spent some time reflecting about her area of research interest. Katie thought carefully about the implications of her decision, talked with trusted acquaintances and friends, and did some additional work looking for existing literature on the suggested topic. The outcome of her deliberation was to go with on-site and off-site conflict resolution in the workplace. With this decision and given her advisor's suggestions, defining the research objective came easily. Katie decided her study would compare the management of on-site and off-site conflict resolution among employees in the workplace.

From Research Objective to Research Questions and Hypotheses

Your research topic has been identified. Your research objective has been defined. What follows next is to convert your research objective into specific research questions. Although this is a critical step in the research process, where it occurs will depend on whether you are using a quantitative or qualitative approach. With both approaches, you will eventually identify specific areas of focus in your study. If you use a quantitative methodology, this step occurs at the beginning, before you begin to gather data. In a qualitative methodology, you more often begin the data gathering with a general research objective and allow the specific research questions to emerge during the course of the study.

Examples of Research Questions

To illustrate the creation of research questions, let's look at some research objectives for both types of studies. For example, a research objective for a quantitative study might be stated as follows: The goal of this study is to compare student preferences and performance in a required research course delivered in online and face-to-face contexts. Research questions from this objective may include the following:

1. Are there differences in levels of participation (face-to-face class attendance or online site log-ins) between students in the online course section and students in the face-to-face course section of a required research course?

2. Are there differences in assessment scores (quiz scores, midterm scores, final test scores) between students in the online course section and students in the face-to-face course section of a required research course?

3. Are there differences in levels of satisfaction between students in the online course section and students in the face-to-face course section of a required research course?

4. Are there differences in overall achievement (overall course grades, retention) between students in the online course section and students in the face-to-face course section of a required research course?

An open-ended research objective for this same topic in a qualitative investigation might be stated as follows: The goal of this study is to explore student preferences and the nature of course engagement among students in a required research course delivered in online and face-to-face contexts.

This enables the researchers to postpone identifying specific research questions until after more information is obtained from the participants themselves. Some examples of research questions that could then emerge include the following:

1. In what ways do students interact with each other?
2. In what ways do students interact with their professors?
3. What themes are evident in students' views of course quality at the end of the semester?

Considering Katie's case. Let's have one final visit with our student, Katie, to see how she moves from the research objective of her study to specific research questions. Katie has a topic related to the management of conflict resolution in the workplace. She also has the following research objective: The purpose of this study is to compare the management of on-site and off-site conflict resolution among employees in the workplace.

At this point, she still has the option of using either a quantitative or a qualitative methodology. Although the word "compare" in her research objective is more often associated with quantitative studies, it doesn't mandate that approach because Katie hasn't yet identified how comparisons will be made. Initial consultation of the literature resulted in a large number of studies related to conflict resolution in the workplace, but she found very few studies that described conflict resolution among off-site employees. Katie now had support from existing literature endorsing the value of pursuing this line of inquiry.

Katie decided on a quantitative study for two reasons. One, she felt that a quantitative methodology was most appropriate to examine the relationship between the two variables of on-site and off-site employees. Secondly, both Katie and her advisor were more familiar with this methodology. Katie reframed her research objective into the following research questions:

1. Are there differences in levels of satisfaction among employees with the management of conflict resolution between on-site employees and off-site employees?

2. Are there differences in levels of satisfaction among employers with the management of conflict resolution between on-site employees and off-site employees?

What About Hypotheses?

Whether the research questions are translated into explicit hypotheses depends primarily on the intent and audience of the research report. In reviewing published research studies, you found that explicit hypotheses were generally found in quantitative research reports. When needed, it is quite easy to translate your research questions into hypotheses.

Imagine that you are doing a study. You have carefully reviewed the relevant literature. It is almost inconceivable that you wouldn't have any idea about how the results would turn out, so you generate hypotheses, educated guesses about the outcome of a study. In the previous section of the book, we described differences among the three types of hypotheses:

- If you believe there would be some differences associated with the factor you are studying and think you can predict the direction of the difference, you need a directional hypothesis.

- If you believe there would be some differences associated with the factor you are studying but are not sure what directions those differences might take, you need a nondirectional hypothesis.

- If you believe there are no differences associated with the factor you are studying, you need a null hypothesis.

Translating research questions into hypotheses is not particularly complex or mysterious—it is just a matter of rewording the questions according to the appropriate model. You go from "Is there?" in the question format to "there is" or "there will be" in the hypothesis format.

For example, let's look at Katie's first research question: Are there differences in levels of satisfaction among employees with the management of conflict resolution between on-site employees and off-site employees? In the directional form, the hypothesis might be as follows: Levels of satisfaction with the management of conflict resolution are higher among on-site employees than off-site employees. In the nondirectional form, the hypothesis could be as follows: There are differences in levels of satisfaction among employees with the management of conflict resolution between on-site employees and off-site employees. As a null hypothesis, it becomes the following: There are no differences in levels of satisfaction among employees with the management of conflict resolution between on-site employees and off-site employees. Hypotheses often add more specificity to the research questions, in effect, forcing you to make a directional, nondirectional, or null prediction.

Reviewing Relevant Literature

Earlier in this chapter, you were advised to search the literature as one of the approaches for finding a general topic for your study. This second foray into the literature comes after you've decided on your area of research. In both quantitative and qualitative approaches, some literature citations are typical at the beginning of the research report to establish its societal context and its importance. The approaches then diverge dramatically.

If you are using a quantitative approach, the major review of relevant literature comes before you begin your study. You will already have identified your specific research questions, thus reviewing the literature is required to justify those questions. In effect you use what has already been done to justify and support what you propose to do. How will your study add to the existing knowledge about the topic? How will your study resolve contradictions in the available literature? How will your efforts link to what has been done previously? How is your study built on historical foundations?

If you are using a qualitative approach, remember that the specific research questions will emerge during the study itself, after you are gathering data. Thus, the review of relevant literature associated with those questions will also come during, not only before you begin, your study. As with a quantitative study, you will do considerable reading and reviewing of the literature to prepare and plan your approach. In addition, you will continually upgrade your reading and reviewing of the literature as the study proceeds and new phenomena emerge.

What follows is a series of do's and don'ts, good ideas and bad ideas, for conducting a review of relevant literature. We'll start with the positives, things that are good ideas when you are conducting your review.

Things to Do

Do it first. In quantitative studies, it is bad form to identify your topic, prepare the research objective, develop your research questions, and then start searching in the literature for support of the questions you've already decide to pursue. We won't claim that this poor practice never happens, but it is hardly desirable for obvious reasons. It would be the equivalent of deciding what you want to discover and then looking for confirming evidence to support what you think you already know. Of course, outside of the realm of science and research, this is what many people do all the time, which is why some media sources self-identify as "liberal" or "conservative" so you know which sources will confirm your favorite beliefs.

Only slight modification is required for this rule to work equally well with qualitative studies. It is correct that qualitative studies both allow and encourage research questions to emerge after interaction with participants has begun. The questions that emerge begin as tentative possibilities. Whether they become the actual research questions will depend both on what continues to be evident with the participants and on related information found in the review of relevant literature. One of the principal challenges of doing this kind of research is suspending preconceptions and approaching your participants with an open mind.

Consider secondary sources. Articles that have the word "review" in their title can be very useful places to begin, as in "Literacy and Non-Native English Speakers: A Review of the Literature." Published books may be helpful, as well, although they may not provide the most current studies. A veritable gold mine for starting the process is often a recently published study related to your topic of inquiry that includes an extensive reference list. In all of these cases, keep in mind that you are going to have to check the original sources yourself. In the first section of this book, we emphasized the risks in relying on secondary sources. One researcher's summary of what another one found may, but may not be, an accurate reflection of what they actually found. Thus, secondary sources have the potential to be excellent starting points for your review of relevant literature.

Include a balanced viewpoint. It is difficult, actually impossible, to imagine a topic in your field of any significance for which there are not conflicting opinions supported by prior research. That's how trail lawyers dilute attacks on their case, by being the first to mention weaknesses before the opposition can do so. If you haven't been able to find any disparate findings, you haven't searched hard enough.

One of the most interesting components of the research process is that in your attempt to investigate a question, you are not necessarily looking to confirm or reject your existing beliefs. Instead, you should seek to advance the base of knowledge in a particular area that may lead to some delightful surprises. One of the ways that you demonstrate your objectivity and thoroughness, which increases your credibility as a researcher, is by reporting not only studies that support where you wish to go or your favored beliefs, but also those that conflict with them.

Use the Internet with caution. Limiting your references to those in traditional print sources would exclude an increasingly important setting for information dissemination. This screening caution is required because the credibility factor for information found on the Internet barely rises above that of information communicated on social media, even if there is appearance of academic respectability. Search engines, such as Google, may be a good first place to start, but only as a means to help you do preliminary investigations.

As with any reference, you are interested in not only what is said, but also the credibility of the source. The majority of information found on the Internet has not been refereed by other professionals, which means the reliability and accuracy of the information may be suspect. Use of Internet searches should be reserved for locating where to find a specific reference or to access information that is published by an established and respected organization, such as the U.S. Department of Education or professional groups within your field.

Online journals that are not indexed in subscription databases are becoming more popular. Many smaller professional organizations publish peer-reviewed electronic journals that can be downloaded directly from their websites. Be forewarned, however, that some online journals can be disreputable, proprietary operations that charge exorbitant fees to review and publish articles, which raises significant concerns regarding the quality of their publications.

Due to the expense of printing hard copy journals, most well-known and well-respected referred journals provide electronic access to current and archived issues through electronic subscription databases. Due to their rigorous professional review process, the credibility of information found in these journals tends to high. Keep in mind, though, under no circumstances should you use any material without making an attempt to corroborate the information.

Identifying the general topic is, of course, not difficult when you're doing the research study on your own accord. For instances in which it is a required task, we suggested three resources for assistance in choosing a general topic—introspection, consulting the literature, and getting help from others. Once you have the general topic area, the research objective and then the research questions come essentially through a process of continuing refinement and adding specificity. How specific you need to be at this stage in planning your research depends in part on whether you will be using a quantitative or a qualitative methodology. A quantitative methodology demands that you have specific research questions identified before you begin the study. In contrast, most qualitative studies begin with a general question, adding specific areas of focus after data are gathered. Not all research studies require the research questions to be stated in the form of hypotheses, but some do. For those cases, we offered some guidelines for translating questions into hypotheses if this format is needed in your study.

There is also a difference in the quantitative and qualitative methodologies regarding when the review of relevant literature is conducted. In quantitative studies, you do the review while you are refining the topic into a research objective and questions. Ultimately, the research questions in quantitative studies are justified by a need to clarify or extend what others have done. In contrast, the review of relevant literature in qualitative studies is ongoing with some expected refinement as you identify your general area of interest and review more literature as specific research questions emerge. In the form of do's and don'ts, this chapter concludes with suggestions for how the review of relevant literature should be conducted and what you are expected to report.

CHAPTER 10

Who Can Tell You the Answer, and How Will You Obtain It?

CHAPTER CONCEPTS

Anonymity

Confidentiality

Higher-risk sampling techniques

Informed consent

Institutional Review Board (IRB)

Lower-risk sampling techniques

Mandated reporting

Privacy

Research ethics

Research risks

Rights of research participants

Selecting data collection tools

Selecting a research design

Voluntary participation

Introduction

When you want to find out something you need to know, one of the most important questions to consider is: Who would you ask? The most obvious choice is to consult with those around you. Let's say you are planning to take your first cruise and are trying to find the best cruise ship, destination, and value. It would be reasonable, under those circumstances, to ask someone for assistance. But what if this person was another first-timer to cruise experiences who was as clueless as you are? It was convenient to ask him because he was immediately available, but he may not have been the best source of information.

Another option would be to ask several different people. You could deliberately seek out those who have had a variety of cruise experiences so you could get the most diverse answers possible and thereby have a better idea of viewpoints among the general population. Needless to say, there are dozens of different methods for selecting the people you will consider in your study, depending on your goals, the type of methodology employed, and practical considerations, such as time, money, and resources. Yet even with these choices, it is mostly a straightforward process to determine who can best tell you what you want to know.

In the previous chapter, you settled on what you wanted to know by developing and framing your research questions. In this chapter, you settle on who is in the best position to help you address those questions, as well as how you will go about getting some answers. The good news is that you are already familiar with the basic concepts needed for this chapter. In Chapter 4, you developed skills to evaluate what has already been done with participants in studies conducted by others. In this chapter, you will move from the past to the future and focus on what will be done within the context of your investigation.

To quickly review, the objectives of your study will probably require getting some information from people. This can be collected through direct sources, such as interviews, surveys, questionnaires, or tests. Information may also be obtained through indirect means, such as observations, content analyses of texts (oral communications, written documents), or secondary analyses of existing data sources (agency databases, data archives). An important decision you must first determine is the target population, the group of people who are most likely to provide you with the most meaningful information.

For example, a professor might want to know how students manage stress while balancing family, school, and work responsibilities. Because students are an extraordinarily large group, a bit of trimming would be needed, defining the people in the target group who could actually be available. Although this makes the study more feasible in many ways, it also creates some additional problems. It has to be reasonable to assume that the relevant characteristics of those who participate will mirror those same characteristics in the target population.

Suppose, for example, that this same professor was associated with a professional organization of university professors who teach in online graduate programs. The plan was to recruit possible participants for the study using contacts with other professors who were part of this association. Do you think this is a good idea? Let's consider some of the possible limitations.

The professor's contacts in the professional organization could indeed provide an accessible research sample, making the study much more convenient to complete. However, it would also supply a group that may not reflect the views of all students, much less graduate students in advanced degree programs. This would be fine, of course, if the professor wished to define the target population as graduate students in online programs.

Often there is another step in selecting the research sample, one that involves choosing people who will actually participate in the study. Ultimately, the participants in your study—the research sample—should match the characteristics of the target population. There is a balance that must often be reconciled between the advantages of lower-risk and higher-risk sampling techniques. With lower-risk techniques, researchers are able to make generalizations with the most assurance, yet higher-risk techniques are more convenient and realistic. Several of the most common sampling techniques are reviewed in Table 10.1.

What we want to do in this chapter is to move, step by step, through a process that helps you address the following questions:

- What should you do before you begin selecting participants for your study?
- How might you select participants?
- Which methods should you follow to obtain the desired information from participants?

Table 10.1 Common Research Sampling Techniques

Category	Type	Process
Lower risk	Simple randomization	Randomly select participants from a master list.
Lower risk	Stratified randomization	Identify subgroups and randomly select participants within subgroups.
Lower risk	Cluster sampling	Sample intact groups, such as households in cities.
Lower risk	Systematic sampling	Systematically select participants from a master list, such as every fifth name on the list.
Higher risk	Convenience selection	Choose readily available participants, such as students enrolled in a class at a university.
Higher risk	Quota selection	Predetermine subgroups and select participants until the desired number is reached.
Higher risk	Purposive selection	Select participants because of known similarities to target population.

Protecting the Participants

Whether in the practice of medicine, education, counseling, or research, there is an overriding mandate: Do no harm! As a researcher, you must make every effort to ensure that research participants are not harmed by anything you do. This is so important and should be the primary consideration before you make any other decisions about who will be used to answer the research questions in your study.

It is obvious that some research studies may have a significant impact on the people who participate in them. It is the researcher's responsibility to anticipate, address, and minimize any risks of harm and provide participants with highly detailed information about identified risks prior to beginning the study. In Table 10.2, we have provided some examples of how participants could be harmed legally, physically, or psychologically in research, as well as ways in which researchers may address and minimize anticipated risks.

We have said that protection of participants should be your first consideration when deciding whom you will select to answer the research questions in your study. We emphasize this not only for pragmatic reasons to save you time and frustration later in the process, but also to honor the rights of participants, as well as the ethical and moral responsibilities of researchers.

Table 10.2 Examples of Anticipated Risks of Harm or Discomfort Among Participants

Type of Harm	Example Study Topic	Possible Ways to Prevent Harm
Legal	A study that compares caretaking strategies used by caregivers of children and adults.	• Inform participants of the researcher's legal obligations to report criminal or illegal activity. • Ask participants not to disclose instances of criminal or illegal activity for which they have not been convicted.
Physical	A study that explores the effect of environmental conditions (room temperature, lighting, noises) on concentration levels.	• Ask participants if there are specific environmental conditions they wish to avoid. • Query participants about sensitivities to environmental conditions under study.
Physical	A study that explores the effect of exercise on stress levels.	• Request an extensive history from participants and remove those with preexisting conditions from the study.
Psychological	A study that explores coping mechanisms among adults who experienced a traumatic event.	• Debrief with participants after their involvement so they may return to normal following distressing recollections. • Provide participants with a list of community resources, if needed.
Psychological	A study that requires participants to participate in an interview or complete a questionnaire about their experiences of being in a long-term relationship with a significant other.	• Inform participants of any sensitive topics that may be addressed. • Provide participants with an estimated time frame for their involvement to reduce anxiety.

 ## Reflective Exercise 10.1

The issues surrounding some research studies are not always easy to resolve. Read the following scenario. Then, work in small groups of three to four individuals to discuss the questions that follow.

Scenario

An elementary school is located in a lower socioeconomic area with few resources available for students. You are the school campus administrator and pleased that a researcher has selected this school as a site for a

study of a new, multimedia instructional program. The researcher will provide all the needed equipment and materials for the program, and, as a reward for participation, the school will get to keep everything when the study is completed.

The researcher felt certain that all students would benefit greatly from this new approach and sent consent forms to parents/guardians of the students. Unfortunately, some of the parents/guardians of the neediest students refused to give permission for their children to participate.

Questions

1. *Would you feel ethically obligated to attempt to persuade the parents/guardians who denied permission for their children to participate and present the potential benefits of this program?*
2. *How far would you be willing to go in your attempts?*
3. *What if a minimum number of participants were required, and without the required number the researcher would choose a different school?*
4. *Are there any conditions under which coercion might seem justified?*

Formal Review Procedures

Sadly, a number of research abuses have harmed research participants. For example, Nazi doctors during World War II conducted painful and unethical medical experiments on thousands of concentration camp prisoners. Many of these horrid experiments resulted in excruciating suffering and death. Another egregious example of research abuse is the Tuskegee Syphilis Experiment conducted by the United States Public Health Service from 1932–1972. During this 40-year study, hundreds of impoverished African American men had syphilis but were not made aware of their condition or treated by researchers. As a result of these abuses, many countries have adopted formal review procedures to address ethics in research that involves humans and monitor their protection.

In the United States, institutional research involving human participants is governed by federal regulations that define rules and responsibilities for reviews of proposed research studies. For example, every college or university has an identified group, often called an Institutional Review Board (IRB), which must review and approve all research involving human participants prior to its initiation. The IRB has the authority to approve, reject, monitor, and require modifications in all research activities to ensure that all human participants are protected from harm. It is your responsibility to determine the specific procedures required by your institution and follow them at all times.

Protection From Harm

Of course, you're not planning a research study that would intentionally place participants in harm's way. You most often will be able to submit your study for IRB review with a legitimate assessment of minimal risk to the participants. It is advisable for you to identify potential risks to participants in your study and include steps that will address these risks and provide protection for participants. For example, demographic questions on a questionnaire might reveal identifying information about participants. You could address this risk by using pseudonyms to safeguard anonymity.

Informed Consent

Informed consent must be obtained from participants, as well as parents and guardians if participants are minors, before the study begins. Informed consent is a process that enables prospective participants to voluntarily decide whether they wish to participate in a research study. According to United States federal regulations, informed consent must

- use language that is free from coercive influence, is understandable to the people being asked to participate, and does not appear to waive legal rights of participants;
- describe the overall experience of participation, including potential risks and benefits;
- communicate any available alternatives to participation;
- convey the extent to which anonymity and confidentiality will be protected;
- explain any voluntary compensation or treatment available for research-related injuries;
- identify contact information for persons who are knowledgeable to answer questions about the study, rights of research participants, and research-related injuries; and
- include verbiage regarding voluntary participation and that participants have the right to withdraw from participation at any time without penalty.

We have provided an example of an informed consent form in Example 10.1.

Example 10.1 Informed Consent Form

By completing this Consent to Participate form, you are giving consent to participate in a research project entitled "Collaborative Digital Literacy Practices Among Adult Learners." The purpose of this research endeavor is to explore the following research questions:

* How do adult learners perceive the effectiveness of collaborative digital literacy practices?
* What are adult learners' levels of interactions with collaborative digital literacy practices?

As part of the requirements in this course, you will engage in five collaborative digital literacy practices during designated times throughout the semester. As a participant in this study, you will complete a short survey before and after each experience to record your familiarity, levels of confidence, and perceived importance with the respective collaborative digital literacy practice. Responding to these questions will take you approximately 15 minutes. With each collaborative digital literacy practice, data related to your levels of interaction will be included in analyses. To maintain confidentiality, pseudonyms will be used during data analyses.

Please read carefully the following information, which explains your rights as a research participant. If you agree to participate in the study, please sign, date, and submit this form. In doing so, it is implied that you have read and understand these rights.

1. You have been asked to participate in a study researching collaborative digital literacy practices among adult learners.

2. You will complete a short survey before and after each experience to record your familiarity, levels of confidence, and perceived importance with the respective collaborative digital literacy practice. Responding to these questions will take you approximately 15 minutes, and there is no anticipated risk to you from participating in this project.

3. There is no anticipated direct benefit to you from participating in this project other than the extent to which you value contributing to your knowledge and expertise towards collaborative digital literacy practices. You may benefit indirectly from the knowledge gained from the research after it is completed.

4. To protect confidentiality, pseudonyms will be used. Your name, professional affiliation, or any other identifiable information will not appear anywhere.

5. You will not be compensated in any way for your participation in this research.

6. Questions about this research may be addressed to Dr. Laurie Sharp at XXX-XXX-XXXX or XXX@XXX.edu. Questions about a research subjects' rights, or research-related injury may be presented to Dr. Anna Fielding, XXX University's Vice President for Research and Compliance at XXX-XXX-XXXX or XXX@XXX.edu.

7. No service of any kind, to which you are otherwise entitled, will be lost or jeopardized if you choose to not participate in the study.

8. Your consent is being given voluntarily. If you decide to participate in the study, you are free to withdraw at any time without any negative effect. Withdrawal from this study will have no impact on your course grade or enrollment in the graduate program. If you choose to withdraw, please discontinue completion of surveys.

To provide consent to participate in this study, please write your full name, today's date, and sign your name before submitting this form.

Thank you for your participation!

Full Name: _____ Today's Date: _____

Signature: _____

Remember also that if your study involves children, assent from the child and consent from the child's parent or guardian is required. Also, additional safeguards are required among other vulnerable populations, such as economically or educationally disadvantaged persons, mentally disabled persons, pregnant women, and prisoners.

Participant Privacy

Respecting the right of privacy among participants in your research study will influence your plans in several ways. In some studies, the responses of the participants can be anonymous. You, as the researcher, might know who participated in the study but would not necessarily know the specific information provided by a participant. An example would be a survey of attitudes that were distributed to participants and returned without identifying information. With some studies, though, anonymity may be a challenge, especially if data collection efforts involve interviewing. As the researcher, you may know the identity of participants, but it is your responsibility to maintain anonymity when reporting data. In all types of research studies, it is usually assumed that the information you obtain will be kept confidential and any information you obtained will not be available for other use.

An exception to the confidentiality rule may be required when in the conduct of your study you might learn about a crime that has been committed or might be committed in the future. This is particularly important if you learned about a situation involving abuse of an individual. If this is a foreseeable outcome of your research, you are required to make that possibility a part of the informed consent information you provide to participants. Example 10.2 illustrates how this may be handled by researchers who are mandated reporters, such as an education or medical professional, as well as those who are not.

 Example 10.2 Mandatory Reporting Information Provided with Informed Consent

Mandatory Reporting

We will keep your data as confidential as possible, with the exception of certain information that we must report for legal or ethical reasons, such as known or suspected child, elder, or dependent adult abuse or neglect. Under state law, we must report such information to the appropriate authorities.

Privacy factors are also addressed in informed consent with the requirement that you inform participants about how records will be secured, how long the records will be kept, and how they will be destroyed when the study concludes. The main goal is simply to inform people of any potential risks they might face, and do so in such a way that their rights and safety are protected.

Selecting Participants

Now that you are convinced how important it is to be cautious and protective of the participants in your study, the next step is to decide who will be included in your study. Once you make such decisions, you face the additional challenges of figuring out how to identify such individuals and then recruit them.

Target Population and Research Samples

As we mentioned, when recruiting participants for your study, the first task is to identify the target population, the group to whom you would like the results to be generalized. Certainly you would hope that your findings apply to a group larger than just those who actually participated in the study, but it would be far too ambitious to think about generalizing to all group members throughout the world. Carefully consider the purpose and context of your study and narrow the target population reasonably.

Once you identify the target population, you are ready to recruit a research sample. Obviously, the participants must be accessible and should also mirror the target population in regard to characteristics that could influence the findings of the study. As the researcher, it is your responsibility to demonstrate the similarities and note possible disparities. This is usually found in the Discussion section of a research report where limitations of the study are acknowledged.

Look back at the common sampling techniques described in Table 10.1. Notice the ways that lower-risk techniques may have to be rejected in favor of those that are more practical. Additionally, almost all qualitative sampling is done intentionally, purposively, and strategically rather than relying on randomization. Some of the main qualitative sampling strategies are summarized in Table 10.3.

Table 10.3 Qualitative Sampling Strategies

Sampling Strategy	Description
Homogeneous sampling	Choosing informants who share common characteristics or who are as much alike as possible.
Maximum variation sampling	Choosing informants who are as different as possible to have a diverse range of experiences and backgrounds represented.
Snowball sampling	Also known as "chain sampling," relying on referrals in which one informant recommends others who might be invited to participate.
Critical case sampling	Also known as "intensity sampling," choosing people based on their likelihood of providing the most relevant, vivid stories related to the topic.
Theoretical sampling	Including informants who do not fit neatly into the model that is developing.
Stratified sampling	Choosing informants based on a particular criterion that represents variations within the larger group.
Deviant sampling	Including informants who represent extreme cases of the phenomenon being investigated.
Random sampling	Randomly selecting informants, or cases, from within a larger group with the hope that they represent the larger population.
Mixed sampling	Perhaps most commonly used, choosing informants using a combination of sampling methods in order to obtain the most robust sample possible.

Remember that lower-risk sampling techniques assume that there is some master list of potential participants in the target population. In your study, even if such a list is available, you may choose to use one of the higher-risk techniques anyway. But, when such a list either does not exist, or cannot be made available to you, the choice between the lower- and higher-risk techniques has already been made for you. As in so many things in life, what is best is not necessarily what is possible. If you encounter problems with selecting participants, you may need to consider modifications with your research questions.

How Many Is Enough?

A common question that novice researchers ask is, "How many participants do I need?" The answer to this question appears quite simple at first glance. You just need enough participants for your research sample to be an accurate representation of your target population. In actual practice, this is not a simple question at all, and new researchers often struggle in trying to find agreement on the minimum number of participants needed.

The goal of having a representative sample is a given. But, the things you need to do toward achieving that goal depend on several factors. One is the type of research you will be doing. Larger samples are expected with quantitative studies than qualitative studies. Among types of quantitative studies, larger samples are expected when you are doing a descriptive survey rather than when your study involves comparing treatment and control groups. If some treatment effect is to be observed, the number of participants needed is influenced by how large you expect the effect to be. If you have used one of the lower-risk sampling techniques, there are statistical tables, even computer software, that provide the optimal sample size if you know the size of the target population. Still another factor is the extent of your resources—the amount of money and time you have to spend on this study. Ultimately, the number of participants you include in your study will involve a judgment call that you make.

General Methods

We are the point where you should be considering which would be the better approach for your research activity, quantitative or qualitative, given that each one has distinct advantages and limitations. Remember, the common feature in all quantitative studies is an emphasis on using numerical descriptions or numerical comparisons, whereas qualitative studies emphasize words or behavior. Your selection of research methodology should be driven by the questions you want to answer, as well as your preferences for methods. In effect, research methods are simply the tools that get the desired job done.

Selecting a Research Design

When choosing among the various quantitative and qualitative designs, the primary consideration is the fit of that choice with your research questions. Obviously, you need a structure that will provide the information you are seeking, but you also must consider practical issues. If the constraints of your setting or resources make it impossible to use what appears at first to be the best design, you will then need to find a viable alternative. Sometimes this involves adjusting or reframing your original research questions to ones that will be a better match for the methodology employed.

Selecting (or Creating) Data Collection Tools

As the researcher, you must also determine whether to use existing data collection tools or create new instruments. The arguments for using existing data collection tools are both practical and philosophical. If you create new instrumentation, you are obligated to establish reliability and validity with the instrumentation and include those results in your research report. Avoiding that extra work is certainly an obvious advantage of using existing data collection tools, which is why most researchers elect to do that as a first option.

There are even better reasons for using existing data collection tools when they can be found. One of the philosophical principles underlying research is the idea of incremental increase in existing knowledge. Each researcher, in effect, stands on the shoulders of those who came before. You can, therefore, see another advantage of using existing tools is these instruments have already been tested and are already in widespread circulation.

The message about the advantages of using existing instrumentation is clear, but there will be instances in which there just isn't an available tool. In these situations, you may be called upon to create, or at least adapt, current measurement tools to assess your results.

Quantitative research designs require some form of measurement of the variables being studied. Because these are quantitative designs, the results of the measurement or observation must be presented in numerical form. Researcher-created surveys, tests, and questionnaires are obvious possibilities, but your choices would also include any type of observation in which counting is possible.

Conversely, qualitative research designs have few limits on what might be included as data. A variety of modalities may be used to gather data for your study in the form of interview transcripts, field notes, video and audio tapes, and so forth. Contingent upon your topic, you may also use personal documents, diaries and journals, official records, photographs, drawings, or essentially anything that bears directly or indirectly on your area of investigation. Similar to an attorney who is trying to prove a case in court with a great deal of evidence, every detail is considered.

Summary and Closing Thoughts

This excursion through the variety of options to select participants for your study has been a long one, but for both quantitative and qualitative studies the primary concern is to find people who can answer the research questions you've identified for your study. Given those questions, we've suggested that your next step is to find out what the requirements are at your institution for conducting studies with human subjects. Voluntary participation is a mandate in meeting human subjects requirements, and you will be seeking volunteers through informed consent whether your study is quantitative or qualitative. Institutional requirements should remain in the forefront as you make decisions about how participants will be selected and what you intend to ask them to do. It is imperative that you maintain rigor with research ethics at all times and protect participants from harm.

If answering your research questions requires a quantitative design, you may be able to choose between sampling techniques that have a lower risk of being unrepresentative, and those that have a higher risk of not reflecting important characteristics, of your target population. The key is whether a master list of all potential participants can be made available to you. If yes, the lower-risk techniques are a far better choice. If no, which we believe will most often be the case, you will need to use one of the higher-risk techniques. With use of a higher-risk technique, you are obligated to provide as much relevant detail as is possible to help readers of your study decide if your sample did in fact provide information that could generalize to the larger group.

When your research questions call for a qualitative research strategy, the most important priority is selecting participants who can answer the research questions that evolve during your study. You will still want to provide readers with sufficient background and information so they can replicate your study, or at the very least, make their own informed judgments about the validity of what you've reported.

Whether your research design is quantitative or qualitative, the Methods section in your research report should describe in great detail the nature of your chosen design, its history and origins, and applicability to your current study. You will also describe, as clearly and accurately as possible, exactly what you intend to do and how you intend to do it. As we have mentioned previously, the descriptions of your methods should have enough detail for another researcher to replicate your study.

CHAPTER 11

You Have the Answer, but What Does It Mean?

CHAPTER CONCEPTS

Negative cases

Protecting data

Quantitative data analysis

Qualitative data analysis

Qualitative software packages

Securing data

Spreadsheet software programs

Statistical analysis software programs

Introduction

O ur goal for this chapter is to provide both a brief, general guide and some specific suggestions for analyzing and interpreting the data you collected. As you've seen in earlier chapters, there are boundaries to what can be provided in the Introduction and Methods sections of a research report. In your research study, you may have a feeling of "too much still to do" even after the data have been gathered. This chapter will definitely help you to lessen the pressure by getting you started with analyzing the results.

By this point, you have already invested some time and effort in planning your study, securing the permissions required to gather the information, and then collecting the data from the participants. Even the thought that these data could be lost is enough to send shivers down the spine of the heartiest of researchers. There is no way you could absolutely guarantee that this could never happen to you—it has happened to each of us at some point in time. But, there are some things you can do to significantly limit your risk with two areas of concern: (1) protecting your data from being lost, and (2) making sure that your data is secure.

Protecting and Securing Data

We'll begin with a brief discussion of factors in data analysis that are important in all research approaches. Our first piece of advice is to be careful with your data. This might sound rather obvious, but you would be amazed at the number of times that researchers have lost significant data because they failed to take appropriate measures. In fact, it has been discovered that 80% of all raw scientific research data collected in the 1990s is gone forever and nobody can figure out where to locate it!

Protecting Data

Things do go wrong, and improbable events do sometimes occur, especially with technology. Devices malfunction, lose their charge, or are erased inadvertently. Hard drives crash. Electricity surges blow out circuits. Hackers steal control of devices. Computer viruses infect files and programs. People forget where they put things, or else believe they are stored on their hardware or in the "cloud" somewhere, even if they can't figure out how to access it.

We all know that we need to regularly back up digital data. But, when is the last time that you actually did it? Our guidance is that you should assume that things will go wrong and have in place a contingency plan for when they do. This is not only sound practice for a researcher, but for any practitioner.

To protect your data against unforeseen calamities, we recommend the following steps:

1. Use two recording devices. We are not kidding. You know how often devices lose their charge or stop working properly. To protect against the likelihood of malfunctions, which will happen, you then have a backup recording device available. Then, if your primary device fails, you still have another option with which to capture data.

2. Take notes, too. Don't rely just on the recording devices. We're not being paranoid here, thinking that your primary and backup devices will both fail (although it has happened, as a few dead parachutists could testify). The data you collect in a qualitative study includes not just what was said or observed, but also the context for these communications. The audio and video recordings will capture most of you want, but not all of it. Some of the things you observe at the time, some of the feelings and thoughts you have during the interviews, are also valuable insights that will help you make sense of the data.

3. Make multiple copies of all essential digital data. Additionally, don't store all backup files in the same place. Keep copies in different safe places. As we mentioned earlier, also make sure you remember to back up your files as you continue your work flow.

4. Make copies of all critical, nondigital documents you may be using in your study. Critical here is defined as anything that could not easily be reconstructed, such as diaries, journals, field notes, videotapes, or photographs. Store copies in a place where accidental harm to them is least likely.

When analyzing data for your research study, you will be working with some information that would be very time-consuming to reconstruct and other information that could not be reconstructed at all. In both instances, it would be foolish not to save yourself the distress that would be inevitable if the "couldn't happen" did in fact happen.

Securing Data

When you received permission to conduct your study, you had to address your protocol for maintaining security of the data. In your protocol, you likely indicated that all data obtained in the study would be kept in a locked office or stored on a password-protected computer. You probably also specified a period of time following completion of the study that data would be stored and then destroyed.

Security is essential for the data in all types of studies. We have access to information about people that may be extremely intimate and potentially embarrassing. Individuals may be identifiable by the images and voices on recordings. Personal disclosures and revelations may also be traceable back to individual participants. They agreed to share information with you, not with anyone who happens to visit you.

Following the instructions we suggested for protecting your data means at least doubling the efforts required to secure it. Possibly the most commonplace violation comes when data are stored on portable electronic devices, such as a computer or tablet. It's convenient—it allows you to work in multiple settings. However, misplacement or theft of portable electronic devices is not a rare occurrence. We certainly encourage you to use portable electronic devices as tools to help with your data analyses, but be extra careful when it contains sensitive data that could compromise the security you promised to the participants in your study.

Analyzing and Interpreting Data

The word "adventure" may seem an unusual word choice when thinking about a research investigation, but it's a rather good description for what is about to follow. Throughout this book we've periodically talked about differences in the quantitative and qualitative methodologies, but nowhere are these differences more evident than in the analysis of the information obtained in the study.

When analyzing data in quantitative studies, you'll find rather structured and prescribed series of tasks. It's akin to a trip you have planned in which the destination is clearly marked on the map along with the routes you'll be taking on the way. You're not positive what you will find when you arrive, but you know precisely how you will get there.

In contrast, analyzing data in qualitative studies has all of the elements of a spontaneous travel plan. You know the general area that you will be visiting, but specific routes, and even the ultimate destination, have yet to be determined. You are operating without a map, in many cases, and only a flexible itinerary.

Quantitative Data Analysis

Could you do the entire analysis for a quantitative study by hand and just ignore using computer software programs? Depending on the type of analysis you are conducting, the answer is that you could, but a better framing of that question would be: Who in their right mind would want to do that? Unless you are stranded on a desert island with no electricity and no battery power for your device, you will want to use some type of computer program to analyze the data in your study. Spreadsheet programs, as well as statistical analysis software, are specifically designed and customized for particular research designs and purposes.

Entering the data. The common feature in all software programs is that you first have to get your data into the program. Typically, there are three ways this can be accomplished. You can

- enter the data directly into the statistical analysis program,
- prepare the data using a spreadsheet program and import the spreadsheet into the statistical analysis program, or
- prepare the data as an ordinary text file and import the text file into the statistical analysis program.

There are advantages and disadvantages for each of these methods. If you enter the data directly into the statistical analysis program, you get to skip the importing step. But, unless you have the program on your computer, the data can only be entered during times when you have access. If you have a small set of data, this may not be a problem, but it will probably not be the most convenient procedure for most quantitative studies.

The utility of using a spreadsheet program, such as Microsoft Excel, as your data entry tool depends on your comfort level with using spreadsheets. Most statistical analysis programs allow you to import data from a spreadsheet. If you routinely use spreadsheet programs, and if you have one available on your computer, this is often a good option because your data will be stored in multiple programs. If you are unfamiliar with spreadsheet programs, there are also all kinds of consulting assistance available through your library, instructional technology department, or tutorials available online.

Sometimes the best way to prepare the data is to create a simple text file. When using this approach, you can use word processing software, such as Microsoft Word, to create the file. Just be sure to select "text only" when you save the file to omit the special formatting.

Checking the data. There is one more task, possibly onerous but absolutely essential, before you are ready to begin analyses. This task requires you to use the raw data to check the accuracy of your data entries. One mistyped numeral could invalidate the entire analysis.

Analysis of quantitative research data may at first appear to be an imposing task, but it actually involves only the ability to follow a series of sequential and logical steps. It is extremely unlikely that you will want to do the calculations without the assistance of a computer program. So, after taking care to be sure your data are protected and secure, the first step is to prepare the data for entry into the selected software program. After the data have been entered, it is a good idea to randomly check entries to ensure precision with data entry. After checking the data and confirming its accuracy, the next step depends on the kind of quantitative design you have used.

Qualitative Data Analysis

Whether you are doing narrative analysis, ethnography, grounded theory, phenomenology, action research, or a case study, there are some general features in common among all qualitative research designs:

1. There is a dynamic interaction between the researcher, the participants, and the data. It is a partnership of sorts in which all three communicate with one another to make sense of a phenomenon.

2. During data analysis, you are trying to represent and describe both the complexity of what has been studied, as well as its variations. The desired outcome of data analyses is to describe comprehensively and fully the phenomenon and to generate new theories and models of practice.

3. During the coding process, you are constantly recognizing, naming, categorizing, comparing ideas and concepts, and looking for common themes.

4. Analysis of themes leads to increased, deeper understandings.

5. The data analytic process is neither rigid nor specifically prescribed. It is constantly evolving in light of what you are discovering.

6. The researcher must be scrupulous, rigorous, honest, and ethical, reporting only what is present in the data.

7. Although subjectivity is acceptable and, at times, honored in data analysis, the researcher's biases and preconceptions are carefully monitored and suspended during the process. New discoveries come from keeping an open mind and putting aside one's biases and prior knowledge as much as possible.

In the analysis of qualitative data, you use coding processes to organize and arrange the information you have accumulated. This involves identifying, classifying, and categorizing ideas and themes. You're involved in a systematic search through the information with a primary goal to reduce it into manageable units.

You'll often see qualitative research characterized as an iterative process, which means data gathered will be examined and interpreted again and again both during and after the analysis phase as you seek the meaning in them. Preliminary interpretations can, and should, lead to additional analyses to confirm or dispute those interpretations and the gathering of additional information.

Analysis during data collection. While you are collecting data, you are listening, observing, participating in the process, as well as processing the experience. You might do an interview, for example, with a helping professional about his ideas regarding sources of stress among individuals who experienced a recent outbreak of violence. During this conversation, he talked about his observations that a number of individuals had been complaining about sleep disruptions, an aspect of the phenomenon that you had not yet considered. This leads you to do a more thorough search of relevant literature on the subject. While analyzing and coding the transcript from the interview, other related themes emerge, all related to overarousal of the sympathetic nervous system that takes place in chronic stress responses. Based on this analysis, you then make some changes in the focus of your research question and your interview protocol that changes the ways in which you approach your next interview.

Every step of the process in qualitative research informs the next one, making data collection, analysis, and interpretation integrally related. A critical component, however, is that the researcher must keep an open mind. Qualitative researchers suspend any preexisting beliefs and ideas that are inconsistent with the data and must be willing to follow the data. In Table 11.1, we offer a set of guidelines to provide some general guidance about things you should be thinking about while gathering qualitative data.

Analysis after data collection. Let's face it—doing qualitative research can be messy. We don't mean this in the bad sense of that term, but in the reality of having a lot of data. You will possibly have transcripts of interviews or written responses to open-ended questions. You may have audio and video recordings. You might have formal documents, such as official records or archival documents. You may have also collected informal documents, such as notes from your observations and analytic memos.

Table 11.1 Guidelines During Collection of Qualitative Data

Narrow your focus	As you listen to interviews, peruse documents, and observe interactions, begin thinking about reducing your original boundaries into more manageable areas of focus. Every study needs to have a stopping place. Some of your questions will have to wait for a follow-up study.
Use what you learn	Empower yourself to make minor and major changes in your direction based on what you learn while gathering the data.
Write, write, write	While you are collecting data, write everything down. Don't trust your memory—write it down. Also, while analyzing and interpreting data, write analytic memos to yourself.
Participant validation of ideas	Participants in qualitative studies are an integral part of the investigative process. They won't do the data analysis and interpretation for you, but they can be a valuable source of assistance while you are doing it.
Check the literature	Don't forget that the review of relevant literature in a qualitative study is an ongoing activity, not something done only when planning your study. New questions and new directions are expected to emerge during the collection of data, and when they do, you will want to know what others have already learned about those questions.
Speculate	While you are collecting data, let your mind roam free. Remember that this is the data collection phase. You aren't locked into any of the ideas that emerge during this period.

A state of disorganization is what can be expected at the beginning of data analysis that is accompanied with a fair bit of apprehension, confusion, and frustration. Our recommendation is to relax and enjoy the ride! One of the wonderful privileges and joys of doing this type of research is that you get to discover something new. But to do so, you must live with disorder for a period of time until you can get a handle on what you are dealing with.

One colleague of ours who specializes in supervising phenomenological research urges qualitative researchers to isolate themselves with the data for at least several uninterrupted days. During this time, he recommends absolutely no distractions or intrusions of any kind—no phones, communication devices, or email—just you and the data literally living together. He suggests that you review all data over and over again, until it seems almost part of you. There is no urgency to organize or make sense of the data at this point, just to take it all in. There will come a time when the data will begin organizing itself and you are merely along for the ride.

Whether you isolate yourself with the data or not, your first job is to bring order to the chaos. You do this by organizing whatever you have collected into some kind of meaningful categories. Exactly how you go about doing this is an individual choice. There are no hard and fast rules. Think about this as if you were preparing to set out on a journey (which, in fact, you are) and that you want to arrange things so you can find them when you need them.

Putting related material into labeled file folders could be helpful. Some people prefer index cards as the basic organizational structure. Storing information electronically using the directory structure on your computing device is another good choice. For example, when you remember that a certain phrase was used in one interview but are having difficulty remembering the interview in which it occurred, you can use the built-in search capabilities of your device to find it. Whatever your preference, your goal is to make it easier for you to locate artifacts and specific pieces of data so that you may easily move information from one place to another.

After organizing your data, you are ready to begin the big job in qualitative data analysis—classifying, categorizing, and making sense out of what you have found. As we described in Chapter 6, qualitative researchers use coding to break up the information into smaller segments, label them, and then use those labels to provide descriptions and broad themes in the data.

The specific objective of the coding process will depend on the type of qualitative study you are doing. Ethnography, for example, will look primarily for rich descriptions, whereas grounded theory will have more focus on identifying themes. Some qualitative designs, such as narrative analysis, will combine both rich descriptions and themes.

The logistics of the coding process will depend on your preference. If you decide on paper and pencil, be sure that your transcriptions of data have wide margins (two inches on each side is recommended). You can use brackets, underlining, highlighting, and so forth to identify the segments and write notes to yourself in the margins. If your preference is to use word processing software, you can use the track changes feature to make comments that discover trends, validate ideas, or make notes about the data. You can also create a table with columns, putting the actual data transcriptions in one column, and using the other column for coding and notes. You should use the technique with which you are the most comfortable.

There are also several software packages that you may find helpful for analyzing qualitative data. Among the most widely used are NVivo, ATLAS.ti, and MAXQDA. There are even web applications, such as Dedoose, that facilitate the storing, organizing, and merging of related qualitative data. Although qualitative data analysis technology tools save a lot of time in the analysis stage, you still have to figure out the codes yourself.

Once you have coded each artifact of your data, you will use these codes to identify potential themes. When identifying the themes, you also need to be alert for negative cases. A negative case is an instance in your data that appears to contradict an emerging pattern. Finding a negative case may require you to revise what you first thought was a theme in your data. If that case appears instead to be an anomaly, its presence in your data must be acknowledged.

At this point in the analysis, you need to find the patterns to identify broad themes across the different artifacts. A pattern is a link that goes beyond a single piece of information. To find the patterns, you will search for the common elements that occur in the data as a whole.

Summary and Closing Thoughts

Successful analysis and interpretation of the information in your study presupposes that you have taken the necessary steps to protect and secure that information. This is not always an easy task given the variety of different types of information you will acquire and the extensive amount of stuff that you will accumulate. Planning in advance how you intend to manage the data is time well spent.

Analysis of quantitative research data may at first appear to be an imposing task, but it actually involves only the ability to follow a series of sequential and logical steps. It is extremely unlikely that you will want to do the calculations without the assistance of some type of software program. After taking care to be sure your data are protected and secure, the first step is to prepare the data for entry into the selected program. Because essentially all of statistical software programs allow data to be imported from a spreadsheet, entering the data first into a spreadsheet program makes sense. And, there are some basic analyses that can be done inside the spreadsheet program itself. If the data have been imported into a statistical analysis program, the next step depends on the kind of quantitative design you have used.

Analysis and interpretation in qualitative research is not something that happens after all of the data have been collected. It begins with the first piece of data you collect and continues throughout the investigation. The analysis during data collection is preliminary and more informal, but it is nonetheless essential. During this analysis phase, you identify the emerging research questions from within your initial research objective and make decisions about what other kinds of data you need to obtain and from whom it can be obtained.

After the data is collected, the coding process becomes a serious endeavor. Coding your information after all data collection is completed is an interesting combination of the subjective and the objective. There are objective factors and rules to which you should adhere. For example, you break the text into segments and mark these segments with codes or category labels. You then review those labels with a goal to reduce them to a manageable number of different identifiers. Next, you identify potential themes and then look for patterns across the different artifacts you collected. How you do this involves an objective process, and what you ultimately find is a result of your subjective impression of the information. In qualitative research investigations, you are not an outside reporter—you are an integral part of the process.

Computer software programs and web applications are available to help you with coding and organizing the information. If you use one of these tools, you will want to be sure that you do not mentally separate yourself from the data. Data immersion is an expected part of the qualitative research process.

CHAPTER 12

Take Your Answers (and Knowledge) and Go Beyond

CHAPTER CONCEPTS

Establishing significance

Noting implications

Supporting findings
with literature

Introduction

You have now reached the finale of your research journey. You have planned and implemented a research study to investigate a specific phenomenon. You have collected and analyzed your data, which hopefully led to some interesting discoveries and significant findings. Your final part of the journey is to now connect your results to the established research objective, as well as situate them in broader contexts.

No matter your research design—quantitative, qualitative, or a combination of the two—you began the journey with a specific objective. You may have expressed this as an objective or statement, or you may have posed questions that you may have later transformed into hypotheses. Regardless, you identified explicit goals at the onset of your research endeavor and carried out a systematic investigation to explore phenomena and satisfy the purpose.

While planning and conducting your study, your research objective should have been at the forefront, the driving force for all of your decision making. Now, your task is to consider the results of your study in relation to your purpose—what exactly do the results of your study mean? Beyond the scope of the study, how do your research findings contribute to existing knowledge?

In Chapter 7, we described all of the typical areas that researchers address in the Discussion section of their research report: summary of findings, implications of findings, limitations of the study, areas for further research, and conclusions for the study. In your research report, you will want to address each of these, as well. Many researchers, particularly novice researchers, find it relatively simple to summarize the findings, identify limitations that were present, and render recommendations for future research studies. The challenge that many researchers encounter is with presenting the underlying meaning of the study by establishing significance with the findings and noting possible implications in connection to their research objective. Our goal in this chapter is to focus on these two areas and provide you with helpful guidelines and suggestions.

Establishing Significance With Findings

Establishing significance with findings is an area in which researchers may encounter challenges. As you know, while conducting a study, researchers have invested much effort and time precisely because they wish to discover something new and meaningful or something useful to their professional practice. They were passionate about their topic from the very beginning, and after consulting much literature, they created and carried out a research plan. After analyzing their data, they know their topic intimately. But, the bottom line is what did they learn that is ultimately useful?

Throughout this book, we have referred to researchers as experts in the sense that they have invested a lot of time becoming knowledgeable about a particular issue, topic, or problem. Researchers invest weeks, months, years, and even decades into one study, whereas a reader may spend only a few minutes. Keeping this perspective in mind may be useful as you approach this part of the research journey.

In Chapter 7, we described three types of significance that researchers may discuss—statistical, practical, or theoretical. As we shift our focus from evaluating the work of others to establishing significance in your own research, let's look at ways in which researchers may do so with respect to quantitative and qualitative findings. In Example 12.1, we have provided an example of each type of significance based on excerpts of recent studies concerning relationships.

[Editor's Note: The following examples are excerpts from third-party readings.]

Example 12.1 Establishing Significance With Findings

EXAMPLE 1 (STATISTICAL SIGNIFICANCE)

Fewer men than women participated in long-term relationships but not necessarily because they did not want to, and men were significantly more likely than women to desire more opportunity for long-term relationships, indicating these patterns may be affected by norms surrounding the social desirability of older and more economically established men. Men may also be conforming to societal expectations that they be more interested in casual sex (Armstrong et al., 2014; England & Bearak, 2014; Hamilton & Armstrong, 2009; Kimmel, 2008) and/or succumbing to a form of pluralistic ignorance resulting from the (false) perception that other men are more interested in casual sex than they are themselves.

Similarly, homosexual men were more likely to engage in hookups and less likely to engage in long-term relationships compared to heterosexual men, but were significantly more likely to desire long-term relationships compared to heterosexual men and not more likely to desire hookups. Cultural scripts associated with hookups and casual sex among homosexual men (Klinkenberg & Rose, 1994), in addition to norms shaping men's behavior more generally may therefore encourage more engagement in hookup encounters while precluding involvement in long-term relationships, despite student's actual interest in those types of relationships

Reference

Kuperberg, A., & Padgett, J. E. (2016). The role of culture in explaining college students' selection into hookups, dates, and long-term romantic relationships. *Journal of Social and Personal Relationships, 33*(8), 1070–1096. doi:10.1177/0265407515616876

EXAMPLE 2 (PRACTICAL SIGNIFICANCE)

This article has explored relationship transitions into shared living or dissolution among adults who had recently become sexually involved with a new partner, using data from the 2006–2010 National Survey of Family Growth. Our study provides some of the first estimates of the trajectories of relationship progression among sexually involved adults. Contemporary relationships in the United States are often marked by sexual intimacy from early on (Finer, 2007; Sassler & Joyner, 2011). Our results show that many of these sexual relationships are short lived. Others progress into shared living within a few months. Contemporary young adults are increasingly experiencing a range of sexual relationships. Our findings highlight how social class, age, and race/ethnicity differentiate relationship tempos. Social inequalities are exacerbated in the very early stages of sexual relationships in ways that might adversely affect the relationship health and well-being of contemporary American adults.

Reference

Sassler, S., Michelmore, K., & Holland, J. A. (2016). The progression of sexual relationships. *Journal of Marriage and Family, 78*(3), 587–597. doi:10.1111/jomf.12289

EXAMPLE 3 (THEORETICAL SIGNIFICANCE)

The theorization of perceived ambivalence is a critical next step in fully articulating how ambivalence operates in family ties (Connidis, 2015). This study further extends our empirical knowledge by demonstrating precisely how individuals discursively characterize family members as exhibiting ambivalence, even as respondents did not use this terminology. First, respondents took stock of what they read as everyday overt contradictory (i.e., both positive and negative) interactions, providing analytical evidence for the presence of ambivalence. Second, respondents perceived overt positive interactions alongside perceptions of covert religious or homophobic beliefs as evidence of ambivalence. Notably, both covert and overt illustrations do not only exist in the present (Suitor et al., 2011) but rather accumulate in nonlinear and dynamic ways across a family history (Bengtson & Allen, 1993; Connidis, 2003; Elder, 1998; Finch, 2007; Kiecolt et al., 2011). These findings push forward the measurement of the broader ambivalence construct, demonstrating the need to capture not only overt affectual, interactional, expressive, and behavioral relationship components (Birditt et al., 2010; Fingerman & Hay, 2004; Gilligan et al., 2015) but also perceptions of others' internal beliefs. Moreover, the clear commingling of the past and present in constructing family narratives moves the field beyond a static construct of present-day ambivalence toward a view of ambivalence as both cumulative and dynamic over time (Connidis, 2015). Perceived ambivalence as revealed via covert and overt evidence across family history opens up new possibilities for the articulation, operationalization, and effects of ambivalence over the life course.

Reference

Reczek, C. (2016). Ambivalence in gay and lesbian family relationships. *Journal of Marriage and Family, 78*(3), 644–659. doi:10.1111/jomf.12308

Obviously, it is much more precise to establish statistical significance in a quantitative study because the parameters were identified prior to the measurement. Quantitative researchers use statistical tests, such as t-tests, ANOVAs, and Pearson's r, to determine differences between groups and the probability of observed differences occurring by chance alone. In the Results section, this is calculated with the p-value, or probability value, and reported in numeric form, such as $p < .05$. In the Discussion section, researchers shift their focus from reporting statistical significance to explaining statistical significance. In Example 1, the researchers did just that by explaining statistically significant findings found between men and women in their relationships, as well as between homosexual and heterosexual men with hookups.

Practical significance is probably the most common way that researchers in the education, health, helping, and social sciences professions describe significance with their findings. Although we provided a quantitative example, qualitative researchers more frequently focus on the practical significance of their results. The researchers in Example 2 pointed out that their exploratory study described the trajectory of romantic relationship progression, which has real-world applications concerning the well-being and relationship health of sexually active adults.

Finally, theoretical significance uses existing models to validate or dispute previously reported findings. In Example 3, this researcher wished to extend postulations of theories for the role of ambivalence among kinship.

With each of the above examples, these researchers incorporated previous literature to strengthen their assertions of significance. In Examples 1 and 3, they supported their discussion with similar claims reported in previous studies. The researchers in Example 2 adopted a different angle because prior research for their topic was lacking. Instead, these researchers used previous literature to provide a context for their investigation. In all three examples, the researchers' goals were to quite simply say how what they found might advance our understandings of the issues or problems under study.

Noting Possible Implications

Recall from Chapter 7 that after discussing the significance of findings, the next logical step is to explore the implications for professional practice. Quite often when people read (or more often skim) a journal article or research report, they first review the abstract, breeze through the review of relevant literature to see if there's anything interesting or novel, and then immediately skip to the implications at the end to see what is relevant or useful.

It's apparent that implications noted in a study must be directly connected to the intended research objective. Let's look at how researchers might describe their implications in both quantitative and qualitative studies. In Example 12.2, we have provided two examples of each to demonstrate these connections from excerpts of recent studies concerning relationships.

[Editor's Note: The following examples are excerpts from third-party readings.]

Example 12.2 Connections Between Implications and the Research Objective

EXAMPLE 1 (QUANTITATIVE)

Research objective	This study investigates this important life transition and assesses how family relationships affect the bereavement experience, for better or worse. This not only will contribute to the literature on linked lives, greedy marriage, and the role of gender in intergenerational relationships but may also inform policy and practice by addressing bereavement as a familial rather than a purely individual, psychological experience.
Implications	This finding may imply that adults' marriages are secure over time and resilient in the face of bereavement, particularly over a period of years rather than weeks or months. For instance, marital quality prior to loss accounts

Jeffrey E. Stokes, "The Influence of Intergenerational Relationships on Marital Qualilty Following the Death of a Parent in Adulthood," *Journal of Social and Personal Relationships*, vol. 33, no. 1. Copyright © 2014 by SAGE Publications.

Reference

Shamai, M., Fogel, S., & Gilad, D. (2016). Experiencing couple relationships in the line of fire. *Journal of Marital and Family Therapy, 42*(3), 550–563. doi:10.1111/jmft.12147

EXAMPLE 4 (QUALITATIVE)

Research objective	… the purpose of our qualitative study was to explore the range of meanings expressed by participants as they talked of being in a dating relationship with someone who was engaging in disordered eating.
Implications	As documented in prior research, partner relationships clearly matter for many individuals who are engaging in eating disorders or disordered eating, and there is a growing recognition of the importance of incorporating partners in research and treatment (Bulik et al., 2011; Fischer et al., 2014). We suggest that an understanding of these relationships will be advanced by close study of the array of developing meanings created not only from the point of view of those with disordered eating but from the point of view of their partners. As illustrated in this study, developing meanings include those about the specific partner, about self, the relationship, what it means to be a partner, and developing understandings of eating disorders.

Reference

Schmit, S. E., & Bell, N. J. (2017). Close relationships and disordered eating: Partner perspectives. *Journal of Health Psychology, 22*(4), 434–445. doi:10.1177/1359105315603478

Notice the similarities between each example. The primary focus of each one is no longer solely focused on components associated with the actual study, such as its specific research design, participants, methodology, or results. No matter the particular type of research design, researchers usually broaden the scope of their work, and attempt to generalize their findings and explain how they can be applied to real-world contexts and problems. Essentially, you are answering the question, "So what?"

Notice also how the researchers in each of the examples used previous literature to further support their implications. With Example 1, the researchers suggested that the quality of marital relationships may be predicated more by internal factors between spouses rather than external dynamics associated with familial members of different generations. These researchers grounded this implication within understandings of the "greedy marriage thesis" that was previously reported in previous literature. In Example 2, these researchers claimed that their study was the first study to measure the length of sexual afterglow and explore its benefits. Under this circumstance, previous literature was nonexistent, so the researchers used literature that reported findings from similar studies. The researchers in Example 3 used previous literature to establish a precedent for implications that propose specific therapeutic techniques for couples who are living in a war zone. Similarly, the researchers in Example 4 cited past studies to corroborate their implication regarding the importance of including partners in the research and recovery of individuals who struggle with eating disorders.

Guidelines and Suggestions

To overcome the challenges that many researchers encounter with establishing significance and noting implications, we offer the following guidelines and suggestions.

Give Yourself Time

In our experience, researchers sometimes feel a bit weary and burned out at this point in their study. Planning, implementing, and writing up the results from a research endeavor takes a great amount of time, sometimes even years. Therefore, when researchers reach the last leg of the journey, they often begin to experience the effects from the demands and responsibilities of conducting research. Once you reach this part of your journey, we encourage you to take a little bit of time—days or weeks—to rest and recharge.

Reframe Your Approach

As demonstrated with the excerpts in Examples 12.1 and 12.2, this part of the research journey is unique. The preceding parts of the journey had a map of sorts that outlined a systematic approach with procedures and a framework for you to follow. However, addressing the implications in your study requires you to be more of an explorer who continues the journey with no map. Although this can be intimidating for some researchers initially, we encourage you to reframe your mind-set and shift your perspective. At this point, you are the expert, armed with information obtained from the research process, who will simply discuss the significance of your findings, as well as their impact or application in the field.

Keep the Purpose of Your Study in Mind

The purpose of your study should be a driving force during your entire study. Sometimes, though, researchers become distracted and lose their focus. We encourage researchers to engage in behaviors and tasks that keep them focused on the central aim of their study, such as maintaining a research journal, debriefing with co-researchers, or referring to their research objective continuously. This is of particular importance when you reach this point because you are, in effect, convincing others about the usefulness of your findings.

Use Previous Literature to Support Your Findings

By the time you reach this point of your research journey, you have consulted a great deal of previous literature. You should have a comprehensive base of literature from which to draw. We provided you with several examples that demonstrated different ways in which researchers use literature to situate their findings among the findings of others. We want to point out that you will likely need to revisit the literature after you collect and analyze your data, especially if your results produce unexpected findings.

We hope these guidelines and suggestions make noting implications less daunting. Don't be distressed if you find yourself spending more time in this part of your research journey—it certainly would not be unusual. As we mentioned previously, this is the part of the research report that many readers will read more closely. In knowing this, you will want to ensure you give adequate and proper attention to each required component.

Summary and Closing Thoughts

Once you have analyzed your data and discovered some findings, your research journey takes a different perspective. Up until now, your focus has been on the study at hand—identifying the research objective, consulting relevant literature, designing a study to investigate the problem, selecting participants, implementing the study, collecting data, and analyzing data. The final part of the research journey requires you to broaden your focus and discuss what it all means.

In the Discussion section of your research report, there are several areas you must address with this new perspective. First, you should restate the research problem and summarize major findings. Next, you should establish statistical, practical, or theoretical significance with your findings and note possible implications in connection to the research objective. Then, you acknowledge any limitations present in your study and recommend areas for further research about the research problem. Finally, you synthesize key points in the conclusion.

Our objective in this chapter was to support you with two areas where many researchers often encounter challenges: establishing significance with findings and noting possible implications. We agree that these two areas can be quite challenging to address because there is an element of risk that the researcher must take. No longer are you relying on what other experts have claimed or following a systematic plan. When you establish significance with your findings and note possible implications, you are asserting the importance of your work and also explaining what it means in real-world contexts. In essence, your efforts and research findings have positioned you as an expert of the research problem, and you have a responsibility to share this information with relevant stakeholders.

We provided assistance with these two problematic areas by providing real examples to examine and evaluate. By using this approach, the different ways in which researchers established statistical, practical, and theoretical significance became clear, as were the ways in which implications were noted. The different tone and style of writing for these areas was obvious in comparison with the previous sections of the research report. Furthermore, our analyses demonstrated how researchers use previous literature to explain, situate, and support their claims.

We concluded this chapter by providing you with helpful guidelines and suggestions to establish significance with your findings and note possible implications in connection to the research objective. These guidelines and suggestions explained techniques that will prepare you to address the Discussion section as a whole and also described specific strategies that will promote your success with attending to these two particular tasks.

We encourage you to keep in mind that good research writing takes much time and practice. It is important that you maintain an appropriate level of self-confidence and a positive mind-set when you encounter new challenges and unfamiliar undertakings. Remember that every researcher who came before you, including both of us, has been in your position. However, our commitment to excellence and passion for research compelled us to persist during times of difficulty and overcome challenging moments.

CHAPTER 13

Some Final Thoughts as Our Journey Comes to an End—and a Beginning

CHAPTER CONCEPTS

Conflict of interest	Ethical dilemmas	Research biases
Core elements of research planning	Imposter syndrome	Research fraud
	Publish findings	Rigorous research methods

Introduction

As we bring our journey to a close, we'd like to take you back to its beginning. As you will recall, we promised an emphasis on practical applications and meaningful content. We said we would provide a step-by-step approach that would enable you to quickly and effectively evaluate research studies that have been published by others. We claimed that learning those evaluation skills would be valuable, in and of themselves, but that they would also provide an important foundation for you to conduct your own investigations now or in the future.

In the material describing how to conduct your studies, we argued that it wasn't all that much different from things you already knew how to do. We implied that all you really needed was to learn how to frame the questions you wanted to answer and approach the data gathering in a more systematic fashion. Of course, there is a little more involved than that.

In the work you have chosen, the stakes can sometimes be incredibly high. Individual lives are changed for the better, or for the worse, by what you are able to do with them. The best practices for your specialization are available—if you know where to look and how to access that information. It is critical to be able to find the most relevant and useful research studies, and, with a critical eye, evaluate whether the findings point toward things you could to do more effectively.

The jigsaw puzzle of total knowledge about your discipline has many missing pieces and perhaps always will. Through your research studies, however, you are in a position to provide some of those pieces, or at least to link them in more helpful ways. This allows you to test ideas in your own practice.

Taking the jigsaw puzzle metaphor just a little further, there is something else we'd like to say about the importance of the research studies you conduct. First of all, no matter how long you study, how diligently you practice, how hard you work, there will always be missing pieces that help explain phenomena, especially those related to the complexity of human behavior. Think about a time when you've been working on one of those puzzles, one with many pieces and no guide to tell you what it is supposed to look like at the end. In the process of putting the puzzle together, you often can reach a point where you can figure out what the puzzle is supposed to be, what it would look like when it was completed, even when some of the pieces are still missing. You can see where we're going with this. Although total knowledge about any important professional activity will probably always remain beyond reach, the more pieces that are in place, the more likely it is that you can understand what the puzzle is about. That is how our professional practices can retain the values of an art while resting on a foundation of science.

In this final chapter, we cover a number of issues that have yet to be discussed, most notably some of the ethical challenges that are part of the research process. We also reiterate how critical it is to safeguard the welfare and privacy of participants. Finally, we cover some of the basics involved in actually publishing your report, whether in an academic journal or elsewhere.

Taking the Research Journey

You will have noticed that we believe the research process is better described as a journey than as a destination. We've introduced you to several widely used research designs for both quantitative and qualitative approaches. Whether you choose to use any one of them to find out something that you'd like to know is your decision, and the same thing applies to whether you actually make use of the tools to evaluate research studies done by others.

In this instance we're going to temporarily put aside the mind-set of the skeptic and be optimistic that you've seen how easily you can make research a part of your personal and professional life. As you might imagine, our descriptions of the options have only scratched the surface of the possibilities. However, the core elements of research planning remain the same across the different designs. These include

- an organizational structure consisting of separate sections (Introduction, Methods, Results, and Discussion), regardless of the actual naming of sections or order in which the content is presented;
- a goal to find answers in the information with numbers in quantitative studies and words in qualitative studies; and
- attention to "what it all means" in contexts beyond the study.

Generalization is often a goal for the findings in a research study. Generalizing beyond the specific information provided was absolutely our goal in selecting the techniques for choosing participants, the basic design strategies, and the analysis techniques we included. Knowing these provides the necessary and essential foundation for learning other, more advanced research methodologies. In effect, it is almost as if we are now saying, "We got you this far—the rest will be on your own." In reality, though, you are not really on your own. As a researcher, you become a member of a professional community with many colleagues, scholars, and practitioners who are available, willing, and capable to provide help when you need it.

We can think of a couple of reasons why you may feel some doubt and uncertainty about your readiness to tackle research activities on your own. For any number of reasons, you could do well enough to pass a research methods course but not retain the information in a meaningful way that allows you to personalize the material. If that's the case, it will be up to you to study more deeply and take responsibility for searching out additional preparation, whether through additional course work, workshops, independent reading, or perhaps recruiting a mentor.

 ### Reflective Exercise 13.1

Discuss in small groups of three to four individuals some of the aspects of actually doing a research study that still confound and confuse you. In other words, share with one another some of the ideas that still don't make sense to you, some of the holes in your understandings, and some of the places where you feel stuck.

After each person has shared some examples, come to a consensus regarding the one or two issues that seem most important to clarify or explain. Bring those back to your instructor or the whole group to compare notes and seek input.

Feeling Like an Imposter

Whether you are a natural at research or a struggling novice, even a little bit of understanding goes a very long way in making you a more accomplished professional. We have explained throughout this book that research skills help you to be a better thinker. They help you to function more systematically in your work. They help you to proceed in a critical, careful way so that you use those methods that are supported by some evidence. They help you to measure the effects of what you are doing so you can decide what sort of adjustments you need to make to become even more effective. Whether you choose to conduct formalized research studies or not, you will still use many of the concepts and skills in order to plan your professional interventions. That is our legacy that we hope to leave with you.

There is one more reason why you might question your ability to master this content, a phenomenon often evident in highly achieving people, called the "imposter syndrome." This is a condition characterized by continuing feelings of inadequacy that persist even in the face of extensive experience or a certain degree of expertise. We can both confess to you, after so many decades of teaching, counseling, researching, and consulting, that there are times that we still feel like frauds, still doubting our capabilities. Such feelings of being an imposter are often accompanied by fears that others will finally discover how little you really know or understand, or how unworthy you are to be a member of this exclusive club.

We wish we could reassure you that such feelings will someday vanish. Alas, we can promise that with experience, they will at least diminish over time. One of the most satisfying, exciting, and stimulating aspects of being a professional is realizing that you will never know enough or be able perform as perfectly as you desire. But, that hopefully won't stop you from constantly growing, learning, and improving your functioning.

 ### Reflective Exercise 13.2

Get together with a small group of three to four individuals to discuss or respond to the following question in writing on your own: What are some of the ways that you most feel inadequate, unqualified, or clueless about some aspect of your professional preparation and practice?

Don't limit yourself to only the role of a novice researcher—describe other ways that you feel doubt and uncertainty. This is obviously a somewhat threatening and difficult discussion to have, so your honesty will depend very much on the trust you feel with others in your group. We have found, however, that such a conversation normalizes the fears and doubts that almost all of us have.

Ethical Issues You Should Know About

Before we leave you, we wish to cover just a few other subjects that must be addressed, beginning with a few of the ethical issues implicit in any research endeavor. There is a myth that research is a completely objective enterprise in which the researchers who conduct the studies are dispassionate and totally free of biases, preconceptions, and prejudgments. Moreover, all the safeguards put in place to minimize experimenter bias and human subjectivity are supposed to ensure that the results obtained are free of influence from those who conducted the study. But of course, that is absolutely impossible! Such biases can be acknowledged, monitored, and even controlled to a certain extent. But, they can never be completely eliminated.

Just as professional practices are influenced by personal attitudes, preferences, biases, ethnicity, gender, religious convictions, political orientations, and moral beliefs, these factors also impact the work of a researcher. What you choose to study, how you decide to study it, and how you report the results will certainly reflect your cherished opinions and entrenched beliefs, some of which you may not even be aware of. It is the nature of human beings to hold strong beliefs about themselves, others, and the ways in which the world works. There are actually very few subjects about which we hold no opinion whatsoever, and many that we feel rather strongly about. One of the salient issues currently circulating in the media and political discourse is what constitutes a "fact" or "truth" and the phenomena of "fake news" in light of competing arguments. It has become a norm that rather than searching for some semblance of reasonably objective information, people so often consume media outlets that only confirm and support their existing beliefs and attitudes. That is one reason why now, more than ever, scrupulous, honest, and rigorous research methods are needed.

Fraudulent Research

There have been a number of cases reported of authors, journalists, and researchers who have resorted to deceit and fraud when reporting the results of their research. Each time this occurs, whether it is a book author who fabricated a supposedly true-life story, a journalist who reported conversations that never took place, or a researcher who fabricated data, the public has often responded with indignation and shock. How could someone ever do something like this, especially someone who holds public trust as a professional? Well, the answer is rather obvious, especially now that organizational political leaders routinely lie on a daily basis and play with so-called facts, as if the truth is a mere suggestion that can be shaped into any form that is most expedient and useful.

Given that many people believe that politicians lie often in their public communications, it is perhaps not any more surprising that certain researchers who have particular personal agendas, would also resort to deception, distortion, or mendacity. After all, they make their living, earn promotions, keep their jobs, and build reputations based on the results they report. Time and time again, we were taught growing up that what matters most is not necessarily how you play the game, but whether you win or not. In school, children learn that there is not exactly a prohibition against cheating as much as there is against getting caught. When athletes and other role models are caught cheating or using banned substances, they respond universally by saying, "What's the big deal? Everyone else is doing it! I just got caught."

Fraudulent research activity can take a number of other forms. Plagiarism has become such a consistent problem, and not just among university students. Some researchers will submit their work to multiple publications, even though they are specifically prohibited from doing so. This same mantra of "anything goes" also extends to the workplace where professionals in every field resort to any means necessary to demonstrate their excellence. Such can become the climate for conducting research, and there's little doubt that it dilutes, if not destroys, the integrity of a profession.

Ethical Guidelines for Conducting Research

Ethical conflicts can become quite challenging because we may owe allegiance to a number of different sources—to our profession, employer, the setting where the research takes place, participants, and even ourselves. There are times when you will be pressured to do things that may be in the best interest of one party, but not in the best interests of others.

Imagine you discover that as a result of some policy adopted by your employer, employees are suffering lowered workplace performance. You have the data to demonstrate this claim. Surely, you would not be so naive as to imagine that your employers would be grateful to you for pointing out their misinformed actions.

Another conflict of interest could easily occur while you are collecting data. For example, a participant you are interviewing seems to be experiencing some distress as a result of your line of questioning. One voice in your head warns you to back off and perhaps cut the interview short. Yet, another voice reminds you that time is running short, you have few other participants scheduled, and you are in danger of missing a crucial deadline.

Still, another situation could occur in which you discover results in your study that not only go against what you had hoped and predicted, but are also decidedly politically incorrect. If you publish your study in its present form, it will provide ammunition against the positions that you most whole-heartedly support.

Finally, imagine that your advisor or supervisor directs you to take a particular direction in your research that you neither feel comfortable with, nor feel is the best course of action. If you follow this advice, you will be going against your own best judgment, as well as compromising the most significant areas of personal interest. If you stand up for your position, it may very well result in alienating those who have power over you and your professional future.

In each of these cases, and many others, you will be faced with ethical dilemmas in which you are required to balance the responsibilities you feel toward different parties. Ultimately, the choice is simple—you must not do anything that puts others in harm's way, even if that means ceasing your research altogether.

Protect the Welfare of Participants

Researchers must make every effort to ensure that research participants are not harmed by what they do, whether that involves an experimental intervention or intrusive question. We addressed the protection of participants in Chapter 10, but it is absolutely vital that researchers keep the welfare of participants in mind at all time. We have provided a Bill of Rights for Research Participants in Table 13.1.

Table 13.1 Bill of Rights for Research Participants

1. *Informed consent.*	All participants have the right to thorough and accurate information about: (a) the purpose and objectives of the study, (b) how the results will be used, (c) possible side effects or personal consequences that may occur, and (d) limits of confidentiality if illegal activities are disclosed.
2. *Protection from harm.*	Researchers must ensure that participants are not harmed in any way as a result of participating in the study. Safeguards should be in place to ensure that participants will not be coerced, exploited, or pressured into doing or saying things that may be hurtful to them. Those who may be "at risk" (unstable, ill, ambivalent) should be excluded.
3. *Right to pass.*	Participants must be permitted to withdraw from the study at any time, without being subjected to coercion or penalty.
4. *Right to privacy.*	Participants have the right to remain anonymous. Any personal data that could possibly identify them should be altered or disguised.
5. *Right to feedback.*	Participants should be treated as co-researchers and collaborators in the process. This includes the opportunity to receive feedback on their participation and results on what was learned from the study.
6. *Respectful relationship.*	Participants volunteer for a study in which they donate their time and energy. As such, the relationship between researcher and participant should be infused with dignity and respect.

How to Publish What You Discover

One of the frustrating aspects of our jobs is that we read the papers and research reports that students submit to us as part of their course requirements, knowing that the audience for these texts may be less than a handful, and often just an audience of one. After going through all the trouble and investment of time, resources, and energy, students spend several months (or years!) working on a research study, and then it is read by only a few people.

If what you have discovered in your efforts was in any way valuable or interesting, don't you feel some compulsion, if not obligation, to disseminate the results so that others might profit from what you've learned? Regardless of how you publish your report, whether in the form of a journal article, conference paper or presentation, web report, monograph, or even a book, you have a professional responsibility to let others know about your efforts. That, after all, is how knowledge and science are advanced in the world.

Excuses for Not Writing

You may not believe that what you have discovered is all that significant, or even useful. You may not have confidence in your voice as a writer, that is, your ability to convey your thoughts in an acceptable form. You most certainly may not understand the mechanisms by which a piece of writing or research can be published. Like most things in life, once you understand the practical elements that are involved in any new and challenging enterprise, the prospect of success is far less daunting than you would imagine.

The main problem that new scholars face is their own internal blocks and excuses for not writing in the first place. We will address some of the more common excuses we hear most often. It is likely these are rather good excuses that successfully prevent you from following through on your best of intentions.

"I don't have time." This is a very good excuse for not writing because, of course, you really don't have a lot of discretionary time. You are busy, overcommitted, and overscheduled, with little time available for extra things. Like you, we are both busy professionals who have families, work responsibilities, and personal commitments. However, we make it a priority to write every day, no matter what. When someone asks either of us how we manage to do this, we don't really understand the question. After all, we find the time to do the things that are most important to us and put off things that matter less. We don't decide whether to brush our teeth in the mornings—we just do it. Likewise, we don't have to make time to write—it is just something that we do every day.

More accurately, it is not that you don't have time to write, but rather that, until now, you have not made this much of a priority in your life. With the additional training and experience you have accumulated through this book, you could make some different choices about how you want to spend your time in the future. If you envisioned from the beginning that you want to publish the product you complete, then you should plan accordingly.

"I'm not a writer." The definition of a writer is someone who writes. It doesn't matter if you write essays in a magazine, best-selling novels, private journal entries, letters or emails to friends, blogs or social media posts, or notes on toilet paper—a writer is someone who writes, usually every week, if not every day.

One of the most valuable ideas is that we make choices about the ways we define ourselves. People constantly make demeaning self-statements, such as, "I'm not good at math," "I've always been lousy in sports," or "I'm not the kind of person who does that sort of thing." Self-statements such as these limit possibilities for the future because they imply that just because someone has usually been a particular way, then that is the way they will always be. Yet, all it takes is one exception to dispute these overgeneralizations. If you try something that you have never been good at before, and try it enough times so that improvement comes with experience, then the self-label no longer applies.

"I'm not good enough." This is probably not so much an excuse but a statement of truth. In all likelihood, you are not good enough to be a skilled, professional writer. It is one thing to be a writer and quite another to be an excellent, successful one. Whereas the former statement takes nothing other than commitment and confidence, the latter takes a tremendous amount of practice, perseverance, and experience.

It takes a certain degree of courage to do something for a period of time that you are not very good at, and perhaps will never be as good as you hope. Even if you don't ever actually publish anything, the process of learning to become a better writer is a worthy and intrinsically enjoyable goal. What will likely happen, however, is that the more you work at your craft, the more mentoring and opportunities to revise you will receive, which will result in valuable learning experiences, and thereby increase the likelihood of publication in the future.

We also encourage you to seek out collaborative opportunities to write. We both have worked individually, as well as with co-authors. Co-authors can provide complementary skills sets, and co-authors who already have a successful track record with publishing know secrets to negotiating the complex system.

"I don't know how to proceed." This is another excellent excuse because it happens to be true. You really don't know how to figure out the most effective ways of preparing a manuscript for publication, selecting the appropriate journal, and submitting the piece in such a way that it will eventually be accepted. This knowledge can only come from experience.

in some small way as a result of your investigative efforts. Clarifying the reasons for why you want to write can help focus where you should invest your energy.

What Do You Have to Say?

This is the key question—what is unique about your message and about your perspective? Think about how you might respond to a colleague in your field who asks you, "What are you researching, and why are you researching it?" After spending considerable time reading the literature related to your research interests, formulating a research question, designing a study that will address your investigation, selecting your participants, carrying through with the plan, sorting and analyzing the data, discussing the results, and considering the implications of what you've discovered, what exactly do you want to tell others that is most meaningful? This is the question your colleagues may be asking, and you need to be very clear about your answer.

Who Is Your Audience?

To decide on the particular form that your published manuscript will take, you must settle on the readers you want to address. Acquisitions editors who work for publishers often complain that one of the most frequent mistakes they encounter from prospective authors is that they send in book proposals that are not well-suited to their target audience. A text publisher cannot easily market their books to the general public. A trade publisher cannot market very effectively to the textbook market. A book written for educational professionals will not be well matched with a publisher who specializes in resources for health professionals.

In a similar vein with a prospective article, each journal or media outlet is designed for specific audiences within each professional field. You have to match not only the subject to the appropriate audience, but also the style and scope of the publication. Additionally, some publications specialize in comprehensive literature reviews, practitioner-focused pieces, or empirical studies with quantitative or qualitative emphases. Some journals are geared for academics, administrators, practitioners, or supervisors. Some journals want a more formally constructed manuscript that strictly follows the academic rules of writing, while others permit a more informal writing tone that may use first person or personal anecdotes. Some journals require extensive citations and documentation of every point, while others permit a more journalistic style. In each of these, and a dozen other dimensions, a specific target audience is defined by each journal.

You will save yourself a lot of time and aggravation if you study the publications you are considering submitting to before you submit something. Look at the kinds of articles or reports that appear in print. Notice how they are constructed and stylized. Identify common issues and subjects that seem popular for this audience. Ask yourself if your manuscript could be adapted and rewritten to fit well in this journal.

It is usually a good idea to select several journals that might publish your study. Get some honest feedback from a mentor or faculty member to find out if your manuscript has a good shot for one of the flagship journals, which are the top-ranked publications in the field, or whether it might fit better in a journal that is less competitive. As we mentioned, some journals have a 90% rejection rate, whereas others may only be 50%. Because it can take up to 6 months or longer to hear a decision, and you are only allowed to submit your manuscript to one journal at a time, overestimating the potential for your manuscript can cost you a lot of time.

What Are Your Strengths and Weaknesses?

It's really important that you be honest with yourself and solicit honest input from experienced mentors who are already well published. How significant is the study you completed? How skilled are you as a writer? How well do you understand what is expected for a published article? How polished is the final piece?

Writing by yourself can be quite satisfying, but it can also be lonely and frustrating. Many first time authors often work with a colleague or two, to pool their skills and knowledge and share the responsibilities for writing. In fact, we encourage novice scholars to invite a peer or colleague to collaborate with them on a project. Not only can this make the process more enjoyable, but often this may result in a reciprocal invitation that can produce double the number of publications.

Either one of us could have written this text by ourselves, but we chose to work together for mutual support and because it makes the work more fun. We can bounce ideas off one another. We can make up for one another's weaknesses and limitations, both as a writer and researcher. We can pool our specialty areas and combine our interests. We can critically respond to each other's ideas. We can split the workload in half. When one of us feels frustrated or blocked, the other can jump in to save the day. We are very different scholars, writers, and practitioners, yet we can combine our talents in such a way that we produce a product that is far better than either one of us could do alone.

Summary and Closing Thoughts

The curtain is coming down, but before the final good-bye, there is just one more thing we'd like you to do. The academic environment has a built-in, seasonal feature to it. Whether it is in the form of a semester, a quarter, a trimester, or some other time structure, there is almost always a clear starting point and a clear ending point. How do you know when you've covered all that you need to cover? It's when the time period allotted comes to an end.

Within the academic environment, there are both good and troublesome features in this seasonal structure. On the positive side, being in an academic environment provides the continuing pleasure of regular new beginnings at multiple times during each calendar year. There is, though, a downside in that faculty structure content for their courses (and plan content for their publications) that will fit into prescribed time slots, rather than what would seem to be a more logical approach of letting the content determine the time required.

We're not going to ask you to remodel the academic environment, but we do think it would be helpful to have a little more closure than is possible with a final examination or final project alone. So, this one last time, we'd like you to form small groups and discuss the questions presented below.

Reflective Exercise 13.4

In small groups of three or four individuals, share your feelings about the following questions. Be candid with each other and take advantage of this opportunity both to learn from and be supported by your peers.

1. *Which parts of this book or your course seemed most relevant for real-world professional practice?*
2. *What did you learn from this book or your course that surprised you in some way?*
3. *What will you do next in order to continue your journey as a researcher, however you define that role in your life and work?*

We are all shaped by our experiences, including those that occurred in a required research class. Once upon a time, we were students and felt a certain reluctance, if not trepidation, in being required to take a research course that we didn't see as all that relevant to our needs or even of much interest. It wasn't until we were well into our professional practice that we began to appreciate just how useful and meaningful the research process was, not just to advance our careers, but to think through challenges, discover new ideas, and address problems that perplexed us.

Isn't there a better way to help a person who doesn't respond to the standard approach? Why is this group of people behaving in a particular way, even though it doesn't seem to be in their best interests? How could I develop a more effective strategy for making a difference? How come we've always done things a certain way? What might happen if I tried something else instead? What seems to be causing this impasse in trying to accomplish our goals? What is the relationship between current practices and success (or failure) rates? These are the sorts of questions that plague us almost every day.

More than anything else, we want to leave you with an understanding that research isn't about how to punctuate a reference list or solve a statistical equation. It's about the excitement of learning new things and finding the answers to questions that make you better able to do your job exceptionally well. It is about finding information you want to know and information you need to know in order to do your job more effectively.

Appendix A: Example Evaluation of a Quantitative Article

Mahapatra, N., & Schatz, M. C. S. (2015). Social networking among health sciences university students: Examining social network usage, social support, and general well-being. *Journal of Human Behavior in the Social Environment, 25*, 618–629. doi:10.1080/10911359.2015.1011253

[Editor's Note: The following is the author's evaluation of the referenced article.]

Introduction Section

Context and Significance

Consider

1. How important is the topic?
2. To what extent is the presentation clear and objective?

Look for

- Personal relevance of the topic
- Sound rationale for investigation of the problem
- Broad societal context for the problem
- Clear portrayal of the general intent of the study
- Evidence of bias in language

The authors, Mahapatra and Schatz, began the article by establishing the importance and relevance of social networking among personal and professional connections through a variety of social networking sites (SNSs). Mahapatra and Schatz established a broad context for the problem by claiming SNSs were an inherent part of the daily social life of many individuals that contribute to social capital among users with commonalities. The authors emphasized that social capital encompasses four features, including social support, which promote an individual's well-being. Mahapatra and Schatz clearly portrayed the intent of their study by providing a literature-based operational definition for SNSs and noting that research concerning two different relationships—(1) SNSs and social support, and (2) the use of SNSs and an individual's well-being—was lacking, particularly among health professionals.

Throughout the Introduction section, Mahapatra and Schatz used language that was free from bias and supported all aspects of context and significance with citations from the literature, which included two articles from peer-reviewed journals (Bauman & Tatum, 2009; Boyd & Ellison, 2008), a paper presented at a professional conference (Mislove, Marcon, Gummadi, Druschel, & Bhattacharjee, 2007), and a working paper (Scrivens & Smith, 2013).

Review of Relevant Literature

Consider

1. To what extent is the viewpoint balanced and appropriately comprehensive?
2. How has attention been given to both historical precedent and more recent work?
3. How coherent is the theme of the review of relevant literature?
4. Where did the researchers appear to emphasize primary, rather than secondary sources?

Look for

- Objectivity with previous research findings
- Accumulation of knowledge reported in the literature with explanations for any gaps in time
- Evidence that previous literature guided the objectives for the study
- Reliance on citation of primary sources

Mahapatra and Schatz provided a review of relevant literature in a section entitled "Background Information." Within this section, Mahapatra and Schatz included two subsections that addressed the variables of their study: (1) Social Networks and Social Support, and (2) Effects of SNSs on Well-Being and Self-Esteem of Users. Within the first subsection, Mahapatra and Schatz delineated findings from two studies regarding how usage of SNSs strengthened social support among student users (Morosanu, Handley, & O'Donovan, 2010; Subrahmanyam, Reich, Waechter, & Espinoza, 2008). Within the second subsection, Mahapatra and Schatz situated the concept of "well-being" in a respected resource (Diener, 2009) and cited seven studies that explored the effects of SNSs and well-being that reported negative effects (Feinstein et al., 2013; Kim, LaRose, & Peng, 2009; Rohall, Cotton, & Morgan, 2002) and positive effects (Gowen, Deschaine, Gruttadara, & Markey, 2012; Kraut et al., 2002; Seder & Oishi, 2009; Valkenburg, Peter, & Shouten, 2006).

All nine previous research studies consulted in Mahapatra and Schatz's review of relevant literature were published in well-known peer-reviewed journals within the fields of higher education, psychology, and sociology, such as *Higher Educational Research & Development, Journal of Applied Developmental Psychology, and Journal of Social Issues*. Thus, their consultation of literature relied solely on primary sources. There were no gaps in the reporting of previous research—the earliest study consulted was published in 2002, which was appropriate for when usage of SNSs was mainstream among the general public. Likewise, the most recent study consulted was published in 2013, which was appropriate because the article was published in 2015. Mahapatra and Schatz's review of relevant literature was free from interpretations and remained objective throughout their reporting of previous research findings.

Objective Statements/Research Questions/Hypotheses

Consider

1. To what extent were the objective statements/research questions/hypotheses clearly stated?
2. How has the review of relevant literature supported development of the objective statements/research questions/hypotheses?

Look for

- Clear understanding of purpose for study
- Researchers' predictions

Mahapatra and Schatz provided a clearly stated research objective for their investigation, which sought to explore relationships between the use of SNSs, perceptions of social support, and perceptions of well-being among undergraduate and graduate students in the health sciences field. Mahapatra and Schatz stated that research for their topic was lacking among health professionals, which was supported by their review of relevant literature, as all studies cited were from other disciplines. With a lack of available literature, Mahapatra and Schatz explained that their study was exploratory survey research; therefore, they did not make any predictions for potential outcomes.

Methods Section Part I: Participants

Target Population

Consider

What was the target population?

Look for

- Whether the target population is also the sample
- Alignment to research objectives

The target population for Mahapatra and Schatz's study included all students enrolled in university health sciences educational programs. Because Mahapatra and Schatz noted the absence of related research in these specific areas, the target population aligned with the intended research objective. Mahapatra and Schatz sought to generalize their findings to this target population.

Research Sample

Consider

Who participated in the study?

Look for

- Enough information so that results can be generalized
- Characteristics that may influence responses
- Unusual characteristics
- Language used to describe characteristics

Participants in the research sample consisted of 146 undergraduate and graduate students enrolled in health sciences educational professional programs. Professional programs included communication disorders, dental hygiene, kinesiology and health, medicine, nursing, pharmacy, and social work. Mahapatra and Schatz shared that although 190 students participated, only 146 had participated completely.

At this point in the research report, there was no additional information included about the research sample. As a survey study, Mahapatra and Schatz included demographic questions on the survey to obtain more specific characteristics among the research sample, such as age, employment status, ethnicity, gender, relationship status, and specific area of study. These findings were reported in the Results section of the research report.

Location

Consider
Where were the participants?

Look for
- Specific information about the setting
- Appropriateness of setting for research objective
- Aspects of setting that may influence findings

Participants in the study were students enrolled at the University of Wyoming. The university is located in Laramie, Wyoming, which is in the southeastern part of the state. Because the research objective was to explore relationships between the use of SNSs, perceptions of social support, and perceptions of well-being among undergraduate and graduate students in the health sciences field, then the research location was appropriate.

Missing from the research report was whether participants were enrolled in programs delivered in face-to-face, online, or other types of learning environments. This information could have a potential influence on findings because online students may be located outside of the geographic area. Additionally, there may be differences in how students who learn in different contexts interact on SNSs with each other.

Time Frame

Consider
When were the data collected?

Look for
- Specific information about the time frame for data collection
- Significant lapses in time or subsequent events that may influence relevance with findings

Mahapatra and Schatz provided a general time frame to describe their data collection efforts. They sent an electronic survey to participants, alone with two reminders that were each 10 days apart.

Mahapatra and Schatz did not specify dates during which data were collected. Their study was published in 2015, so it is likely that the data were collected two or three years prior to publication. However, this information is not known for sure, which does present questions regarding possible lapses in time or subsequent events that could have influenced relevance with their findings.

Rationale for Sampling Technique

Consider

Why was this sample collected?

Look for

- Utilization of sampling techniques to accurately represent the target population
- Appropriateness of sampling techniques to achieve research objective

It is obvious that Mahapatra and Schatz selected this research sample because they intend to generalize their findings to the target population. Therefore, creating the research sample at a university setting was an appropriate way for the researchers to achieve their research objective.

Sampling Techniques

Consider

How was this sample collected?

Look for

- The manner in which participants were selected
- Descriptions of advantages and risks associated with selected sampling technique

Although it was not explicitly stated, Mahapatra and Schatz used convenience sampling to create their research sample. Both researchers were faculty members within the Division of Social Work at the University of Wyoming during the time of the study, so they had access to students. However, Mahapatra and Schatz did not discuss advantages or risks associated with their sampling technique. This was necessary to ensure that the research sample was truly representative of the target population.

Methods Section Part II: Procedures and the Tools

Procedures: Sufficient Detail

Consider

To what extent did the researchers provide sufficient detail about the procedures implemented in the study?

Look for

- Complete information and sufficient detail for each step in the procedures
- How permissions to conduct the study were sought and obtained
- How participants were informed about the study
- How participants provided consent
- The time frame for data collection
- How data were collected and analyzed
- Enough information was provided to replicate the study

Mahapatra and Schatz addressed the procedures for data collection somewhat sufficiently. They first received permission to conduct the study from the Institutional Review Board at the University of Wyoming. Next, they mentioned that a pilot study was conducted, but no additional information about this process or its outcomes were included. Mahapatra and Schatz then sent an e-mail to potential participants inviting them to participate. In this recruitment e-mail, potential participants were informed about the study and permitted to provide consent. Mahapatra and Schatz also stated that participation was incentivized with a drawing for five gift certificates to the university's bookstore by mail. All data were collected anonymously via the online survey, which was created in Survey Monkey™. Mahapatra and Schatz's time frame for data collection was 20 days: the recruitment e-mail was sent, a reminder e-mail was sent 10 days later, and a final reminder e-mail was sent 10 days after the first reminder email. Although the researchers provided enough information to gain a general idea of data collection procedures, more information about the pilot study was needed, particularly if any subsequent revisions were made to the study's procedures or survey. Mahapatra and Schatz described their procedures for data analysis sufficiently. They calculated descriptive statistics (i.e., means and percentages) and inferential statistics (i.e., correlation coefficients) with Predictive Analytics Software. By doing so, Mahapatra and Schatz could note trends in the data, as well as identify any possible relationships among variables.

Procedures: Relevant to the Researchers' Objective for the Study

Consider

How are the procedures relevant to achieve the research objective of the study?

Look for

- Type of research design
- Appropriateness of research design
- Relevance of procedures to the research objective

Mahapatra and Schatz's research design and procedures were relevant to achieve the research objective. They described their study as "survey methodology," which sought participation through a research sample that seemed representative of the target population. Mahapatra and Schatz elicited participation only from individuals who used SNSs. Based on the procedures for data analyses, it is evident that the study's research design was quantitative. With a quantitative research design, the researchers were able to collect and analyze data for the identified variables in the study—usage of SNSs, relationships maintained through SNSs, perceived social support, and general well-being. Although a qualitative research design could have provided rich data for a topic that lacks a strong base of literature, the selected quantitative research design was highly appropriate for exploratory purposes.

Data Collection Tools: Sufficient Detail

Consider

To what extent did the researchers provide sufficient detail about the data collection tools used in the study?

Look for

- Complete information
- Sufficient detail for each data collection tool
- Focus is on measurement

Mahapatra and Schatz provided sufficient detail about the data collection tool used in the study. They included subsections in their research report to describe each of the six separate sections for the survey instrument administered online using Survey Monkey™: (1) usages of SNSs, (2) perceived social support, (3) general well-being, (4) quality of relationships maintained through SNSs, (5) level of self-disclosure on SNSs, and (6) demographic information. Mahapatra and

Schatz's descriptions revealed that the first five survey sections contained items that were grounded in literature with which to measure each variable. For example, the first section consisted of three items to measure usage of SNSs that were based on previously developed survey items (Valkenburg, Peter, & Schouten, 2006). Two of these items included response categories, and one item required a self-reported number. The researchers then calculated a composite score by calculating the product for the three reported number scores to describe each respondent's usage of SNSs. One of the survey sections, Self-Disclosure, was not grounded in literature and asked respondents to self-report their level of self-disclosure on SNSs.

Data Collection Tools: Relevant to the Researchers' Objective for the Study

Consider

How are the data collection tools relevant to achieve the research objective of the study?

Look for

- Reported metric or technique to establish consistency (reliability) with findings
- Reported metric or technique to establish truthfulness (validity) with findings

Mahapatra and Schatz did not explicitly report reliability or validity with the survey instrument as a whole. They reported a variety of reliability (e.g., internal consistency reliability, test-retest reliability correlation) and validity (e.g., content, construct) metrics for the Perceived Social Support and General Well-Being sections. All of the survey items required participants to self-report information; therefore, establishing reliability and validity with the entire instrument was necessary to promote credibility with the study's results. Internal consistency should have been calculated for the survey instrument as a whole to ensure reliability. In addition, because the survey measured five variables (i.e., usages of SNSs, perceived social support, general well-being, quality of relationships maintained through SNSs, and level of self-disclosure on SNSs), employing a factor analysis to determine the dimensions that were measured with the survey would have further strengthened its validity.

Results Section

Sufficient Detail

Consider

How did the researchers present the findings with sufficient detail?

Look for

- Explanations for unanticipated events
- Detailed descriptions of collected data
- Complete information for findings
- Proper reporting for descriptive and/or inferential statistics
- Appropriate use of visual displays

Mahapatra and Schatz reported their findings using descriptive and inferential statistics. They used six tables to summarize descriptive statistical information for types and frequency of visits to specific SNSs, characteristics of participants, areas of study among participants, levels of self-disclosure shared, frequency of usage, and rate of usage. The titling of several tables was somewhat confusing, though. Tables 1, 5, and 6 all had the same title but showed different information. Similarly, Table 3 included additional information that was not noted in the name of title. Mahapatra and Schatz also reported inferential statistics for two statistically significant relationships identified with linear regression analyses: (a) usage of SNSs and perceived social support, and (b) general well-being and usage of SNSs. The reporting of inferential statistics was sufficient—the test statistic (i.e., r value) and probability value (i.e., p value) were included. However, it is not clear if the data set met the four assumptions required for use of parametric statistical testing.

With respect to the reporting of descriptive statistics, more detail was needed. The majority of findings were reported as percentages and did not include the number of respondents. Therefore, if a reader wanted to determine the number of participants associated with a specific reported finding, they would have to perform a calculation.

Relevant to the Researchers' Objective for the Study

Consider

To what extent are the results relevant to achieve the research objective of the study?

Look for

- Relevance with results to the research objective
- Absence of interpretations
- Explanations for information that is not relevant to the research objective

Mahapatra and Schatz's reporting of results were free from interpretations. All reported information aligned with the research objective, which was to explore relationships between the use of SNSs, perceptions of social support, and perceptions of well-being among undergraduate and graduate students in the health sciences field. This section of the research report did not contain extraneous information irrelevant to the research objective.

Discussion Section

Clear Presentation

Consider

How did the researchers present the discussion with clarity?

Look for

- Clear demarcation between the summary of findings, implications, limitations, future areas of research, and conclusions
- Logical flow and coherence with ideas

Mahapatra and Schatz's Discussion section included three subsections: Implications, Conclusion, and Funding. The latter subsection simply recognized a specific funding source that supported the study. The first part of the Discussion section provided a rationale for the study, summarized findings, and included the researchers' interpretations of the findings. The presentation of information addressed was clear and logically flowed from idea to the next.

Relationship to Study Objectives

Consider

To what extent does the discussion relate to the objectives of the study?

Look for

- Relevance with discussion to the research objective

Including a rationale for the study in the first part of the Discussion section set the stage for relevance of areas addressed in the discussion with the study's research objective. All information included in this section was clearly connected to the research objective.

Summary of Findings

Consider

How did the researchers present a summary of findings?

Look for

- Logically follows the Results section
- Elaboration beyond the actual findings
- Consistency with reported findings (no exaggerations, omissions of data, avoidance of value-laden terms)

Mahapatra and Schatz's summary of findings logically followed the Results section. They supported some of their findings with findings reported in a previous study (Choi & Chung, 2013) to demonstrate similarities (i.e., rate of usage, importance of social support) and differences (i.e., frequency of daily visits with SNSs). Mahapatra and Schatz also cited four other studies that reported similar findings with one of their statistically significant findings—usage of SNSs and perceived social support (Clayton, Osborne, Miller, & Osberle, 2013; Huxhold, Fiori, & Windsor, 2013; Maghrabi, Oakley, & Nemati, 2013; Rau, Gao, & Ding, 2008).

After the summary of findings, Mahapatra and Schatz included an interpretation that elaborated beyond the actual findings and stated the study showed "that the reliance for online interactions did not discourage or limit their offline relationship experiences" (p. 627). Although the reported findings may have suggested this as a possibility, this interpretation seems exaggerated, especially because the size of the research sample was so small. Moreover, because Mahapatra and Schatz demonstrated where their findings differed from those reported in previous studies (Feinstein et al., 2013; Rosen, Whaling, Rab, Carrier, & Cheever, 2013), their interpretation appeared overstated.

Implications of Findings

Consider

How did the researchers address implications of findings?

Look for

- Establishment of statistical, practical, or theoretical significance
- Detailed descriptions of how the findings contribute to the purpose of the study, as well as a broader societal perspective

Mahapatra and Schatz did not explicitly establish significance in their discussion. They did report two statistically significant findings in the Results section to which they implicitly referred to the practical significance of each in the Discussion section. First, they contended that students may benefit from interacting with SNSs after completing their academic programs as a way to maintain connections. Mahapatra and Schatz also indicated that their findings pointed to ways in which educators might consider incorporating SNSs during learning experiences as a way to foster continuous learning. Finally, Mahapatra and Schatz noted that their findings suggested that SNSs usage may reduce stress among students enrolled in academic programs.

Although Mahapatra and Schatz outlined these implications, a stronger link to their contributions to the research objective was needed. Additionally, using existing literature to support each implication would have further explained how their results applied to real-world contexts.

Limitations of the Study

Consider

How did the researchers acknowledge limitations of the study?

Look for

- Identification of possible problems with the design of the study

Mahapatra and Schatz did not acknowledge any limitations with the study. Limitations should have been acknowledged with the research sample (e.g., small number, same location, combined undergraduate and graduate students) and research design (e.g., information was self-reported).

Areas for Further Research

Consider

How did the researchers suggest specific areas for further research?

Look for

- Specific suggestions about how future studies could be designed to complement the findings of the current study

Mahapatra and Schatz did not suggest specific areas for further research. Because no study within itself is sufficient to provide the universal answer, the researchers should have suggested ways that subsequent studies could extend, replicate, or validate their findings. As an exploratory study, it makes sense that future researchers should replicate the study to confirm the validity with findings, as well as conduct follow-up investigations on a wide variety of related topics.

Conclusions of the Study

Consider

How did the researchers present conclusions of the study?

Look for

- Clear statements regarding how the research questions or objectives were supported by the results

Mahapatra and Schatz concluded their research report with clear statements as to how their research objective was supported with the results of their study. The researchers cited existing literature that was referenced in their introduction (Bauman & Tatum, 2009), which connected their final ideas with the starting point. Mahapatra and Schatz also cited literature to make a broader connection between the findings of their study and human behavior (Dale, Smith, Norlin, & Chess, 2009).

Appendix B: Example Evaluation of a Qualitative Article

Stanton, A., Zandvliet, D., Dhaliwal, R., & Black, T. (2016). Understanding students' experiences of well-being in learning environments. *Higher Education Studies, 6*(3), 90–99. doi:10.5539/hes.v6n3p90

[Editor's Note: The following is the author's evaluation of the referenced article.]

Introduction Section

Context and Significance

Consider

1. How important is the topic?
2. To what extent is the presentation clear and objective?

Look for

- Exploration of new phenomena, as well as how people experience them
- Personalized style of writing
- Continuing interactions among data gathering, literature reviews, and research questioning
- Personal relevance of the topic
- Sound rationale for investigation of the problem
- Broad societal context for the problem
- Clear portrayal of the general intent of the study

Stanton, Zandvliet, Dhaliwal, and Black (2016) described how their research topic aligned with a new international initiative that focused on promoting well-being among students in college- and university-based learning environments. Stanton et al. cited the original source that advocated for this initiative (Okanagan Charter, 2015) and cited several existing studies with which to emphasize the importance of addressing students' well-being in educational contexts (Conley, Durlak, & Kirsch, 2015; Seligman, Ernst, Gillham, Reivich, & Linkins, 2009). Stanton et al. also pointed out that little research existed regarding how classes and curriculum could be designed to foster well-being among students. They also contended that their findings would benefit those who design learning experiences, such as faculty members and instructors, as well as health care practitioners who serve in higher education contexts.

Stanton et al. addressed the context and significance of their study clearly and established its importance with existing literature. It is clear that they intended to conduct a qualitative investigation to explore well-being in higher education learning contexts among students' experiences. The researchers began this section with a direct quote from a student, which added an element of personalization. At this point in their research report, however, it is not clear how their topic is personally relevant to them.

Review of Relevant Literature

Consider

1. To what extent is the viewpoint balanced and appropriately comprehensive?
2. How has attention been given to both historical precedent and more recent work?
3. How coherent is the theme of the review of relevant literature?
4. Where did the researchers appear to emphasize primary, rather than secondary sources?

Look for

- Preliminary review of relevant literature
- Balanced and sufficiently comprehensive review of relevant literature
- Includes contemporary and historical studies, with outcomes from these studies synthesized
- Reliance on citation of primary sources

Stanton et al. addressed the Review of Relevant Literature in a section entitled "Literature Review." Within this section, the researchers noted that available literature for investigations of well-being from students' viewpoints in higher education contexts was scant. They cited and briefly described one related qualitative study (Hammond, 2004). Next, Stanton et al. noted that available literature was also scant for studies that explored the impact of specific well-being interventions. They cited and briefly described studies that explored the inclusion of well-being interventions in curricula (Conley et al., 2015; Seligman et al., 2009), specific learning experiences (Ewert & Yoshino, 2011; Rowe & Stewart, 2011), and teaching practices (Adriansen & Madsen, 2013).

The literature included in this section were all primary sources published from 2004–2015. Because this topic is relatively new, this span of time demonstrates a good balance of older and newer works. Each cited study was also published in well-known and respected peer-reviewed academic journals in the fields of education and health care practice, such as *Prevention Science, Oxford Review Education, Journal of Adventure Education and Outdoor Learning, Health Education,* and *Innovative Higher Education.* However, closer inspection of each of these cited studies revealed that two utilized youth as participants, not adults (Rowe & Stewart,

2011; Seligman et al., 2009). This raises questions regarding the relevance of their inclusion. Moreover, the briefness of the literature review was not sufficient enough to cover the topic. The researchers could have included more information from the Okanagan Charter (2015) document to explain the initiative or cited literature to support well-being in general. By doing so, the reader would have access to more relevant literature concerning the research topic.

Objective Statements/Research Questions

Consider

1. To what extent were the objective statements/research questions clearly stated?
2. How has the review of relevant literature supported development of the objective statements/research questions?

Look for

- Preliminary identification of a guiding research question(s)
- Guiding research question(s) served as general framework that guided the study initially
- Sufficiently open-ended to facilitate exploration of themes that emerge during the study

Stanton et al. stated that the preliminary guiding purpose of their study "provides insight into how future learning experiences in higher education may be designed to enhance well-being and learning" (p. 90). They also noted that the goal was to identify features of learning experiences that can be implemented to foster well-being among students in higher education contexts. The stated purpose and goal of their study was open-ended and provided a general framework that guided the exploration of emerging themes throughout the investigation.

Methods Section Part I: Participants

Target Population

Consider

What was the target population?

Look for

- Whether the target population is also the sample
- Alignment to research objectives

Based upon Stanton et al.'s stated purpose and goal for this study, the target population was students in higher education contexts. The target population is well aligned with the intended research objectives of the study.

Research Sample

Consider

Who participated in the study?

Look for

- Enough information so that results can be generalized
- Characteristics that may influence responses
- Unusual characteristics
- Language used to describe characteristics

Participants in the study included 25 undergraduate students and 4 graduate students who were seeking degrees offered in the Faculties of Health Sciences, Science, Education and Arts and Social Sciences. Within the Methods section, no additional information about participants was provided. This descriptive information may have highlighted characteristics that potentially influenced responses, such as age, brief summaries of educational background, gender, cultural background, and other pertinent personal attributes.

Location

Consider
Where were the participants?

Look for
- Specific information about the setting
- Appropriateness of setting for research objective
- Aspects of setting that may influence findings

Participants in the study were affiliated with Simon Frasier University in Burnaby, Canada. The researchers indicated that the university's enrollment consisted of 25,000 undergraduate students and 4,000 graduate students at the time the study was conducted. Of the total enrollment, Stanton et al. reported that approximately 54% were female and 20% were international students. It can be assumed that all participants resided close to the university because they participated in focus groups and interviews. Because Stanton et al. sought to generalize their findings to students in higher education contexts, the setting seems appropriate to achieve the goal of the study.

Time Frame

Consider
When were the data collected?

Look for
- Specific information about the time frame for data collection
- Significant lapses in time or subsequent events that may influence relevance with findings

Stanton et al. stated that data were collected between November 2013 and February 2016. The researchers did not indicate any significant lapses in time while data were collected. Additionally, because the study was published in 2016, it is reasonable to assume that no subsequent events occurred that may have in influence on the relevance with findings.

Rationale for Sampling Technique

Consider
Why was this sample collected?

Look for
- Utilization of sampling techniques to accurately represent the target population
- Appropriateness of sampling techniques to achieve research objective

Stanton et al. explicitly stated that purposive and convenience sampling techniques were used. These techniques were appropriate to accurately represent the target population: students in higher education contexts. Moreover the university had implemented a Healthy Campus Community Initiative during the time of the study was conducted. This initiative engaged more than 100 faculty members with identifying and sharing ways to create conditions that promoted well-being among students. Based on this factor, participants would have likely experienced some of these conditions, which enabled the researchers to achieve their stated research goal.

Sampling Techniques

Consider
How was this sample collected?

Look for
- The manner in which participants were selected
- Descriptions of advantages and risks associated with selected sampling technique

Although Stanton et al. explicitly stated the sampling techniques utilized, they did not describe the procedures that followed to create the research sample. It is unclear if the researchers invited all students affiliated with the university to participate or if they limited participation to students with whom they were familiar. Without this information, it is impossible to evaluate advantages and risks associated with their selected sampling techniques.

Methods Section Part II: Procedures and the Tools

Procedures: Sufficient Detail

Consider
To what extent did the researchers provide sufficient detail about the procedures implemented in the study?

Look for
- Complete information and sufficient detail for each step in the procedures
- Description for positionality and the role of the researchers
- How the researchers gained entry to the research site
- Steps taken to secure any required permissions
- How participants were informed about the study
- How participants provided consent
- How data were collected
- Established protocols for documenting and/or recording data
- Transcription methods used for nontextual data
- Data analysis strategies
- Explicit descriptions of coding procedures, including the codebook and analytic memoing
- How interpretations were made
- Information about data saturation
- Enough information was provided to replicate the study

Stanton et al.'s descriptions of procedures was somewhat detailed. They provided adequate information concerning the role of the researchers by explaining that three of the researchers (Alisa Stanton, Rosie Dhaliwal, Tara Black) were members of the university's Healthy Campus Community initiative who worked in partnership with David Zandvliet, a learning environments researcher at the university. All four researchers were employed by the university, so it can be inferred that they each had reasonable access to the research site. Stanton et al. did not describe the steps taken to secure permission from the university. They likely sought approval from the university's Institutional Review Board because their study involved human subjects research, but this was not explicitly stated. The researchers did note that participants provided consent before participating, but they did not explain the consent process.

Stanton et al. described data collection and analyses procedures somewhat sufficiently. They conducted five focus groups and three semi-structured interviews, but they did not provide more specific information about the design of these processes, such as length of time, who conducted the sessions, or the composition of participants during each session. Data were recorded via audio recordings during the focus groups and interviews. Four open-ended questions were asked, along with clarifying questions. Audio recordings were transcribed and data were analyzed using constant comparative methods as described by Maykut and Morehouse (1994) and Lincoln and Guba (1985). Stanton et al. indicated that two readers conducted separate analyses to code data into initial categories, which were then grouped together by meaning. However, it was not clear if the readers were two of the researchers or other individuals. Themes among categories were developed during the last stage of analysis, during which analytic memoing documented relationships among themes. Stanton et al. also noted that analytic memoing was used to describe relationships between themes and theoretical frameworks; however, this was confusing because no theoretical frameworks for the study were described or explicitly identified. Information about data saturation was also missing, so it is unclear if the researchers set out to conduct the specific number of focus group sessions and interviews or if there was a point when data saturation was reached.

Although Stanton et al. had several areas within their descriptions of procedures that included sufficient detail, the missing and vague areas would prevent another researcher from replicating this study.

Procedures: Relevant to the Researchers' Objective for the Study

Consider

How are the procedures relevant to achieve the research objective of the study?

Look for

- Type of research design
- Appropriateness of research design
- Relevance of procedures to the research objective

Stanton et al. employed a qualitative research design that elicited data from focus groups and interviews to ascertain students' perspectives about their experiences with well-being at the university. This type of research design was appropriate to achieve the purpose of the study, and the procedures were relevant to realize the stated research goal.

Data Collection Tools: Sufficient Detail

Consider

To what extent did the researchers provide sufficient detail about the data collection tools used in the study?

Look for

- Complete information
- Sufficient detail for each data collection tool
- Focus is on description

Stanton et al. obtained data by asking the following four open-ended questions during focus groups and interviews: (1) What does well-being mean to you? (2) What comes to mind when you think of well-being in relation to your learning experiences? (3) Do you have a story to tell related to this? (4) Do you think it's important to consider well-being in relation to your learning experiences? Although the researchers intended for the research questions to be general in nature, the latter two could potentially elicit a limited response. However, the researchers indicated that they also posed clarifying questions throughout the focus groups and interviews, although they did not provide any examples.

Data Collection Tools: Relevant to the Researchers' Objective for the Study

Consider

How are the data collection tools relevant to achieve the research objective of the study?

Look for

- Reported technique to establish consistency (reliability) with findings
- Reported technique to establish truthfulness (validity) with findings

Stanton et al. did not explicitly state how they established reliability and validity with the study. However, these techniques were implicit within their descriptions in the Methods section. For example, triangulation was evident through the use to two readers during data analyses and analytic memoing. This could have been strengthened with more explicit references, as well as with employment of additional techniques. For example, reflexivity could have been addressed with the information regarding the roles of the researchers by postulating potential biases or inclinations that could influence interpretations.

Results Section

Sufficient Detail

Consider

How did the researchers present the findings with sufficient detail?

Look for

- Detailed descriptions of collected data
- Complete information for findings
- Appropriate use of direct quotations and data excerpts

Stanton et al., included seven subsections in the Results section that addressed the study's themes. The researchers provided a brief preliminary narrative to describe the structuring of this section of the research report. No specific information was provided regarding the collected data, though. The subsections in the Results section were: (1) Understanding Well-Being in Learning Environments, (2) Pathways to Well-Being in Learning Environments, (3) The Importance of Social Connection and Learning in "Relation," (4) Social Connections are Created through Learning Experiences, (5) The Role of Participation and Flexibility in Well-Being and Learning, (6) Learning for Purpose: Making a Real and Valued Contribution, and (7) Deep Learning is Connected to Happiness. Each subsection included a balance of direct quotations and descriptive narrative. Direct quotations were italicized and included information about the respondent, such as "Student F-13, 4th Year" (p. 95). This presentation of data was efficient and written in a very clear and understandable manner.

Relevant to the Researchers' Objective for the Study

Consider

To what extent are the results relevant to achieve the research objective of the study?

Look for

- Relevance with results to the research objective
- Absence of interpretations
- Explanations for information that is not relevant to the research objective

All of the information included within the Results section was relevant to Stanton et al.'s research goal. All seven themes derived directly from participants' experiences and provided insights for their perspectives toward well-being in higher education learning contexts. Within several subsections, the researchers offered interpretations of findings. The information in this section should have been limited to summaries of findings that resulted from data analyses.

Discussion Section

Clear Presentation

Consider

How did the researchers present the discussion with clarity?

Look for

- Clear demarcation between the summary of findings, implications, limitations, future areas of research, and conclusions
- Logical flow and coherence with ideas

Stanton et al. began the Discussion section with a brief summary of findings, followed by implications of findings, which were addressed in separate paragraphs. A separate section entitled "Conclusions" was the last section of the research report. With these included areas, there was a logical flow and coherence with ideas. Stanton et al. cited existing literature to support implications made within the Discussion section.

Relationship to Study Objectives

Consider

To what extent does the discussion relate to the objectives of the study?

Look for

- Relevance with discussion to the research objective

Stanton et al. made strong connections between information presented in the Discussion section and the research goal of the study. They began this section by stating their findings provided "insights into students' lived experiences of well-being" in higher education contexts and also suggested ways in which well-being can be promoted within academic learning experiences (p. 96). Stanton et al. concluded this section by reiterating the importance of continued research in this area.

Summary of Findings

Consider

How did the researchers present a summary of findings?

Look for

- Logically follows the Results section
- Elaboration beyond the actual findings
- Consistency with reported findings (i.e., no exaggerations, omissions of data, avoidance of value-laden terms)

Stanton et al.'s summary of findings logically followed the Results section. Findings reported were consistent with what was presented in the Results section and were free from exaggerations. This would have been a more appropriate place for the researchers to insert their interpretations that were included in the Results section. By doing so, their findings would have set a strong foundation that buttressed their implications.

Implications of Findings

Consider

How did the researchers address implications of findings?

Look for

- Establishment of statistical, practical, or theoretical significance
- Detailed descriptions of how the findings contribute to the purpose of the study, as well as a broader societal perspective

Stanton et al. established theoretical significance by stating their findings aligned with Self-Determination Theory (Ryan & Deci, 2000), which is a model widely used to describe psychological needs that correlate with well-being and motivation. Stanton et al. also contended that their findings supported findings from a previous study (Hammond, 2004), thereby establishing practical significance. Moreover, Stanton et al. used previous literature to support application of their findings in real-world contexts among higher education settings (Harward, 2014; Keeling, 2014; Okanagan Charter, 2015). This demonstrated how their findings contributed to both the goal of their study and more broadly to higher education contexts.

Limitations of the Study

Consider

How did the researchers acknowledge limitations of the study?

Look for

- Identification of possible problems with the design of the study

Although Stanton et al. stated that the study was exploratory, they did not acknowledge specific limitations of the study. Therefore, it is impossible to identify possible problems with the study's design. For example, a conceivable limitation with the study could be that participants were all students at the same university and may have similar attitudes and perspectives towards well-being specific to this location.

Areas for Further Research

Consider

How did the researchers suggest specific areas for further research?

Look for

- Specific suggestions about how future studies could be designed to complement the findings of the current study

Stanton et al. referred to their study as "an initial exploration" and made a general suggestion that future studies should investigate learning experiences, teaching practices, and instructional design features that promote well-being among students (p. 97). Stanton et al. also asserted the importance of future studies balancing these inquiries from those that consider well-being among faculty who implement such practices. These suggestions identified essential areas for further research that complement the findings of the study.

Conclusions of the Study

Consider

How did the researchers present conclusions of the study?

Look for

- Clear statements regarding how the research questions or objectives were supported by the results

Stanton et al. addressed the conclusions of the study in a separate section entitled "Conclusions." Within this section, the researchers made clear statements that connected the research goal with their findings. Moreover, the researchers cited recent literature to indicate the timeliness of their topic due to the release of an international initiative (Okanagan Charter, 2015) and works that have indicated a need for focusing on well-being within higher education contexts (Harward, 2014; Keeling, 2014).

Appendix C:
Reading and Writing
Academic Reports
Overview of APA Style

W hat exactly is academic writing, and how does it differ from other forms of prose, discourse, and published communications? Regardless of your level of familiarity, our experiences as seasoned faculty members have shown us that students are rarely introduced to the APA style of writing in a meaningful way. Typically, they encounter a professor who instructs students nonchalantly to submit a written paper using the APA style of writing with little to no support in what this actually means. Therefore, students often find themselves in a "sink or swim" scenario for which they feel very underprepared.

The American Psychological Association (APA) style is the most commonly used style of writing in published research reports within the education, health, helping, and social sciences professions. It is essentially a set of accepted writing rules and guidelines for publishers to establish clarity, consistency, and uniformity among written material. The *Publication Manual of the American Psychological Association* outlines the rules and guidelines for the APA style, and the most recent edition should be consulted for the most current standards and practices. During the time we wrote this book, the 6th edition was the most current *Publication Manual* and our source of authority for the information we present in this appendix.

At this point, you might be asking whether you should obtain a copy of the *Publication Manual*. If you are a professional who is reading this book for personal or professional learning purposes, you probably do not to own a copy of the *Publication Manual*. You may simply need to borrow one for occasional consultations. If you are an undergraduate student, it wouldn't hurt to obtain your own copy, especially if writing in APA style is expected in your classes. If you are a graduate student, we strongly encourage you to not only obtain your own copy and read it from cover to cover, but to keep it close by for frequent references. We assume that obtaining a copy of the *Publication Manual* would be a requirement of all graduate students enrolled in graduate programs. However, there may be cases where this expectation has not been made explicit to students. Please keep in mind that the information in this appendix is only intended to familiarize you with the APA style. Under no circumstance does it serve as a substitution for more specific knowledge that is required for you to be successful in your academic journey.

This may also be a good time for us to caution you regarding information accessed online. Whereas some websites may be good, reliable points of reference, such as Purdue Online Writing Lab (OWL), others may have incorrect or outdated information. Even software programs with citation tools are not 100% accurate. It never ceases to amaze us that students are often more willing to trust an unfamiliar source rather than themselves! Remember—one important part of being a competent and critical consumer of research is accepting that nothing can replace your own efforts and thinking.

Basic Stylistics

Our goal here is simply to familiarize you with a few stylistics that you will encounter when reading texts written in APA style. By doing so, we hope to remove the fear of the unknown and prepare you to be a competent consumer of published research reports.

APA Style Is Clear and Succinct

Are you an avid reader who appreciates a detailed, well-written text? Some texts often contain extensive, descriptive wording, such as the following:

> *A large number of people enjoy reading and conducting research regularly. As a general rule, these individuals are not themselves researchers by profession, nor would these individuals really ever enjoy being a full-time researcher in a professional setting. Many individuals who enjoy reading and conducting research probably enjoy learning about new approaches, ideas, methods, and ways of thinking within*

> *their professional realm. By doing so, they increase their professional knowledge and understandings, which in turn leads to improved professional performance.*

This is exactly the type of writing you will not come across in a published research report written in APA style.

Now, this might go against how you have been trained with academic writing. We are quite confident that you have received comments from former teachers and professors on submitted written assignments that noted "more detail was needed." As a result of these experiences, many individuals have been conditioned to produce longer, lengthy pieces of writing that are chock-full of descriptive details, and often, extraneous information. Somewhere along the way, the adage of "more is better" became applicable to academic writing.

We are not saying that teachers and professors who have provided such feedback to students were incorrect or that these evaluative approaches were without merit. Depending on the task, it may very well have been exactly what was needed to improve student performance. What we are saying, though, is that lengthier, wordy explanations are not an aspect of the APA style of writing. APA style is clear and succinct. Keep in mind that clear and succinct does not necessarily mean that a paper written in APA style is shorter. There are a large number of published research reports that consist of a great number of pages with written text! It does mean, however, that writing in APA style states information in a clear and succinct manner.

Let's reexamine our previous example. If we took these same ideas and wrote them in APA style, it might look like this:

> *Many individuals who are not professional researchers enjoy reading and conducting research because they are able to develop their professional knowledge and understandings. These efforts often lead to improved professional performance.*

Notice how the ideas presented in both examples are basically the same—people who are not researchers by trade enjoy research because it helps them perform better professionally. Just as we have demonstrated, the primary objective of research report writing in APA style is to present readers with information in a distinct and precise manner.

APA Style Is Organized

The APA style of writing uses several organizational features to present information in a logical manner. In a published research report, these features greatly enhance the readability of the writing and act like a road map for readers. Thus, readers are able to easily navigate to desired parts of a research manuscript.

One particularly useful organizational feature in APA style of writing is the levels of heading. Levels of heading are similar to the hierarchical, linear structure you likely used to outline papers in your former English classes. Both outlining and APA style utilize a top-down progression where sections of equal importance are noted with like identifiers. However, unlike outlining, which uses Roman numerals and lettering, APA style uses elements of typography, such as alignment and font style, to identify sections with five different levels. We have demonstrated how each of the five levels of heading looks within an excerpt of text in Figure 1.1.

As you can see, levels of headings enable readers to determine the content of the information being presented in a published research report, as well as locate desired information easily. In our example, the first heading informed you, the reader, that the ideas presented in this text excerpt were concerned with being competent consumers of research (Level 1 heading). As you continued to read, the next heading indicated a narrowing of the main idea toward the discipline of education (Level 2 heading). Within this discipline, the main idea continued to narrow, as demonstrated by the remaining headings, to address teachers (Level 3 heading), classroom teachers (Level 4 heading), and classroom teachers within the elementary grade levels (Level 5 heading).

Tables and Figures

Published research reports that use APA style may present information relevant to their study in tables and figures. Tables and figures are excellent ways for researchers to communicate information to readers visually, rather than textually. Tables generally present large amounts of numerical and textual information that are organized in rows and columns. Figures encompass all other visual representations, such as charts, drawing, graphs, and photographs.

Tables and figures can be extremely helpful for readers of published research reports to gain a better understanding of information presented. To illustrate our point, let's take a closer look at tables. As we mentioned previously, tables primarily display numbers and text that a reader needs to make sense of information described in the research report. Tables are most often used in the Results section of a published research report and present data that has been collected or findings from data that has been analyzed.

Competent Consumers of Research ← This is a Level 1 heading. Level 1 headings are the main sections within a paper that uses APA style of writing Level 1 headings are centered, boldface, and use upper- and lowercase.

Individuals in education, social sciences, helping professions, and health professions must be competent consumers of research. Consulting research is how an individual stays current within their respective professional discipline. Although these professional disciplines have similarities regarding the publication of research, each professional discipline is unique. With this in mind, there are unique characteristics and features regarding research endeavors.

Discipline of Education ← This is a Level 2 heading. Level 2 headings are the next level of heading Level 2 headings are left-aligned, boldface, and use upper - and lowercase.

Within the discipline of education, various educational stakeholders should be competent consumers of research. Educational stakeholders include teachers, school campus administrators, school district administrators, and other professionals who engage in educational decision-making.

Educational stakeholders who are teachers. ← This is a Level 3 heading. Level 3 headings are the next level of heading Level 3 headings are paragraph headings that are indented, boldface, use lowercase, and end with a period.

Teachers should be competent consumers of research who consult current published reports related to teaching and learning. Teachers include classroom teachers, campus specialists, and other instructional professionals who teach students. These reports may include instructional methods, assessment approaches, as well as any other texts regarding the improvement of pedagogical practices.

Classroom teachers. As the primary instructor ← This is a Level 4 heading Level 4 headings are the next level of heading Level 4 headings are paragraph headings that are indented, boldface, italicized, use lowercase, and end with a period.

among a group of students, classroom teachers should be concerned with published research reports that describe teaching and learning practices for all learners. Classroom teachers generally teach groups of students who vary by ability, culture, ethnicity, gender, and socioeconomic staras.

Elementary grade level classroom teachers. ← This is a Level 5 heading Level 5 headings are the next and final level of heading. Level 5 headings are paragraph headings that are indented, italicized, use lowercase, and end with a period.

In addition to teaching and learning practices, teachers in the elementary grades may also be interested in consulting research reports that describe community partnerships, developmental trends among children, and parental involvement.

Figure 1.1 Examples of Levels of Headings

Let's pretend you are reading a research report about dog breed preferences among different types of professionals. This particular research report (which is fictitious) presents findings from a study conducted among 1,000 different types of professionals to investigate their preferences of dog breeds. While reading the Results section of the research report, you come across a table (see Table 1) and the following text:

As shown in Table 1, participants (n = 1,000) encompassed a wide variety of professionals within the education, health, helping, and social sciences professions. Results for dog breed preferences indicated by participants were reported using the following seven groups acknowledged by the American Kennel Club:

- Sporting Group (Labrador, Golden Retriever, Cocker Spaniel);
- Working Group (Boxer, Great Dane, Doberman Pinscher);
- Terrier Group (Westie, Scottish Terrier, Bull Terrier);
- Nonsporting Group (Poodle, Bulldog, Dalmatian);
- Herding Group (Collie, German Shepherd, Sheltie);
- Hound Group (Beagle, Bloodhound, Dachshund); and
- Toy Group (Yorkie, Pug, Chihuahua).

As shown in Table 1, the most favored types of dogs among the majority of participants were from the Working Group.

After reading the text, what do you do? Keep reading and limit your understandings to what was reported by the researcher? Or, do you explore the data presented in the table and then compare/contrast your analyses with those of the researcher? We are hoping that you stated the latter, not the former. We want to emphasize that a competent consumer of research reads all of the information presented in a published research report critically. By doing so, they develop deeper understandings of the content with which to evaluate the quality of information presented and confirm any accuracies and possible inaccuracies with analyses of reported information.

In our example, what if the researcher who authored the published research report did not elaborate on the data provided in the table? The researcher would have missed the opportunity to point out specific groups of dogs that were most favored and least favored among each professional who participated. For example, data showed that police officers favored dogs from the hound group. This finding suggests that police officers prefer dogs that bear a resemblance to a vital aspect of their occupation: the reliance on instinct and investigation to "sniff out" who may have committed a crime. Similarly, data revealed that coaches favored dogs from the nonsporting group the least. This finding suggests the disposition that coaches have towards competition may influence their preference toward dogs

Table 1 Example of APA Table

Dog Breed Preferences

	Sporting Group	Working Group	Terrier Group	Nonsporting Group	Herding Group	Hound Group	Toy Group
Education							
Coach	511	222	54	2	29	177	5
Teacher	126	292	201	53	79	36	213
Principal	299	367	42	156	111	22	103
School counselor	47	253	56	91	49	341	163
Social Sciences							
Archaeologist	101	301	54	99	112	309	24
Lawyer	15	279	40	212	58	294	102
Police officer	58	303	77	20	75	411	56
Political scientist	38	245	180	177	186	75	99
Helping Professionals							
Church pastor	36	265	163	61	290	62	123
Life coach	49	251	57	202	166	58	217
Psychologist	33	286	113	127	11	196	234
Social worker	23	387	143	159	8	32	248
Health Professionals							
Dentist	173	298	12	230	35	45	207
Dietician	285	303	238	21	28	26	99
Nurse	202	380	92	68	42	30	186
Physician	288	377	20	21	6	267	21

that are more athletic. Depending on the objective of the research study, interpretations such as these could be valuable and lead to stronger implications and conclusions. Thus, those who read research must be critical readers who look beyond the face value of reported information, consider possible limitations of the research design, and appraise interpretations and conclusions made by the researcher.

Citation of Sources

You have probably either read or written a paper that uses APA style and are somewhat familiar with the citation of sources. However, we assume that you might not feel completely competent. Therefore, we are going to review vital aspects regarding citation of sources in APA style.

To start, sources are cited two different ways in APA style: (1) within the body of the report, and (2) at the end of the report. Both ways are equally important and greatly assist readers with evaluating the content and quality of information. Let's talk about sources that are cited at the end of the research report first.

All sources that a researcher refers to and cites within their research report are listed at the end of report. Typically, a Level 1 heading labeled "References" indicates the beginning of this list of references. Each type of source provided in this list—books, peer-reviewed journal articles, corporate or governmental reports, dissertations, website information—has a specific APA citation form. Each citation form includes pertinent information about the source, such as the author and date of publication. This information serves two purposes: (1) it communicates to the reader the sources that the researcher referenced in their research report, and (2) it provides the reader with the information needed to retrieve a cited source. We have provided a few examples in Figure 1.2 of the most commonly cited sources that a researcher in the education, social sciences, helping professions, and health professions may cite in a published research report.

As competent and critical readers of research, we encourage you to look at the list of references before reading the report. When you review the sources listed, ask yourself the following questions to evaluate their quality:

- What specific sources did the researcher cite? Are these sources credible, recognized, and reputable among professionals within the discipline?
- What is the publication date of each source? Are these sources accepted as the most current and valid among professionals within the discipline?
- Did the researcher cite seminal sources that are widely accepted as the most influential within the discipline?
- Did the researcher cite print and Internet sources? What are the quality standards for each source?

We want to emphasize that the quality of published research reports varies greatly, particularly among sources that are not peer-reviewed. Therefore, readers must be skilled with conducting an evaluation of the sources cited to make judgments regarding the strength of evidence presented within a given research report.

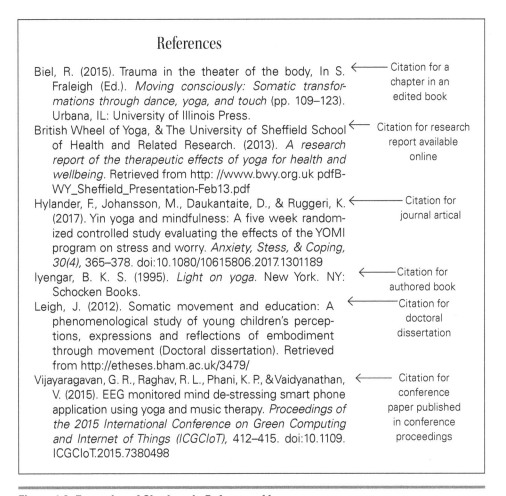

Figure 1.2 Examples of Citations in Reference List

The sources listed in the reference list at the end of a published research report are also cited within the text of a research report by author and year of publication. We have provided an example of in-text citations in Figure 1.3. As a reader encounters information in a research report, the in-text citation provides them with the information needed to locate the source in the reference list. By doing so, the reader can determine the quality of the source and access it if necessary. All sources cited in text should appear in the reference list, and the reference list should not contain citations that are not located within the text. Oftentimes, you may not be familiar with a specific source that the researchers cited. In these cases, you might need to access these sources and evaluate their quality to determine whether they support information presented within the research report.

According to Dyson and Freedman (2003). "… writing is a developmental process" (p. 967). A lot of research and literature have attempted to formulate a model that describes the processes during the acts of writing (e.g., Emig, 1967, 1971; Flower & Hayes, 1981; Graves, 1983, 1994; Hayes & Flower, 1980, 1986; Murray, 1968; Rohman, 1964; Zoellner, 1969). However, Dyson and Freedman noted that "… there is no 'writing process,' but a flexible process, one influenced by the kind of writing being attempted, the writer's purpose and the simational conditions" (p. 974). Feachers of writing typically implement a process approach during writing instruction that prescribes the successive use of specific processes of planning, drafting, revising, editing and publishing during the acts of writing (Lacina & Silva, 2011). Although this model for the acts of writing has been described as "recursive" (p. 133), it is often applied as a prescribed, linear process within the context of the classroom. This narrow perspective towards the acts of writing disregards the theoretical understandings that (a) writing is developmental and (b) the processes that a writer uses during the acts of writing is flexible. Thus, teachers of writing potentially lack an understanding for the various processes at work during the acts of writing among each student writer, and writing instruction potentially becomes narrow, rigid and inflexible. Munay (1985) noted that the processes associated with the acts of writing vary with each writing task and should take into consideration each writer's personality, cognitive style and experiences.

Figure 1.3 **Examples of In-Text Citations**

Once you begin reading a given research report, you are evaluating the strength of evidence that the researchers present more rigorously. As you encounter in-text citations, potential questions you might ask are:

- Did the researchers present information from each source accurately?
- Does the information cited from each source reinforce claims, ideas, and implications?
- Are the sources relevant to the topic of the research study?

List of Journal Articles Used

Example 3.1	Ruberton, P. M., Gladstone, J., & Lyubomirsky, S. (2016). How your bank balance buys happiness: The importance of "cash on hand" to life satisfaction. *Emotion, 16*(5), 575–580. doi:10.1037/emo0000184
Example 3.2	Jeong, H. I., & Kim, Y. (2017). The acceptance of computer technology by teachers in early childhood education. *Interactive Learning Environments, 25*(4), 496–512. doi:10.1080/10494820.2016.1143376
Reflective Exercise 3.2	Several journal article titles listed
Example 3.3	DeMatthews, D. E., Edwards, Jr., D. B., & Rincones, R. (2016). Social justice leadership and family engagement. *Educational Administration Quarterly, 52*(5), 754–792. doi:10.1177/0013161X16664006
Exercise 4.1	Smith, L., Mao, S., & Deshpande, A. (2016). "Talking across worlds": Classist microaggressions and higher education. *Journal of Poverty, 20*(2), 127–151. doi:10.1080/10875549.2015.1094764
Exercise 4.2	Verdinelli, S., & Kutner, D. (2016). Persistence factors among online graduate students with disabilities. *Journal of Diversity in Higher Education, 9*(4), 353–368. doi:10.1037/a0039791
	Langi, F. G., Oberoi, A., & Balcazar, F. E. (2017). Toward a successful vocational rehabilitation in adults with disabilities: Does residential arrangement matter? *Journal of Prevention & Intervention in the Community, 45*(2), 124–137. doi:10.1080/10852352.2017.1281053

Reflective Exercise 5.1	Pooler, J. A., Morgan, R. E., Wong, K., Wilkin, M. K., & Blitstein, J. L. (2017). Cooking Matters for Adults improves food resource management skills and self-confidence among low-income participants. *Journal of Nutrition Education & Behavior, 49*(7), 545–553. doi:10.1016/j.jneb.2017.04.008
	Verrill, L., Wood, D., Cates, S., Lando, A., & Yuanting, Z. (2017). Vitamin-fortified snack food may lead consumers to make poor dietary decisions. *Journal of the Academy of Nutrition & Dietetics, 117*(3), 376–385. doi:10.1016/j.jand.2016.10.008
	Stickel, A., Rohdemann, M., Landes, T., Engel, K., Banas, R., Heinz, A., & Müller, C. A. (2016). Changes in nutrition-related behaviors in alcohol-dependent patients after outpatient detoxification: The role of chocolate. *Substance Use & Misuse, 51*(5), 545–552. doi:10.3109/10826084.2015.1117107
Reflective Exercise 5.2	McMillan, C., & Jenkins, A. (2016). "A magical little pill that will relieve you of your womanly issues": What young women say about menstrual suppression. *International Journal of Qualitative Studies on Health & Well-Being, 11*(1), 1–12. doi:10.3402/qhw.v11.32932
	Simmonds-Moore, C. A. (2016). An interpretative phenomenological analysis exploring synesthesia as an exceptional experience: Insights for consciousness and cognition. *Qualitative Research in Psychology, 13*(4), 303–327. doi:10.1080/14780887.2016.1205693
Example 6.1	Woodford, M. R., Joslin, J. Y., Pitcher, E. N., & Renn, K. A. (2017). A mixed-methods inquiry into trans* environmental microaggressions on college campuses: Experiences and outcomes. *Journal of Ethnic & Cultural Diversity in Social Work, 26*(1–2), 95–111. doi:10.1080/15313204.2016.1263817
Example 7.2	Isacco, A., & Mannarino, M. B. (2015). "It's not like undergrad:" A qualitative study of male graduate students at an "all-woman's college." *Psychology of Men & Masculinity, 17*(3), 285–296. doi:10.1037/men0000021
Example 7.3	Kenny, R., Dooley, B., & Fitzgerald, A. (2016). Developing mental health mobile apps: Exploring adolescents' perspectives. *Health Informatics Journal, 22*(2), 265–275. doi:10.1177/1460458214555041
	Chiu, C., Hu, Y., Lin, D., Chang, F., Chang, C., & Lai, C. (2016). The attitudes, impact, and learning needs of older adults using apps on touchscreen mobile devices: Results from a pilot study. *Computers in Human Behavior, 63*, 189–197. doi:10.1016/j.chb.2016.05.020
	Zahry, N. R., Cheng, Y., & Peng, W. (2016). Content analysis of diet-related mobile apps: A self-regulation perspective, *Health Communication, 31*(10), 1301–1310. doi:10.1080/10410236.2015.1072123

Example 7.4   Juhasz, A., & Bradford, K. (2016). Mobile phone use in romantic relationships. *Marriage & Family Review, 52*(8), 707–721. doi:10.1080/014949 29.2016.1157123

Miller-Ott, A. E., & Kelly, L. (2016). Competing discourses and meaning making in talk about romantic partners' cell-phone contact with non-present others. *Communication Studies, 67*(1), 58–76. doi:10.1080/10510974. 2015.1088876

Sprecher, S., Hampton, A. J., Heinzel, H. J., & Felmlee, D. (2016). Can I connect with both you and my social network? Access to network-salient communication technology and get-acquainted interactions. *Computers in Human Behavior, 62*, 423–432. doi:10.1016/j.chb.2016.03.090

Reflective   Hartman, C. L., Evans, K. E., & Anderson, D. M. (2017). Promoting adaptive
Exercise 7.2   coping skills and subjective well-being through credit-based leisure education courses. *Journal of Student Affairs Research and Practice, 54*(3), 303–315. doi:10.1080/19496591.2017.1331852

Cholewa, B., Schulthes, G., Hull, M. F., Bailey, B. J., & Brown, J. (2017). Building on what works: Supporting underprepared students through a low-cost counseling intervention. *Journal of Student Affairs Research and Practice, 54*(3), 261–274. doi:10.1080/19496591.2017.1331445

Example 12.1   Kuperberg, A., & Padgett, J. E. (2016). The role of culture in explaining college students' selection into hookups, dates, and long-term romantic relationships. *Journal of Social and Personal Relationships, 33*(8), 1070–1096. doi:10.1177/0265407515616876

Sassler, S., Michelmore, K., & Holland, J. A. (2016). The progression of sexual relationships. *Journal of Marriage and Family, 78*(3), 587–597. doi:10.1111/jomf.12289

Reczek, C. (2016). Ambivalence in gay and lesbian family relationships. *Journal of Marriage and Family, 78*(3), 644–659. doi:10.1111/ jomf.12308

Example 12.2   Stokes, J. E. (2016). The influence of intergenerational relationships on marital quality following the death of a parent in adulthood. *Journal of Social and Personal Relationships, 33*(1), 3–22. doi:10.1177/0265407514558962

Meltzer, A. L., Makhanova, A., Hicks, L. L., French, J. E., McNulty, J. K., & Bradbury, T. N. (2017). Quantifying the sexual afterglow: The lingering benefits of sex and their implications for pair-bonded relationships. *Psychological Science, 28*(5), 587–598.

Shamai, M., Fogel, S., & Gilad, D. (2016). Experiencing couple relationships in the line of fire. *Journal of Marital and Family Therapy, 42*(3), 550–563. doi:10.1111/jmft.12147

Schmit, S. E., & Bell, N. J. (2017). Close relationships and disordered eating: Partner perspectives. *Journal of Health Psychology, 22*(4), 434–445. doi:10.1177/1359105315603478

Appendix A   Mahapatra, N., & Schatz, M. C. S. (2015). Social networking among health sciences university students: Examining social network usage, social support, and general well-being. *Journal of Human Behavior in the Social Environment, 25*, 618–629. doi:10.1080/10911359.2015.1011253

Appendix B   Stanton, A., Zandvliet, D., Dhaliwal, R., & Black, T. (2016). Understanding students' experiences of well-being in learning environments. *Higher Education Studies, 6*(3), 90–99. doi:10.5539/hes.v6n3p90

Appendix C   Sharp, L. A. (2016). Acts of writing: A compilation of six models that define the processes of writing. *International Journal of Instruction, 9*(2), 77–90. doi:10:12973/iji.2016.926a

Index

Printed in the USA
CPSIA information can be obtained
at www.ICGtesting.com
LVHW082018030124
767915LV00003B/5